Tribal Cultural
Resource Management

Heritage Resources Management Series

Series editor Don Fowler, University of Nevada, Reno
Sponsored by the Heritage Resources Management Program
Division of Continuing Education, University of Nevada, Reno

Books in this series are practical guides designed to help those who work in cultural resources management, environmental management, heritage preservation, and related subjects. Based on a series of successful workshops sponsored by the University of Nevada, Reno, the books are designed to be "workshops between book covers" on important strategic, legal, and practical issues faced by those who work in this field. Books are replete with examples, checklists, worksheets, and worldly advice offered by experienced practitioners in the field. Future titles in this series will deal with assessing historical significance, management of archaeological sites, working with native communities, and other topics.

Volumes in the series:

Tribal Cultural Resource Management
The Full Circle to Stewardship

Darby C. Stapp and Michael S. Burney

A Division of Rowman & Littlefield Publishers, Inc.
Walnut Creek • Lanham • New York • Oxford

ALTAMIRA
P R E S S

A Division of Rowman & Littlefield Publishers, Inc.
1630 North Main Street, #367
Walnut Creek, CA 94596
www.altamirapress.com

Rowman & Littlefield Publishers, Inc.
A Member of the Rowman & Littlefield Publishing Group
4720 Boston Way
Lanham, MD 20706

12 Hid's Copse Road
Cumnor Hill, Oxford OX2 9JJ, England

British Library Cataloguing in Publication Information Available

Library of Congress Cataloging-in-Publication Data

Stapp, Darby C., 1954–
   Tribal cultural resource management : the full circle to stewardship / by Darby C. Stapp and Michael S. Burney.
      p. cm.—(Heritage resources management series ; v. 4)
   Includes bibliographical references and index.

   1. Indians of North America—Antiquities—Collection and preservation. 2. Cultural property—Protection—United States. 3. Historic preservation—United States. 4. Indians of North America—Politics and government. I. Burney, Michael S. II. Title. III. Series.
   E77.9 .S73 2002
   363.6'9'08997073—dc21   2002003942

Printed in the United States of America

♾ ™The paper used in this publication meets the minimum requirements of American National Standard for Information Sciences—Permanence of Paper for Printed Library Materials, ANSI/NISO Z39.48—1992.

ISBN: 978-0-7591-0105-0

CONTENTS

CONTENTS

FIGURES AND TABLES

Figures

Tables

FIGURES AND TABLES

FOREWORD

Before I begin, the reader should know that I am a member of the Confederated Tribes of the Umatilla Indian Reservation (CTUIR), where I am also the manager of the Tribe's Cultural Resources Protection Program. Over the years we've watched many archaeologists come and go in Indian Country; very few of them stay. This book is the product of years of teaching to and learning from two seasoned white archaeologists who stayed, Michael Burney and Darby Stapp. For fifteen years Michael and I have shared ideas and then figured out ways to implement the best of them. Darby came along later, but in a relatively short amount of time, through torturous meetings and lengthy golf games, I think I know where he stands. After reading this book, I can finally say that we—the tribes—made them realize that there is another way of doing things, that there is a purpose beyond research.

We knew early on that the Indians and the archaeologists were going to have to work together someday to protect cultural resources. We just didn't know how. We always knew it would be a challenge because this was not a popular idea in Indian Country back then. All the archaeologists we knew or knew of were determined to dig up, research, and analyze everything in their path. Collectors and looters were out there, too, and developers were here to stay. Cultural resource management needed to catch up, and the big agencies were looking the other way. It was time for the tribes to take things into their own hands. But we needed help from a few good archaeologists in the non-Native world. In walked Michael. It was 1987.

The Council of Energy Resource Tribes sent Michael to Mission, Oregon, to help us develop a cultural resource program. He saw that a bridge between the worlds of Indians and archaeologists was possible—it just needed to be built. As he began to pull us into his vision, the tribes and their belief system also began to work on Michael. Eventually, the tribes bought off on the vision and pushed me in front to start to pursue the program. Our team was small at first. It included the one person who truly believed in me, Paul "Bucky" Minthorn, then a policy analyst for the Tribe. Bucky knew the cultural resource laws forward and backward and drilled them into me. Every day I would get a lesson. Michael Burney was the other team member. He stayed around and taught me everything he knew about paper, organization, and protocol. I learned my lessons about paper and protocol very well. I've been told that my organizational skills are something to be desired. So, in time, I hired a staff.

We started a cultural resource program that was run by small contracts. Then some larger contracts and a few tribal dollars. Now, in 2002, we are a very large cultural resource program with almost thirty staff members. In *Tribal Cultural Resource Management: The Full Circle to Stewardship*, Darby and Michael say in chapter 6, "Tribal government support is an absolute must. No tribal cultural resource protection program can exist without it. Tribal politics can hinder and even prevent a successful program." This is absolutely correct. People always ask me: "How do you do this, Jeff? How can you work around the tribal politics?" Well, I don't. I have very strict rules to follow. Because of the structure of the CTUIR and a written policy and procedure manual, I can work much more effectively at developing strategies because the tribal policies have already been established.

Many representatives from other tribes don't have the freedom I have. They can't go out and form cultural resource programs and hustle money to support these, so it's a little slower for them than it was for me. The way my tribe is set up makes me look good. I have an infrastructure to work with. The CTUIR had the foresight to set up a system that allows individuals to maximize their abilities in order to maneuver in the outside system.

Let's address the concept "coming full circle." For me, coming full circle means coming together with the ones who were here before, to be one with the spirit and the mind. A couple of generations ago, communication with our ancestors was severed by the U.S. government. In the eighteenth century, the U.S. government policy seemed to be driven toward elimination or termination of American Indian cultures. But in spite of 200 years of assimilation, we managed to keep our belief system alive. To the dismay of the U.S. government and its attempts to outlaw our language, our religion, and our belief system, assimilation didn't work. As we have always said, "We shall live again."

Today, we *are* coming back. We are reconnecting with the ones who were here before through cultural resources management. For Indian people, this work feeds the spiritual part of the body. We understand the knowledge of our past generations, and through those who were here before we know our purpose. Our purpose is to make decisions that will bring us (all of us) better water, better air, and a better way of life. Before the non-Indians took away our responsibility to manage the land and our cultural resources, we were like ecosystem managers. Sometimes I drift back in time and wonder what happened to our people. What law did we break; what did we do wrong? Now, today, I stand proudly in front of federal agencies and tell them what laws *they* have broken and what wrongs they have done. And they have to listen, they have to consult, because it's required by federal law.

Darby and Michael write, "An effective way to exclude Indian people from cultural resource plays on their having no credentials." This is very true. For years we were told we weren't qualified to do our work, so we started to provide training for tribal members that certified them as cultural resource technicians. There wasn't a school to send them to, so we developed our own course and invited Ph.D.'s from universities into the field to teach our young people. This was an annual event for a while; now we teach it on an as-needed basis.

Darby and Michael talked a lot about "action anthropology" and I would say, "Well, what is that?" I wasn't sure what this concept was until I attended and coauthored a paper at the Society for Applied Anthropology in 1998. I found that the anthropologists claiming to be action anthropologists were actually out helping groups, like Indian tribes, meet their needs and goals. I was amazed to find myself interested in the anthropologists who were at the conference there. They were different—not archaeologists—there was no attitude or arrogance that seemed to rub me the wrong way. There was something more pleasing here than at other conferences. I realized that action-oriented anthropology should be one of our goals.

A big mistake made by archaeologists and anthropologists of the past is that they would come to the tribes with a problem and, later, leave with answers that would help them write their report or book or somehow further their career. We sat, watched, and asked, "What's up with that?" Today we are seeing a change. We have been able to influence people like Darby and Michael, who now feel good about themselves because they are helping others make decisions that affect our spiritual places. Those decisions will affect the future of all of us. Archaeologists and anthropologists are starting to come full circle. For years they had learned by excavating our past, reading about our existence, and talking to our elders. Now they are actually working with the tribes to reach common goals, and the tribes are benefiting.

This book may be one of the most important books ever published on the subject of tribal cultural resource management. It certainly is the first one that represents the efforts of two white guys taught by Indians. Here's the way I see it. Two white guys, with graduate degrees, listened and learned and are making a difference. And I have learned a lot from working with these guys, too. We have come together in a unique way to help other people make decisions. We have experimented; now it's time to spread the word. I hope this book creates a new understanding between the Indian people and the archaeological community, one that will affect others in a healing way.

The book teaches that we can work together to protect cultural resources. We need to slow archaeologists down and make them listen—listen not just to us but to those whose lives they are excavating. And in turn, we need to be less judgmental toward the individuals themselves. After all, the basic difference between us is one of worldview.

We have learned to use the white man's system to get where we want to go. Friends like Darby and Michael have assisted us in coming back full circle to place (sacred sites), to our original responsibilities of taking care of the land and our cultural resources. Coming full circle perpetuates a belief system, like bringing breath back into a dying animal. This book will surely be a guide for cultural resource managers and the future of archaeology.

Jeff Van Pelt
Manager
Cultural Resources Protection Program
Confederated Tribes of the Umatilla Indian Reservation
Mission, Oregon

PREFACE

We wrote this book to share our experiences of the past twenty-five years working with federal agencies, Indian tribes, and the cultural resource management profession. During the last fifteen years, we have each served as cultural brokers mediating between two, sometimes vastly different, cultural groups. One of us (MSB) worked with the Confederated Tribes of the Umatilla Indian Reservation in Pendleton, Oregon, helping to protect tribal resources managed by federal agencies, including the Bureau of Indian Affairs, the U.S. Forest Service, and the U.S. Department of Energy at the Hanford Site in southeastern Washington State. The other (DCS) worked with the U.S. Department of Energy at the Hanford Site to assist it in complying with federal regulations that require the protection of the resources within Hanford's boundaries. A great deal of our compliance work involved working with local bands and tribes to clarify and understand their concerns, interests, and expectations.

Over the years, the two of us developed a conflict-based relationship, which helped us understand our respective clients' needs and how best we could help meet those needs. We struggled to understand what needed to be done to protect the resources and what could reasonably be done, given the circumstances at the time. We experimented with ways to get our clients to do what we thought should be done to achieve their goals. Through it all—the heart-thumping highs and the heartwrenching lows—we learned a lot. We learned about bureaucracy, Indians, and how they can work against each other. But we also learned how they can work with one another to protect the resources and the native cultures that depend on their stewardship.

We've written this book to help in the struggle to protect, preserve, and make accessible the cultural resources that are important—no, essential—to native peoples and their ancestral way of life. Really, we've written it for those *in* the struggle: the current and future cultural resource management professionals working for agencies and tribes, tribal members, and others who value the preservation of the resources enough to fight for their conservation and future availability. To all those folks out there, we have but three words of advice: Don't give up!

We have no pretensions of claiming ideas put forth in this book as our own. How could we? For the past fifteen years, we have had countless conversations with tribal elders, tribal archaeological protection employees, State Historic Preservation Office staff, state and federal agency cultural resource management personnel, archaeologists, anthropologists, and the like. Many of these individuals have made contributions toward advancing tribal participation in the field of anthropology and archaeology. So, you see, it would be impossible to try and trace the genesis of any idea or strategy contained herein. Rather, it's a cumulative process of trial and error between these, at times, vastly different groups. To those colleagues and friends who have worked with us, trying to understand the various dimensions of cultural resource management with a tribal twist and the commensurate need for stewardship, we thank you. A Ho!

Darby C. Stapp
Richland, Washington

Michael S. Burney
Taos, New Mexico

Part I

TRACING THE ROOTS OF TRIBAL CULTURAL RESOURCE MANAGEMENT

About one century ago, American society chose to take action to stem the loss of the country's heritage resources. Over the years, the government, communities, archaeologists, American Indians, and others worked to improve the laws and approaches to preserving, protecting, and accessing important resources. By the mid-1970s, these efforts matured to the point where a new profession, commonly referred to today as cultural resource management, appeared.

By many measures, the young field is off to a good start. Public awareness of cultural resources—historic buildings, archaeological sites, historical places, and American Indian sacred sites—is on the rise. People value these resources, which provide ties to their ancestry, contain important information, and teach people about their past, about the past of others, and about the places they live. In many ways, the growing awareness of the importance of cultural resources and the need to manage them has paralleled the increase in environmental awareness, though natural resource management has achieved much greater public awareness to date.

Professional and avocational archaeologists really led the charge to protect archaeological sites and materials for many decades, so it is not surprising that cultural resource management evolved early on to serve professional interests. Recent involvement, however, by descendent communities such as American Indians, African Americans, Asian Americans, and smaller groups within the Euro-American community are challenging cultural resource professionals to rethink some of the field's goals, methods, and decisions. The synergy resulting from the interaction of groups with different perspectives on the value of resources found across the landscape is strengthening the field and improving cultural resource preservation, protection, and access.

1

Our focus is on one large descendent community, American Indians, and the role they have played in the development of cultural resource management. Probably more than any other group, American Indians were impacted by the destruction of their lands and resources as a result of economic development across the nation during the twentieth century. The damming of rivers for irrigation and hydropower destroyed many ancestral areas, as has the growth of urban centers and towns across the country. Even cultural resource professionals, in their quest to salvage sites, have impacted American Indians by collecting the remains of their ancestors for museum collections, excavating sacred places to learn about the past, and failing to value places and resources for the roles these play in contemporary and future Indian culture.

By the late 1960s, this situation had become so dire to American Indians that something had to change. The American Indian political movement was soon underway (Josephy, Nagel, and Johnson 1999). The U.S. government responded with laws, regulations, and executive orders, which required agencies and cultural resource professionals working on federal lands or with federal moneys to involve Indians in the decision-making process. The result of this involvement has been a transformation of the field of cultural resource management.

Through their direct involvement, American Indians have shown that archaeological sites and other components of the cultural landscape—sacred areas, traditional places and resources, and the graves of ancestors—are not merely sources of data about the past, but are holy, sacred, and important parts of their ongoing way of life. This recognition has led many land-managing agencies to adjust their role as cultural resource managers to that of cultural resource stewards. The agencies now give more attention to preserving, protecting, and making cultural resources accessible to those who need them.

We've taken the following approach in writing this book. First, we provide a context for the history of American Indian involvement in cultural resource management, from the beginning to the present day. We feel that such a context will help to provide a common understanding and help us move forward together, rather than apart. Second, we try to capture the gist of Indian perspectives on the sacredness of cultural resources to their way of life; this can help cultural resource professionals and others better understand the importance of the resources to living people.

Third, we share our experiences and perspectives on the challenges of Indians working with agencies and cultural resource professionals to preserve, protect, and make accessible resources important to them. We hope our thoughts will help others working in cultural resource management so that the relationships can continue to grow. If we are to be successful in saving important places and resources for the future, the various constituencies who value these resources will need to unite. Together we can accomplish more than we can separately.

Organization of the Book

We've divided *Tribal Cultural Resource Management: The Full Circle to Stewardship* into three parts. In part I, chapter 1, we define, to the extent possible, tribal cultural resource management and present our approach in writing this book. In the next three chapters, we give context to the development of tribal cultural resource management by tracing the development of archaeology and anthropology as it relates to American Indians. We use these chapters to illustrate the ways that anthropologists and archaeologists have helped—and, in some cases, hindered—tribal efforts to protect places important to them. To conclude part I, we present in chapter 5 a history of the Confederated Tribes of the Umatilla Indian Reservation Cultural Resource Protection Program to illustrate the many points made in previous chapters.

In part II we focus on the present and discuss a number of topics that are important to tribal cultural resource management. Chapter 6 provides ideas and suggestions for starting a cultural resource protection program within a tribal structure. Chapter 7 discusses a key ingredient to working with tribes and agencies: consultation. Chapter 8 presents the cultural landscape concept and the status of this concept within the current cultural resource management structure. Chapter 9 discusses the stewardship concept and the shifts that are needed to transition from management to stewardship.

In part III, chapter 10, we highlight the accomplishments that tribal cultural resource management has made up to now and identify the obstacles and threats that remain.

CHAPTER ONE
DEFINING TRIBAL CULTURAL RESOURCE MANAGEMENT

We have written this book primarily for those in cultural resource management. Our goal is to help non-Indians better understand how American Indians view their important places and remains and to help American Indians better understand how archaeologists look at these places and remains. Archaeology students, tribal technicians, agency officials, university professors, and tribal leaders and managers will all find something here that will help them accomplish their goal of protecting resources.

This is not a cookbook on how to work with tribes, nor is it a sourcebook on the history of tribes and cultural resource management. Rather, we designed the book to cover an immense amount of territory in an easy-to-read format. The intent is to stimulate readers to think about their own experiences and situations and to develop approaches that are appropriate for them.

The reason for this is simple. As we discuss later in this chapter, there is no "Tribal Cultural Resource Management" per se. Every situation differs. You need to adapt to your situation. For example, in part I, we trace the development of ideas and events in the history of cultural resource stewardship as we have seen it develop; you may view the development in your area similarly, or it might have been quite different. We will have been successful if this book causes you to think about such matters in a new light. We also provide examples of how tribes, archaeologists, and agencies have interacted in the past and provide suggestions for working together in the future. We will have been successful if the book gives you either models to follow or ideas on how to improve your own interactions.

In the end, we try to convey in an informal and enjoyable fashion what tribal cultural resource management is all about. If you like the applied anthropology and archaeology of working with non-Indians and Indians, then tribal cultural resource management is for you. In the end, it's not all work, but a tremendous learning experience and, oftentimes, a whole bunch of fun.

We hope the book will also be useful to those outside cultural resource management. There is something in here for anyone working with American Indians in any area—natural resources, fisheries, health, economic development, and so on. The book can provide food for thought for anyone involved in an intercultural situation, especially those involving dominant societies and indigenous peoples.

What Are Cultural Resources and What Is Cultural Resource Management?

Cultural resources are many things to many people. Cultural resources include places that have some historical connection with people, be they old living sites, spiritual places, or economic places. Cultural resources typically include archaeological sites; old buildings; areas noted in oral traditions; places where traditional resources such as foods and medicines were, and are, gathered; and related features such as trails and roads. Some will even argue that natural resources themselves—the water, the salmon, and the plants—are cultural resources that must be protected. Our focus in this book will be more on the former, more restricted, definition, though the underlying spirit of the book—stewardship—certainly argues for narrowing the gulf between cultural and natural resource management.

Cultural resources pertain to all cultures and all time periods. Many professionals are interested in resources related to American Indians, from the earliest peoples of North America to those alive in the present day. Many in the North American cultural resource management field are also interested in cultural resources related to Euro-Americans, Asian Americans, African Americans, and others. Generally, their interest is directed toward resources that are fifty or more years old, but not necessarily so. Cape Canaveral, home of the U.S. space program, is an example of a resource having great historical value to the nation, though less than fifty years old.

A large part of cultural resource management relates to identifying, evaluating, and documenting old buildings and engineered structures such as bridges. These are generally valued for their stylistic attributes, their technological uniqueness, their association with important people, or their

importance to a community or cultural group. This aspect of cultural resource management can, and often does, have relevance to American Indians, but we do not focus on these topics. Our focus is more on archaeological places, traditional use areas, and cultural landscapes.

Cultural resource management calls on society to take an active role
in preserving and protecting cultural resources so that they are not lost
forever. There can be a variety of reasons why people want to preserve,
protect, and access resources, which we will go into in more detail later.
But in all cases, it is because the resources are valued by someone.

Cultural resources must be managed because they are threatened. Primary threats include development, looting, erosion, and inadvertent impact
from recreationists. American Indians have also viewed archaeologists as an
additional threat, who potentially will rob them of their resources.

Cultural resource management involves providing access to resources,
although this is a more recent development than preservation and protection. Access can mean a variety of things, from providing on-site access for
ceremonies, to on-site access to extract resources, to simply providing information about the resources and their meaning. Access issues often pertain to descendant communities, but they are also relevant to the general
public, who may want to visit sites and learn from them. Helping to develop access protocols and information that are appropriate for the public
is also in the purview of cultural resource management.

Who Are the Participants in Cultural Resource Management?

Cultural resource management involves a number of players, both inside
and outside the profession. Inside the profession we see cultural resource
managers who generally work for federal agencies or state or local governments that are responsible for managing the resources on specific lands
or in areas impacted by the organization. Examples include a National
Forest, a Bureau of Land Management Region, a state Transportation
Department, or a local county planning department.

Other professionals serve in a regulatory role, usually for one of the
state or tribal historic preservation offices or the Advisory Council on
Historic Preservation. Sometimes this role is advisory, and other times
they function as part of a regulatory review process.

Many professionals work in the private sector for businesses that bid on cultural resource–related projects and are awarded contracts to do the work. In a practice commonly referred to as "contract archaeology," these firms can work for corporations that conduct ground-disturbing projects on federal land or with federal moneys. They can also work directly for agencies and governments that choose not to do the work in-house. Increasingly, American Indians are managing cultural resources on their reservations as tribal historic preservation officers. Tribal programs often hire cultural resource professionals to do the work, while training tribal members at the same time.

American Indians and other groups that are descended from the people associated with a given set of resources have a specific role to play in cultural resource management. As will be shown in later chapters, the formality of this role is relatively recent. In essence, agencies must consult with descendant communities about the resources being managed so they can understand the threats facing the resources and how the agency intends to manage the resources. In particular, the agency must consult with the community about any activities it is considering that might impact cultural resources. The descendent community has the right to inform the agency about any interests, concerns, or expectations its members have about the activity; the agency is obligated to take this input into consideration when making decisions. American Indians, in some cases, have additional rights because of their unique historical and legal positions.

Certain public and special interest groups, such as historical societies, also have a right to be consulted by an agency that is responsible for managing cultural resources. Any individual or group can indicate to an agency that it has interests in the management of resources under its purview. As long as the request is legitimate, the group should be afforded "Interested Party" status, which will open the door to consultation. The agency must consider the input from tribes, other descendant communities, interested parties, and the public and weigh all input in the context of the importance of the activity to the agency's mission and the general benefits to society.

What Is *Tribal* Cultural Resource Management?

We have titled the book *Tribal Cultural Resource Management*. Where does that expression come from and what does it mean? The term refers to the concept of tribes formally managing cultural resources that are important to them. The concept dates to approximately 1980, when tribes started stressing to agencies how important it was that their sacred natural and cultural resources be protected, not molested. This emphasis on providing protection and conservation of the resources through stewardship stands in sharp contrast to the prevailing concept in cultural resource management, which emphasizes the research value of cultural resources and the primary goal of using cultural resources to learn about the past and the way cultures change.

These differing views have split the cultural resource management field into two fundamentally different camps: academic-influenced cultural resource management and Indian-influenced cultural resource management. Naturally, the term *tribal cultural resource management* became an easy way to refer to cultural resource management that is conducted by, or heavily influenced by, American Indians.

Just as the cultural resource management field was created by federal legislation, so, too, did legislation stimulate tribal involvement and participation. The 1970s set the stage, as the Red Power movement started tribes toward self-governance. When major irrigation and other federal projects began to be planned on, or adjacent to, Indian lands, opportunities arose for tribes to get involved in cultural resource compliance. But nothing quite enabled tribal involvement like legislation and executive orders that required consideration to be given to Indian concerns.

In the 1980s, tribes began to emerge with their own archaeological protection programs (hereinafter, referred to as tribal programs). With additional legislation significant to Indian tribes being passed from approximately the mid-1980s through the 1990s, more tribes became active in archaeological consulting and contracting. Beginning in 1996, there are now more than thirty tribes that have achieved their own Tribal Historic Preservation Offices. These tribes make up the National Association of Tribal Historic Preservation Officers.

A problem with the term *tribal cultural resource management* is the misconception that there is but one tribal perspective. In other words, that all Indian tribes speak with one voice. This is simply not true. To begin with, there are currently 562 federally recognized, sovereign Indian tribes in the United States alone. Besides the federally recognized Indian tribes, some additional tribes are recognized only by states, such as the

Potawatomi in Michigan. In addition, there are bands and tribes recognized by neither the states nor the federal government; the Wanapum Band, residing at Priest Rapids, Washington, is an example.

Each tribe maintains an independent status. Further differentiating tribes is their history of population movement and the differing degrees of acculturation, both of which influence the ways in which cultural resources are viewed and therefore managed. For these reasons, when we use the term *tribal cultural resource management,* we do not mean to imply a singular model for how tribes view cultural resources. There are no formulas for agencies to follow to consult with tribes when attempting to obtain tribal approval for federal undertakings. Rather, we strive to provide some history of how tribes got involved in cultural resource management, some approaches that tribes or agencies have taken to resolve cultural issues, and some ideas on how everyone can work together in the future. We hope you will be stimulated by some of our words to develop strategies for the situations in which you find yourself. Our experiences indicate that when agencies, cultural resource professionals, and tribal representatives choose to work together in an honest and respectful manner, there can be compromise, reconciliation, and mutual satisfaction.

That being said, we can point to some common values that many tribes have expressed over the years. The importance of protecting and preserving the sacred landscape, natural and cultural resources, and human burials for the long term are three values that come to mind. There are similarities in the approaches tribes have taken to managing their cultural resources. Some tribes prefer to keep their cultural resource activities more in-house, thereby retaining greater privacy. Other tribes prefer, initially, to hire non-Indians to begin an archaeological program and maintain it. In the latter case, tribal members are employed as part of the tribal archaeological program, too. Would it be a *tribal* program if they weren't?

Recurring Themes

Several recurring themes arise throughout this book. One is that cultural resource management is more about people than about places and artifacts. While this might seem obvious, we will show that as the profession developed, this concept got lost. At some point archaeologists forgot that sites and places were still important to living peoples. Archaeological sites were the remains of people long gone, and it was the professional's job to bring the lost cultures back to life. Today, we have come to realize that many of the places and resources are ancestral to peoples living today and important for their cultural continuity.

This brings us to our second theme: cultural resource stewardship. In the past, under the research paradigm, if a resource got in the way, it could be mitigated by "data recovery." One could excavate the site, analyze the data, and report the results, and the "problem" was taken care of. Now that we realize that people need these resources for their cultural survival, we must find ways to protect the resources. Instead of solely focusing on what the archaeological record can tell us about the past, we are starting to focus on using our methods and techniques to help sustain these places, thereby benefiting those whose past, present, and future depends on them.

Our final recurring theme is that people who care about cultural resources must be involved if the resources are going to be preserved, protected, and made accessible. One main reason is to combat bureaucratic inertia; agencies and bureaucrats, no matter how well intentioned, perform better when outsiders hold them accountable. But there is another, almost as important, reason for outside involvement: diversity of ideas. Whether one is developing approaches to protect sites or ways to present information to the public, ideas developed in isolation pale in comparison with those developed in cooperation with others. That's a simple fact.

CHAPTER TWO

THE EARLY YEARS: ARCHAEOLOGY AND AMERICAN INDIANS, 1492 to 1960

W e begin this chapter by describing the early years of archaeology, the initial attempts to preserve the archaeological record, the changing status of American Indians, and the role that anthropologists played in working with Indian groups. The time period spans from 1492 to about 1960.

Following a brief introduction to the beginnings of archaeological research in North American, we move on to the efforts by the archaeological community to preserve the archaeological record through excavation, analysis, and reporting. While American Indians often see the focus on salvage archaeology as little more than organized looting, these archaeological pioneers did plant the seeds for respect of the archaeological record and were instrumental in passing legislation that started the nation on the path to a conservation ethic.

We then provide a brief overview of the development of anthropological research on Indian culture. We close the chapter with a summary of how the professional communities involved Indians in the management of resources important to them. We link many key events that occurred between the early 1800s and 1960 in table 2.1.

The Development of a Professional Archaeology

Most, if not all, cultures manage in some fashion those places that are important to them spiritually, economically, and culturally. Modern societies establish laws, while traditional societies tend to establish codes of behavior that dictate access, use, and maintenance. American Indians certainly cared for their sacred places long before the advent of European settlement and continued to do so until they were overwhelmed by the dominant society.

11

Table 2.1 National, Native American, Archaeological, Anthropological, and Cultural Resource Management Events, 1803–1959

Year	National/ International Events	Native American Events	Anthropological Events	Archaeological Events	Cultural Resource Management Events
1803	Louisiana Purchase completed				
1804	Lewis & Clark expedition begins				
1812				American Antiquarian Society formed	
1819		Civilization Act passed			
1821	Hudson's Bay Company and North West Fur Company merge				
1824		Bureau of Indian Affairs (BIA) created			
1828		"Removal Period" begins			
1830		Indian Removal Act passed		Lyell's *Principles of Geology* published	
1831		"Trail of Tears" begins			
1836		Supreme Court upholds treaties			
1838		"Trail of Tears" ends			
1839			Morton's *Crania Americana* published		
1841	Oregon Trail migration begins				
1842			Ethnological Society formed in New York		
1845	Term "Manifest Destiny" coined; Texas annexed				

Year			
1846	Oregon obtained from Great Britain		Smithsonian Institution established
1848	Mexican cession; California Gold Rush begins		Squier and Davis issue *Mounds Report*
1849	U.S. Department of Interior created		BIA moved from War Department to Interior
1851		Reservations become basic Federal Indian policy	Morgan's *League of the Iroqois* published
1856		Navaho resettlement begins	
1859	Darwin's *Origin of Species* published		
1860	Abraham Lincoln elected president		
1861	Civil War begins	Sand Creek Massacre	
1862	Homestead Act passed		
1865	Civil War ends	Reservation schools established under Christian organizations	
1867	U.S. purchases Alaska		John Wesley Powell floats Colorado River
1869	Transcontinental Railroad completed	Board of Indian Commissioners created	
1871		U.S. Congress ends treaty making	
1872	Yellowstone becomes first National Park		
1876		Custer's Last Stand	
1877	Desert Land Act passed	Nez Perce War; Lakotas cede Black Hills	

Table 2.1 National, Native American, Archaeological, Anthropological, and Cultural Resource Management Events, 1803–1959 (Continued)

Year	National/ International Events	Native American Events	Anthropological Events	Archaeological Events	Cultural Resource Management Events
1879			Bureau of American Ethnology established	Archaeological Institute of America founded	
1881		Jackson's *A Century of Dishonor* published			
1882	Buffalo Bill's Wild West Show opens				
1885		Geronimo surrenders			
1886			Cushing report on Pueblo pottery issued		Great Serpent Mound purchased for protection
1887		Indian Allotment Act enacted (Dawes Act)			
1888			*American Anthropologist* first published	Wetherill brothers discover Mesa Verde	
1890		Wounded Knee massacre of 146 Indians			
1895	Henry Ford mass produces automobiles				
1898	Spanish American War begins				
1901			Koeber establishes anthropology department at UC Berkeley		
1902	Newlands Act passes		American Anthropological Association formed		

Year			
1903	Wright Brothers' first flight		
1906			Antiquities Act enacted; Mesa Verde National Park created
1910		Boas establishes anthropology at Columbia University	
1911	Structure of atom discovered		Congress charters Archaeological Institute of America; Machu Pichu discovered in Peru
1912	Titanic sinks		"Piltdown Man" discovered
1914	World War I begins		
1916			National Park Service created
1919	World War I ends	National Research Council forms Anthropology Division	
1920	U.S. women granted right to vote		
1923	American Indian Defense Association founded		
1924	American Indians granted U.S. Citizenship		Kidder publishes *Introduction to Southwestern Archaeology*
1925			Folsom site discovered
1927			First Pecos Conference held
1928	*Meriam Report* released summarizing failures of U.S. Indian policy	Mead's *Coming of Age in Samoa* published	
1929	"Great Depression" begins		
1932			Clovis Site discovered

Table 2.1 National, Native American, Archaeological, Anthropological, and Cultural Resource Management Events, 1803–1959 (Continued)

Year	National/ International Events	Native American Events	Anthropological Events	Archaeological Events	Cultural Resource Management Events
1933	U.S. Prohibition ends				Historic American Building Survey authorized
1934		Indian Reorganization Act enacted		Society for American Archaeology formed	U.S. National Archives created
1935					Historic Sites Act enacted
1940				Stone Age paintings found in France	
1941	Japan attacks Pearl Harbor; U.S. enters World War II		Society for Applied Anthropology formed		
1944		National Congress of American Indians founded			
1945	World War II ends	End of Indian New Deal (1934–1945); Termination Period begins			River Basin Survey Program begins
1947		Collier's *Indians of the America's* published			Reservoir Salvage Act
1948				Taylor publishes *Study of Archaeology*	
1949	China becomes communist	Hoover Commission calls for total assimilation of American Indians		Libby publishes radiocarbon dating method	National Trust for Historic Preservation Chartered
1950	Joe McCarthy begins communist "witch hunt"	Urban Relocation Program begins			Pipeline Salvage Program begins

1954   Report says cigarettes   U.S. House passes
        cause cancer   Termination Resolution
1955   Rosa Parks refuses to give
        up seat on bus in Alabama
1956   Korean War begins   Indian Resettlement and
1958   NASA founded   Indian Termination
                                      Acts enacted

The United States, as a young country, did not come to terms with its need to manage important places until the latter part of the nineteenth century. Occasionally, at the local level, communities and individuals took action to protect places that were especially important to them. For example, a Deerfield, Massachusetts, community in 1846 worked to preserve "Old Indian House," the last remaining Indian structure from the site of a 1704 massacre, but this was an exception, not the typical situation.

Archaeology as a profession developed in a similar manner to other natural and physical sciences in America. To understand why archaeology is as it is today, it is useful to look at this development. In *A History of American Archaeology* (Willey and Sabloff 1993), archaeological curiosity in North American is divided into several periods, described in the following sections.

Speculating about the Origins of Artifacts and Indians (1492–1840)

The first period lasted from 1492 to 1840 and is referred to as the Speculative Period:

> The collection of virtually all the archaeological data uncovered during this period, with a few notable exceptions, was incidental to other pursuits. Archaeology was not established as a vocation or a discipline until well after 1840 and did not even become a popular avocation until the beginning of the 19th century. However, there were mounds and artifacts and a wide variety of antiquities, as well as the Indian population, which could not be ignored, and speculation about all of these was rife. (Willey and Sabloff 1993, 21)

Early interest focused on the mounds of the Ohio and Mississippi, as well as on other oddities that appeared from time to time. Examples included such diverse studies as the origins of the mounds, the relationship of the mounds to present-day Indians, Thomas Jefferson's well-controlled excavation, and excavations in Aztec sites in Mexico.

As noted in the previous quote, Euro-Americans' fascination with Indian culture can be traced to the arrival of Europeans in the New World. This early interest was directed at the origins of the Indian population. Speculations ranged from the Lost Tribes of Israel, the lost continent of Atlantis, Scandinavia, migrations from Asia by boat, and ultimately, Asian migrations over the land bridge (Willey and Sabloff 1993, 25–26).

In 1812, an archaeological enthusiast started the American Antiquarian Society, the first archaeological society formed in America. By 1820, the society was publishing a journal, *Transactions*, in which various discoveries and studies were published. The significance of this society was that it brought together people with an interest in archaeology, whereas before they had generally worked on their own.

The Euro-American fascination with human remains can also be traced back to this period. Thomas Jefferson had encountered numerous graves during his excavation, noting that the mounding process was related to the successive interment of one burial upon another over time. Skeletal analysis also traces its roots to this period. An early physical anthropologist, S. G. Morton, analyzed skulls from ancient mounds, as well as skulls from recently deceased Indians, and learned that both were of the same people. Results were published in Morton's book *Crania Americana*, in 1839.

Classifying and Describing the Archaeological Record (1840–1914)

Archaeological research began in earnest after 1840. From 1840 to 1914, American archaeology was in what has been called a Classificatory-Descriptive Period:

> [T]he principal focus of the new period was on the description of the archaeological materials, especially architecture and monuments, and rudimentary classification of these. Throughout this period, archaeologists struggled to make archaeology into a systematic, scientific discipline. They did not succeed, but they laid the foundations for many of the achievements of the 20th century. (Willey and Sabloff 1993, 42)

Mounds in the Ohio and Mississippi river valleys still piqued the interest of many of these early investigators. Efforts that focused on who the mound-builders were, where they came from, and where they went kept investigators—largely, amateurs—busy. During the early years of this period, archaeology was generally organized at the local level, with local societies being the common organization.

Before long, however, the local amateur gave way to the professional employed at universities and large museums. In this way, archaeology paralleled the other sciences and grew as universities grew across the country. This process of professionalization led to a more organized approach toward the treatment and study of archaeological remains than had existed previously. Two centers of archaeology emerged, the Smithsonian Institution in Washington, D.C., in 1846 and the Peabody Museum at Harvard University in Massachusetts in 1866.

Research during this period focused on a number of areas. The Hopewellian mounds continued to interest archaeologists, as did shell mounds, for which analogues had been found in Europe. The antiquity of humans in the New World stimulated new research, much of which involved human remains. The concept of excavating stratigraphically became commonplace, and artifact analyses began to reveal differences between lower and upper levels of sites, which, of course, were associated with different time periods. Investigators started looking at the stylistic variations of ceramics, stone tools, and manufacturing techniques for more clues about the past.

By the end of this period, an impressive array of research was ongoing at archaeological sites throughout North American and Central America. Expeditions to western North America and elsewhere brought new insights each year. Sites were being found and classified according to the features and artifacts they contained. The spatial distribution of artifact styles was becoming clear, as was the nature of artifacts themselves. The *Bureau of American Ethnology Annual Reports* contained large and impressive descriptions of antiquities, such as never had been seen before. Not surprisingly, prolific archaeologists and physical anthropologists soon emerged as the leaders of the field.

The Concern for Chronology (1914–1940)

Building on the foundation constructed during the previous period, in which there was at least a minimal understanding of artifacts and sites, archaeologists now focused on building cultural chronologies across the continent. This period, formally known as the Classificatory-Historical Period, is described as follows:

> Stratigraphic excavation was the primary method in the drive for chronological control of the data. It was introduced to American Archaeology in about 1914, and in the next two decades, spread to most parts of the New World. . . . Whereas earlier classifications of artifacts had been merely for the purposes of describing the material, they were now seen as devices to aid the plotting of culture forms in time and

space. Besides artifact classifications, American archaeologists also began culture classifications. (Willey and Sabloff 1993, 88)

By digging stratigraphically, whereby the remains of the older cultures were found below those of more recent cultures, archaeologists could focus on the artifacts from discrete time periods and cultures. Then by comparing the types and styles of artifacts found at particular times and particular places, they began to describe the nature and extent of the cultures. Projectile point typologies and ceramic styles and designs were most amenable to these types of efforts. For example, if the distribution of a highly stylized projectile point such as a Folsom could be shown to be throughout the American West in deposits dating from 9,000 to 10,000 years ago, archaeologists could say Folsom people lived in that area at that time.

One of the most well-known chronologies produced in the Southwest in 1927 was the Pecos Classification. Archaeologists working in the Southwest were called together to develop a general scheme and to standardize terminology. The chronology that ultimately emerged was as follows:

- Basketmaker: lacks pottery and intensive agriculture; primitive forms of corn, squash, slab-lined cists; wood and mortar houses in circular depressions; *atlatl*;

- Modified Basketmaker: beans and new type of corn; pit dwellings lined with slabs; gray pottery; bow and arrow;

- Developmental Pueblo: trend toward single-story, multiroom pueblos built of masonry; kivas; black-on-white pottery and corrugated cookware; cranial deformation; cotton fabrics;

- Great Pueblo: multistoried masonry pueblos; elaborate black-on-white pottery and polychrome pottery; mosaic work in turquoise; and

- Regressive Pueblo: large pueblos; elaborate painted wares; lead glaze paint; murals in kivas show new life forms (Kidder 1962, 40).

Many methodological and technological advancements also characterized this period. Identifying the soil stratigraphy required new skills and expertise, and methods to excavate in this way had to be developed. Techniques to refine artifact and style typologies were popular.

Museums were the main employer at that time, with a few major universities also employing archaeologists. The early decades of the twentieth century were the era of large-scale research excavations, modeled after those conducted in the Old World. The classic archaeological expedition would depart with a cadre of students for a summer dig in the Southwest or Midwest and excavate for months. If in the Southwest, as the Yale and Harvard excavations were, local tribal members would supply the labor force required to move the large volumes of dirt.

Reconstructing Culture (1940–1960)

By the 1940s, archaeologists had developed a basic understanding of the chronologies and distributions of archaeological cultures in most areas of North America. Now their efforts turned again to understanding what the sites and artifacts could tell them about the people. Termed the Classificatory Period—the Concern with Context and Function—the period is described by Willey and Sabloff (1993, 132) as focused in three areas:

- Inferring the function of artifacts to gain insight to social and cultural behavior;

- Identifying the settlement pattern to infer relationships with the natural environment and the social and economic environment; and

- Seeking to understand the relationship between culture and the environment, an endeavor that popularly became known as cultural ecology.

Dating methods improved during this period, the most notable being carbon-14 dating, which could provide absolute dates to archaeologists, with reasonable error. Geological dating methods also helped. Other techniques such as aerial photography became available.

This period was marked by many debates over the goals and limitations of archaeology. Cultural anthropologists tended to dismiss the value of archaeology for its limitations to truly recover information about cultures. Archaeologists attacked others as doing nothing but chronicling the past or, at best, writing history—not contributing to a broader under-standing of culture. In the meantime, most archaeologists in North America and Central America were working away, recovering more data, and contributing new information about artifacts, sites, and the past.

Development of Archaeological Stewardship

Archaeologists have a long and varied tradition of working to conserve ar-chaeological sites. Many of these efforts, particularly during the early years, focused on effecting federal legislation. We'll cover just the high-lights of these efforts and refer the reader to Don Fowler's overview of ar-chaeological conservation efforts for a more thorough treatment (Fowler 1986).

By the late 1880s, the young archaeological community began to rec-ognize that the archaeological record was disappearing. America's treas-ures were disappearing at the hands of private collectors, as well as muse-ums seeking to build collections. Working with politicians, archaeologists began a tradition of lobbying for legislation to protect archaeological in-terests. The result in 1906 was the American Antiquities Act, signed into law by President Theodore Roosevelt. This act required people to obtain permits to conduct archaeological investigations on federal lands, estab-lished penalties for those diggers caught without a permit, and gave the president the authority to establish National Monuments in areas that possessed archaeological, historical, and natural values.

Considerable archaeological work was undertaken during the Depres-sion, as government funding for public works projects found its way into archaeologists' hands. One piece of legislation that Congress did pass at this time was the Historic Sites Act of 1935. This legislation authorized the National Park Service to record and document important places in the nation's history. It also enabled the Park Service to purchase and interpret properties. Places important to American history were the focus, but so were American Indian–related properties, confirming that they, too, were considered part of "American history."

New questions energized the field and brought on a whole new era of growth, stimulated by Depression-era funding through the Civilian Conservation Corps, Works Progress Administration, and the Tennessee Valley Authority (McManamon and Wendorf 2000). Several leading archaeologists of the time had recognized that the nation was about to embark on a massive program of building hydroelectric dams and reservoirs. Knowing that these projects would destroy prime archaeological sites, which were typically found in the major river valleys to be dammed—virtually all of which had never been investigated archaeologically—these leaders again worked with their political friends to pass new legislation requiring surveys and excavations prior to construction. This legislation, known as the Reservoir Salvage Act of 1960, was eventually passed.

The Inter-Agency Archaeological and Paleontological Salvage Program was created in 1945, along with the Smithsonian Institution River Basin Surveys that ended in 1969 (Jennings 1985; Snyder, Hull-Walski, Thiessen, and Giesen 2000). Two notable examples of this time are the Missouri River Basin Survey (Latham 2002) and the Columbia Basin Survey (Sprague 1973). These efforts to save or "salvage" archaeological information prior to reservoir construction—and after 1956, highway salvage archaeology—made up the most important federally funded involvement with archaeology until the mid-1970s (McGimsey 1998, 20).

In addition to reservoir work, the 1950s saw the emergence of energy-funded archaeological work. Considered the direct forebear of cultural resource management, the San Juan Project proposed in the mid-1950s consisted of a series of gas pipelines across northern New Mexico, Arizona, and California, including the Navajo Indian Reservation. Due to efforts by Dr. Jesse Nusbaum, the Navajo Nation tribal chairman, and the El Paso Natural Gas Company, funding was provided for an archaeological inventory. Fred Wendorf, who was experienced working with Nusbaum on the San Juan Project (see further on), followed suit, introducing highway salvage archaeology in 1954 in New Mexico (McGimsey 1998). In addition to reservoir and pipeline salvage archaeology there was highway salvage archeology, emergency archaeology, and rescue archaeology (McManamon and Wendorf 2000).

Anthropological Interest in American Indians

Interest in American Indians parallels the interest in archaeological remains reviewed earlier. From the first contact, Europeans speculated on the origins of these new people they encountered. Before anthropology emerged as a formal discipline in North America, one man, Lewis Henry Morgan, was working closely with Indians in New York State. His *League of the Iroquois* (Morgan 1851) was one of the first ethnographies of non-Western people ever produced. His fieldwork contributed as well to his later works on kinship systems and cultural evolution.

In 1879, John Wesley Powell, the geographer who had explored the Colorado River in the early 1870s, began the Bureau of American Ethnology at the Smithsonian Institution. Powell's goal was to produce ethnographies and collect linguistic data before the Indian disappeared. Most anthropological work at this time was sponsored by museums. University anthropology would not become a major force for decades.

And finally, there were anthropologists who occasionally helped implement government policies directed at solving the "Indian problem." An example was Alice Fletcher, who worked with the Nez Perce and Omaha tribes to distribute lands under the Dawes Act (Mark 1988).

Franz Boas, a German anthropologist, accepted a position with Columbia University in 1896, where over the next few decades he would gain a reputation as the Father of American Anthropology. Boas is often credited with the four fields approach to the study of culture: ethnography, archaeology, linguistics, and physical anthropology. He also believed strongly in good fieldwork. Over the next two decades, Boas trained a large number of students, most of whom were sent out to Indian communities across the continent to document Indian culture. As these students moved on to their own university positions, they promoted the Boasian agenda for yet another generation. Much of this agenda focused on American Indians, and during this era, graduate students and young professors published hundreds of ethnographies and thousands of research studies on American Indian culture.

Since the 1800s, the tribes not targeted for extermination had been subjected to government agents, teachers, and missionaries on a campaign to eradicate all traces of Indian culture, including traditional economics, language, social structure, law, and religious beliefs. Indian people were instructed that they must become completely acculturated to the non-Indian way of life if they had any hopes of surviving and prospering under their newly experienced domination.

In addition to research, a small number of anthropologically trained individuals worked with a movement that focused on protecting the treaty

Anthropology's Debt to American Indians

American Anthropology owes a special debt to American Indians, who have served as the object of study since its inception. This point was summarized well over forty years ago by Irving Hallowell, a noted social scientist of his day.

It seems to me that among the more recent influences, the impact of the Indian on modern anthropology should not be omitted. The social sciences as they have developed in the United States during the past half-century have attained an unusual prominence in American culture. Among these[,] anthropology in its modern form was just getting underway about the time the frontier closed. It was in the 1890s that Franz Boas began to teach at Columbia University and to train students in fieldwork. Boas was a specialist in studies of the American Indian and a majority of his early students followed in his footsteps. Indeed, practically all the chief authorities on North American Indian ethnology, archaeology, and linguistics have been American. A historical accident? Of course, but that's the point. It is only recently among the younger generation that more attention is being devoted to people in the South Seas, Africa, and Asia. But it was the study of the Indians, and the problems that emerged from the investigation of the Indian as a subject, that gave American Anthropology a distinctive coloring as compared with British, French, and German Anthropology. (Hallowell 1957, 254–55, quoted in Medicine 2001, 331)

rights of Indian people, as well as on their simple right to exist and maintain their culture. Oliver LaFarge, for example, a writer trained in anthropology at Harvard, joined the Board of Directors of the Eastern Association on Indian Affairs (later called the National Association on Indian Affairs) in the 1920s; other members included prominent anthropologists and archaeologists. One of these directors, Herbert Spinden, explained the organization:

Our work began with the land-grabbing Bursum Bill [a 1922 bill that would validate non-Indian claims to Indian lands], then it passed to the trachoma situation [a rampant eye infection that caused blindness] and to other problems of health and economy confronting the surviving first families of America. The pressing business in each case was to obtain and spread knowledge of the situation, accurate knowledge, to persons who could help. (McNickle 1971, 77–78)

A similar organization, the American Indian Defense Association, formed in 1923 and was led for many years by John Collier. Although not an anthropologist by training, Collier gained a good understanding of Indian culture by working with the New Mexico pueblo groups. It was John Collier whom President Franklin D. Roosevelt appointed to run the Bureau of Indian Affairs in 1933. Collier revamped the Bureau and brought in anthropologists to assist in designing and implementing programs to benefit tribes. He also was the architect of the Indian Reorganization Act of 1934, although the Act in its final form differed significantly from what Collier wanted. In any event, the road to assimilation was slowed as the result of people such as Oliver LaFarge and John Collier, who joined organizations composed of people who believed that American Indians had a right to exist—exist, that is, as American Indians.

Applied anthropology has its U.S. origins in New Deal humanitarian liberalism and progressive industrial management ideology:

> The field of applied anthropology got its start in the United States during the Collier administration. Although Collier was the first Indian Commissioner to go out and meet with Indian people in the field to hear their grievances and wishes, he and his staff designed the program to respond to them, and anthropologists were hired to help tribes make use of its benefits. (Lurie 1999, 110)

Collier created an applied anthropology unit of three anthropologists, "charged with the duty of making studies of the existing political, and power, and traditional structure on the reservations, with the idea that the information thus obtained would be helpful in designating the form of government that they would set up under the procedures called for in the Indian Reorganization Act of 1934" (Nash 1973, 25).

These "New Deal anthropologists" were funded by, and responsible to, the federal government, not tribes. Outcomes of the Indian Reorganization Act certainly reflect this fact. But these anthropologists were among the many scholars and intellectuals that Collier—and Roosevelt, more generally—brought out of the academy and into the more "applied" settings of the New Deal. Collier's concept of orienting anthropology toward the goals of what he thought were progressive reforms to strengthen self-determining communities was precedent-setting.

In addition to Collier's work in the Bureau of Indian Affairs, there were other applied programs between about 1936 and 1946 with the Technical Cooperation-Bureau of Indian Affairs and the Soil Conservation

Service. Some 70 to 80 studies were undertaken of the Middle West, the Southwest, the Dakotas, the Northwest, and the Navajo Reservation, "to be the basis for administrative decisions, administrative organization of soil conservation programs, and other aspects of the behavioral sciences" (Nash 1973, 26). Behavioral science, undertaken between 1942 and 1946, resulted in five tribal studies pertaining to the Papago (today the Tohono O'odham), Zuni, Hopi, Sioux, and Navajo.

Another stimulus to anthropological work was the Indian Claims Commission, a tribunal created by Congress in 1946 (AILTP 1988). Through this forum, tribes were able to make monetary claims for the loss of tribal lands related to non-Indian western expansion. For the next few decades, the government and tribes hired anthropologists primarily to determine the nature and extent of tribal activities as part of the claim process (Barney 1974). These efforts resulted in an extensive amount of research on many tribes by anthropologists, archaeologists, and historians (Manners 1974).

American Indian Involvement in Archaeological and Anthropological Efforts

There are many examples of Indian involvement in archaeological and anthropological efforts. Indeed, most ethnographic and linguistic efforts required some degree of involvement because the data had to come from the people themselves. There was cooperation by Indians, but the significance of this cooperation is not well understood. Were these individuals working alone? Did they have tribal support? Was there debate within the tribe about whether such information should be shared? We simply do not know much about this area, except to say that for whatever reason, anthropologists have a long tradition of establishing relationships with individuals who serve as consultants. While there are well-documented cases of anthropologists being tricked, this appears to be the exception, not the rule; though, undoubtedly, informants did not reveal all their knowledge to anthropologists. American Indians, like many others, have knowledge that should not pass beyond the family, the community, or the group.

Archaeologists and physical anthropologists had an easier time collecting their data; they just went and got it—at least, prior to the 1960s. If there was Indian involvement, it generally came in the form of paid labor. This was especially true during the early years, when large-scale excavations were the norm. Indian labor could be procured for low prices.

A well-known, if unique, example of cooperation is Ishi, the Californian Indian who appeared out of nowhere, near starvation, in 1911. Alfred Kroeber, a Boas student teaching at Berkeley, brought Ishi to the University museum where he lived for several years, sharing knowledge about his people, his toolmaking, and his language (Kroeber 1964).

A more direct form of involvement emerged in the case of reservoir work, when native cemeteries were relocated. In this case, assuming the people felt that the interred were better off being moved than flooded out, they cooperated with agencies and archaeologists to locate the cemeteries and, in some cases, provided tribal members to remove their relatives.

Although these grave-removal projects were conducted in cooperation with tribes, these examples are dwarfed by the hundreds of cases where burials were removed without the knowledge and consent of local Indian people. These cases are well documented, and there is no need to review them here. Archaeologists have long considered human remains archaeological data, and many still do (Echo-Hawk and Echo-Hawk 1994; Mihesuah 2000; Sprague 1993).

While it is important to view the work of people in the context of their times, to understand why American Indians view anthropologists and archaeologists as they do, one needs to read books such as the *Mismeasure of Man* (Gould 1996) and *Skull Wars* (Thomas 2000). For an in-depth understanding of a specific case, one can read *Give Me My Father's Body* (Harper 1986), the story of the little Eskimo boy who was brought to New York from Greenland to be studied by the American Museum of Natural History. The recent disclosure that Ishi's brain was removed against his wishes and kept at the Smithsonian for eighty years simply says something about the way scientists in the Western tradition are; they cannot change in a few generations. Whether these individuals were wrong or just living in the context of their times, their actions simply make it hard for Indians and anthropologists and archaeologists to work together, especially when manifestations of these early behaviors continue today (Downey 2000). As long as people believe the quest for knowledge supersedes indigenous peoples' (or anyone's, for that matter) right to control and manage their resources, we will have problems working together.

While we can cite many examples of American Indians cooperating with archaeologists and anthropologists, this has occurred primarily along a one-way street. Cooperation almost always occurred to help the professionals meet their goals. How many times did the professionals knock on the door, asking what could they do to help Indians improve their condition? Not often.

We should note in closing that there have been American Indians in both archaeology and anthropology, Arthur C. Parker (Thomas 1955), Francis LaFlesche (Green 1969), Robert K. Thomas (Pavlik 1998), and Bea Medicine (Medicine 2001) being four notable examples. Behind these men and women are many examples of indigenous people who have crossed, straddled, and leaned upon the fence between the professional and native worlds—not always a very comfortable place to be.

CHAPTER THREE
ARCHAEOLOGY, ANTHROPOLOGY, AND AMERICAN INDIANS, 1960 TO 1980

Indian involvement in managing cultural resources started changing in Indian Country in the 1960s. In fact, many things started to change in America in the 1960s. The nation was torn apart by the Vietnam War, the Civil Rights Act passed, race riots shook the country, and environmental quality suddenly emerged as an issue. Anthropologists and archaeologists underwent a revolution, along with other social scientists, changing their focus to questions of how and why things happened instead of when and where they happened. Indian rights activists were demonstrating across the nation, and the public became more aware of American Indian issues. Key events during this period are identified in table 3.1.

The Archaeological Community in the 1960 and 1970s

The 1960s and 1970s were real boom times for archaeologists. At the start of this period, universities were hiring, and it was common for graduate students to be hired for tenure-track positions before their dissertations were even completed. This generation of archaeologists and anthropologists had little experience outside academia. True, many had participated in River Basin surveys and excavations, but the focus was salvage archaeology, recovering data to learn about the past.

Through more legislation, a new market opened for anthropologists who were trained in archaeology: cultural resource management. In some respects this was an evolution of the salvage archaeology market described in the last chapter; there was, however, a significant difference. Whereas the salvage archaeology operated out of a centralized Washington, D.C., office (Interagency Archaeological Services and its various predecessors

Table 3.1   National, Native American, Archaeological, Anthropological, and Cultural Resource Management Events, 1960–1979

Year	National/ International Events	Native American Events	Anthropological Events	Archaeological Events	Cultural Resource Management Events
1960	President Kennedy elected	American Indian Chicago Conference held			Reservoir Salvage Act enacted
1961	Berlin Wall built				
1962	Carson's *Silent Spring* published; Cuban Missile Crisis occurs				
1963	President Kennedy assassinated				
1964	U.S. involvement in Vietnam escalates; Civil Rights Act enacted				
1965		Termination Era ends; Self-Determination Era begins			Land & Water Conservation Fund Act enacted
1966					National Historic Preservation Act enacted
1967			Vine Deloria attacks anthropology		Office of Archaeology and Historic Preservation created within National Park Service
1968	Martin Luther King assassinated	American Indian Movement founded	American Anthropological Association issues Ethics Statement	Binfords publish *New Perspectives in Archaeology*	
1969	Man lands on moon	Alcatraz occupied			
1970	Kent State students shot during war protest				National Environmental Policy Act enacted

Year				
1971		Brown's *Bury My Heart at Wounded Knee* published		Nixon issues Executive Order 11593
1972	Watergate scandal begins	Bureau of Indian Affairs Building occupied		
1973	Abortion legalized in U.S.	Wounded Knee takeover		Archaeological and Historic Preservation Act (Moss-Bennett) enacted
1974	President Nixon resigns	Columbia River Intertribal Fish Commission started	Lipe publishes Conservation Archaeology article	
1975	Microsoft started	Indian Self-Determination and Education Act enacted; Pine Ridge occupation begins		
1976		Indian Health Care Improvement Act enacted		American Folklife Preservation Act and Federal Land Management Policy Act enacted
1977				The *Airlie House Report* published
1978		American Indian Religious Freedom Act enacted	American Museum Association passes resolution on Human Remains; Margaret Mead passes	
1979	Iran takes American hostages			Archaeological Resources Protection Act enacted; 106 Regulations issued

33

and successors), the new cultural resource management responsibilities fell squarely on the shoulders of the various agency field offices. This is an important point. As we explain further in chapter 9, one of the principles of stewardship is that it be managed at the administrative level where the resources reside.

This section begins with the changes that were occurring in academic archaeology, followed by the emergence of tribes into the management of cultural resources.

A "New" Direction for Academic Archaeology

Archaeology in the 1960s underwent a revolution of sorts, similar to that in the other social sciences. The concern was no longer chronology, function, or the spatial distribution of styles. Rather, archaeology now stressed the search for cultural process. Questions concerning the definition and distribution of artifact styles, the cultures that settled a region over time, and the lifeways as indicated by archaeological remains were no longer in vogue. Now the interest was on how and why things happened in the past: How did humans respond (or adapt) to population increase, to environmental change, to technological innovation?

The "New Archaeology" created much turmoil in academic archaeology, dividing the profession along "new" and "old" lines. New questions to be answered and new approaches to excavating and analyzing data led to a wholesale discounting of prior work, requiring a whole new surge in excavations across the land and a widespread disregard for the value of previously made collections that sat on shelves in archaeology departments and museums across the country. Furthermore, the shift from the old to the New Archaeology (and anthropology) meant that the new research had even less direct relevance to American Indians.

For example, Lewis Binford, widely recognized as the father of the New Archaeology, identified the following "big" questions he saw as most important for archaeology to pursue (Binford 1983, 26–30):

- What were the behavioral characteristics of our earliest ancestor? When did the *typical* behavior—language, living in small monogamous families, food sharing—that separates us from other animals come into being and how can we understand its development?

- What are the origins of agriculture and what were the conditions that led man to settle down and start producing food within smaller and smaller pieces of space? Why did it happen in different parts of the world, all within a fairly narrow time period (2,000 years)?

- What are the origins of civilization? What made agriculturally based societies become increasingly complicated, politically and bureaucratically? What caused the tremendous increase in specialization—in crafts, in social roles—that characterizes ancient and modern cities?

The New Archaeology was not simply pursuit of these new questions, but a fundamental shift in the value of archaeology and methodological approach. The purpose of archaeology—at least, for the New Archaeologists—was to discover laws of human behavior. Presumably, though they rarely explained how, such laws *would* be useful to those of us living today and into the future. Concerning method, the New Archaeologists focused on the hypothetico-deductive form of reasoning: formulate the hypothesis, deduce some prediction that can be observed, then perform the observation to see if the prediction is true or false. If true, the hypothesis is confirmed; if not, it is disconfirmed (Salmon 1982, 34).

To illustrate confirmation, consider the following attempt to support the hypothesis: "A prolonged drought in years prior to the abandonment of Grasshopper Pueblo caused its abandonment." One deductive implication of the hypothesis is the statement "There was a prolonged drought at Grasshopper in the years prior to abandonment." While this period of drought is not directly observable, its indicators, such as tree ring data, are so reliable that the presence of drought may be counted as an observable prediction; and in fact, the indicators show that the drought occurred. It is quite obvious, however, that only limited support is given to the causal hypothesis, for though we may confidently assert the existence of the drought, what is at issue is whether or not the drought *caused* abandonment. It could not have caused abandonment if it did not occur, but its occurrence may have been only incidentally, and not causally, related to abandonment. Thus the claim that abandonment was caused by drought is not strongly supported by the evidence that there was a drought. (Salmon 1982, 34)

This approach stood in marked contrast to that used in prior periods, when researchers derived conclusions based on the data they recovered from archaeological sites. Interestingly, the New Archaeology brought many archaeologists to the reservation. If the questions of the New Archaeology had made archaeology less relevant to American Indians, the archaeologists' search to understand the nature of archaeological remains brought them somewhat closer. As Binford explained:

> We need sites that preserve for us things from the past; but, equally, we need the theoretical tools to give meaning to these things when they are found. . . . if we intend to investigate the relationship between statics and dynamics, we must be able to observe both aspects simultaneously; and the only place we *can* observe dynamics is in the modern world, in the here and now. . . . I myself have worked on this linkage problem with the Nunamiut, a group of Eskimo caribou hunters in Alaska, and with the Navaho, who are sheep herders in the American Southwest; and I have several students working with the !Kung Bushmen in southern Africa. All these pieces of fieldwork are designed to study in a direct way the linkages between the things we find as archaeologists and the various behaviors that resulted in the production, modification and eventual disposal of those things. (Binford 1983, 23–24)

Thus, the 1960s and 1970s brought a new group of anthropologists—this group trained in archaeology—to the reservations, seeking information about how Indians made things, how they structured their activities, how they disposed of things, and so on. Some were watching to see how Indian activities resulted in artifacts on the landscape, while others were learning how to make things such as pottery so they could do "experimental archaeology." All of these activities continued to have one thing in common, the archaeologists were seeking information from the natives so that they (the archaeologists) could try to answer questions that they (the archaeologists) thought useful. Few ever thought to ask the natives what questions they might have for the archaeological record or how archaeological tools and knowledge could be used to help the Indian. We've belabored the points about the New Archaeologists primarily because many of the archaeologists who would move into cultural resource management have been heavily influenced by the New Archaeology movement. Such influence affected the way they would interpret their responsibilities to the resources; archaeological sites were data banks needing to be exploited for information and preserved for future investigations.

The Emergence of Cultural Resource Management

As discussed in the last chapter, during the 1940s and 1950s salvage archaeology developed at a centralized level in Washington, D.C. In the next few decades, salvage archaeology evolved into cultural resource management, sometimes called *compliance* archaeology. It also became decentralized. Whereas previously archaeology operated out of the Washington offices of the National Park Service, increasingly archaeology operated out of the lower levels of different federal agencies. In the Forest Service, forests took on the responsibility; in the Bureau of Land Management, districts took on the responsibility; and so on.

As with the prior period, the catalyst was federal legislation. Four events stand out. The National Historic Preservation Act of 1966 created the National Register of Historic Places and initiated a system for reviewing federal projects that to this day is the foundation of cultural resource management. The National Environmental Policy Act of 1969 also created a system where impact to the environment, including the cultural environment, had to be considered in deciding whether a project should be conducted. Executive Order 11593 in 1973 called for federal agencies to inventory their lands for cultural and historical sites. And the Archaeological and Historic Preservation Act of 1974, known also as the Moss-Bennett Bill, added additional fuel by authorizing federal undertakings to commit up to 1 percent of project costs for mitigating archaeological remains.

In response to these actions, by the mid-1970s new markets opened for archaeologists just as the academic market was starting to close. Federal agencies such as the U.S. Forest Service and the Bureau of Land Management started hiring large numbers of archaeologists to inventory their lands and evaluate sites. Even smaller agencies had the need. The Bureau of Reclamation, for example, hired its first archaeologist in 1974. Some agencies hired archaeologists as employees, others as contractors. Most contractors at this time came from universities, as the volume of work had yet to create the need for private contracting firms.

Conducting surveys for archaeological sites was something the current generation of archaeologists was relatively well trained for, at least when it came to prehistoric resources. Attention to historic sites lagged, and attention to places important to living peoples, such as American Indians, was never really considered until later. Research focused on sampling strategies, predictive modeling, and developing settlement patterns to understand how the prehistoric peoples had lived. Site forms evolved over the years, but the focus was always the same—documenting what was there, not the condition of the resource (except in a very cursory way).

The archaeologists hired by federal agencies to manage the resources were especially challenged. Cultural resource stewardship was a new business, much different from the archaeological research for which most had been trained. Setting up site files, working with agency personnel to review projects and find ways to avoid various types of impact, evaluating sites for National Register eligibility, setting up facility databases, protecting sites, working with the public—these were all new roles for an archaeologist trained to elicit information about the past.

Conservation Archaeology

About this same time conservation archaeology—the conservation and preservation of prehistoric and historic resources—generated interest. Building on a long, if minor, tradition of conservation-thinking archaeologists (Fowler 1986), Bill Lipe's paper entitled "A Conservation Model for American Archaeology" (1974) led many to think about the need to conserve archaeological sites, not just exploit them for insights about the past or about cultural processes. Lipe's fundamental point was, if archaeology and society did not

Personal Reflections on CRM: Part I

For those having participated in the last thirty years of cultural resource management (CRM), the following comments sent to us by Evan DeBloois, former Federal Preservation Officer for the U.S. Forest Service and now the Utah NAGPRA coordinator, will ring familiar.

Having spent over thirty years doing archaeology, salvage archaeology, cultural resource management, and heritage resource management for the second-largest land-management agency in the nation, I have witnessed much of the evolution of what is called cultural resource management. Although that evolution varies somewhat depending on where one was sitting during the process, it is clearly a many-headed beast. I was hired by the Forest Service in 1970 to initiate an "archaeology" program for the Intermountain Region. The direction and focus was academic in nature—identify important archae-

(Continued)
ological resources and prescribe a program to protect, preserve and interpret them. In 1970 NHPA Section 106 had not been translated into regulations, historic sites and traditional cultural properties were not yet of agency concern, and project [impact] on prehistoric sites did not set the priorities. We focused on the biggest and the best, inventoried areas where we expected to find lots of sites, and developed research driven projects that were designed to generate scientific data about prehistoric resources.

After a few years of this approach, 36 CFR 800 appeared for the first time and agency priorities began to shift. Historic properties assumed a high priority position and prehistoric archaeologists began to grapple with not just historical archaeology, but historic architecture. In general, this did not result in the hiring of historically trained specialists, but added new responsibilities to existing employees. Projects and their potential [impact] began to dominate other types of archaeology. "Cultural resource management" began to be the descriptor of choice for this focus, replacing "salvage archaeology." Management direction was to carry out a program that met minimal legal sufficiency. Devoting resources to doing "academic" research or research that did not contribute directly to "project clearance" was inappropriate and for many years, unacceptable. Any request for funding that was not directly related to project clearance was rejected during the budget process. Changes in the program are usually driven by legal challenges, not resource needs. Lawsuits captured management attention and frequently resulted in program modification when reason and research could not. Train wrecks brought reforms when reports of unsafe conditions did not.

change the way they did business, before long there would be no more archaeological sites for archaeologists to study, for the public to enjoy, or for American Indians to maintain as part of their cultural tradition.

Not all archaeologists would support the conservation ethic; some archaeologists reacted with fear and anger. Clearly, the study of prehistory and history without excavations was considered detrimental to archaeology as a scientific discipline, just as relinquishing possession of human remains without undertaking rigorous study was sacrilegious and detrimental to biological anthropological science.

Although a segment of disgruntled archaeologists emerged, for the most part, the conservation message resonated with many. Archaeologists working for agencies as cultural resource managers now had a new agenda under which they could explain their purpose. University archaeologists had a new "hot topic" with which they could make a name. The National Park Service could use the new agenda to reinvigorate its work. And the Society for American Archaeology could answer the call and gather prominent archaeologists together to move the concept forward.

Contract Archaeology

Demand for archaeologists increased again with the energy crisis of the latter 1970s and early 1980s. Agencies—particularly in the West, where energy resources predominate—were faced with hundreds of requests for drilling permits to explore for oil, mine coal, and extract other resources. Each permit needed a cultural resource investigation, meaning an archaeologist had to conduct background research; inventory the proposed area to be impacted, including access roads to be constructed; and propose recommendations for any archaeological materials threatened by the projects. Where large areas were to be mined or new dams constructed, substantial work would be required.

Federal agencies, attempting to comply with historic preservation legislation, began administering to "compliance archaeology," employing Class I Overview (summaries of site records and literature), Class II (sample) inventories, Class III (100 percent) inventories, testing for National Register of Historic Places eligibility, and mitigation or data recovery programs. The emphasis was on the preservation of data through systematic inventories and careful and precise excavations, not on the preservation of sites.

This is not surprising. Excavating had always been the trademark of archaeology. Recovering, analyzing, and publicizing human remains had always been part of, almost a symbol of, archaeology. If archaeologists weren't looking for sites to dig, or digging a site, what would they do? Consequently, archaeological sites were vigorously excavated whenever the situation—that is, "mitigation"—allowed. The logic was simple: By archaeologists recording and excavating sites, these would be "preserved." And preserved they were. State Historic Preservation Office libraries received technical reports weekly, and today thousands can be found in each library.

Eventually, agencies were unable to meet the demand in-house and contracted for archaeological services. By this time, even universities were swamped with work and could not meet the demand. Soon emerged the archaeological contracting firm, mostly small firms owned and managed by archaeologists.

State and federal agencies were ill-prepared to deal with the rapid increase in archaeological work. Suddenly, variations in cultural resource forms and report preparation standards became obvious, as did inventory, testing, and mitigation standards. Agencies tried to standardize methods and reporting; the attempt met with varying degrees of success.

By the late 1970s, archaeology had evolved into a new form. Terms varied from cultural resource management, to archaeological resources management, contract archaeology, and others. Research-oriented archaeology continued in the universities, but the new form of archaeology became the primary source of funding for graduate students and jobs for degreed individuals (Green and Doershuk 1998, 124; Knudson 1986). Whereas university research and teaching positions had been the primary employers for archaeology students in the past, now federal and state agency positions and private sector contracting firms provided opportunities for graduate students and those just completing their degrees.

The big business of "contract archaeology," or "client-oriented archaeology," expanded into a multimillion-dollar-a-year industry. It was reported in the late 1980s that "Well over $300 million . . . is spent on archaeology in the United States" (King 1987). Hester (1996, 70) reported that compliance-related archaeological investigations numbered 55,000 annually at a cost of some $50 million. Characterizing the archaeological contracting industry, Meighan (1986) published *Archaeology for Money*. There was money if you were quick enough to make it, and smart enough to keep it. The window of financial and experiential opportunity was not open long, however, and it was never open to tribes, not even a crack.

The Anthropological Community in the 1960s and 1970s

The anthropological community witnessed a number of similar changes during the 1960s and 1970s. Perhaps most relevant for us was the reemergence of applied anthropology, defined "as the utilization of anthropological theory and methods, especially those of socio-cultural anthropology, to achieve practical ends" (Winthrop 1991, 16). Many anthropologists were attracted to the idea that they could apply their knowledge and skills to real-life situations.

Applied anthropology had been heavily affected by World War II and the subsequent Cold War. Global conflicts had created a demand for people who understood and could work with peoples in countries under siege by the world powers. Anthropologists helped meet this demand, with training that was well suited to the government's needs. The orientation, however, to use knowledge about a people for the government's needs, not the people's needs, was a divergence for the profession. Over time, influenced by the action anthropologists and others, applied anthropology moved back toward the community-based studies for which anthropologists had been known before the war. Such studies accelerated with passage of the National Environmental Policy Act, which stimulated more work in the form of social impact assessments, work for which applied anthropologists were well suited.

Sol Tax and his action anthropology were an important influence on the development of applied anthropology during this period. Tax and his students and colleagues developed the action concept by working with a variety of cultural groups, but mostly with American Indians, and most notably with the Fox (Gearing 1960, 1970). In this regard, Tax was building an anthropological tradition of helping Indian communities, not just studying them.

Tax's development of action anthropology was an important step forward for anthropology's involvement with disenfranchised cultural groups. For Tax, the action anthropologist was a facilitator to a cultural group, perhaps helping the group identify the problems from its own perspective; anthropologists would then help develop solutions that made sense to the tribal members. For example, the anthropologist might provide technical expertise, share ideas for solutions, or help find financial resources for the group. The role was more like that of a consultant, rather than the more typical role of the anthropologist as principal investigator, designing the research and implementation on his or her own.

Sol Tax's help in organizing the 1961 American Indian Chicago Conference is a prime example. In 1960, tribes were under assault, termination and urban relocation being the current strategies deployed by the government to assimilate Indians into the mainstream culture.

Tax, well aware of these problems and a lack of Indian unity in coping with them, came to Denver [to the National Congress of American Indians annual meeting] with an offer to coordinate an all-Indian gathering that he called the "American Indian Charter Convention." The idea was to review Indian affairs since the Merriam Report [A 1928 report on the abominable conditions on reservations and a call for a complete overhaul of the Bureau of Indian Affairs and of national Indian policy (Meriam 1928)] and see if Indian people could agree on a document setting forth their recommendations as a policy guide to the incoming presidential administration. He based his proposal on his concept of action anthropology, enabling disaffected and distressed groups to take charge of their own destinies in their own way. (Lurie 1999, 109–110)

The meeting occurred in Chicago in June 1961, attended by more than 500 people, representing at least 90 tribes. In commenting on one impact of the meeting, Nancy Lurie, an assistant to Tax, said:

Ironically, while the American Indian Chicago Conference was the largest and most representative gathering of Indian people to that date and had far reaching and lasting effects, some younger activists have not even heard of it. In a way, this is a gauge of its success. Ideas taken for granted today in Indian country were discussed and debated in 1961 in an atmosphere of distrust, the result of the divisive effects of the Indian policy of the 1950s. Once Indian people from across the country began to communicate with each other, they discovered they shared deeply held values as a basis for further action. (Lurie 1999, 108)

Some anthropologists followed in this action anthropology tradition and went off to work with tribes to better their condition (e.g., Schlesier 1974). By the 1980s, however, the concept was waning. Most anthropologists these days miss the significance of the action anthropology concept, thinking it but one variation of applied anthropology; a distinction without a difference. Its distinction, if subtle, was profound, as described by a student of Tax:

Rather than making a study of the Indians as described by outside authorities and then handing back the analysis to those same authorities to implement as they wish, the action approach entails a stage-by-stage evaluation of the community's problems as presented by its members, and a feedback of these developing ideas to the client group together with a clarification of alternative paths of action among which the community could choose. (Ablon, as quoted in Lurie 1999, 110)

To Ablon's description, we would add one other key point: self-sustaining. The goal was not just to develop programs to solve problems identified by tribes using solutions developed with tribes, but also to develop programs that could be staffed and maintained by tribes. This, we will see, would be a key element in the soon-to-emerge tribal cultural resource management paradigm.

Tax was also clear about the important benefits action anthropology would have to scholarship more generally. He emphasized the need for a flow of knowledge from the community or work site into the university. Anthropologists could bring back knowledge gained from their field experiences and integrate it into the theoretical state of anthropology. In this way, anthropology would be better grounded in the reality of cultural life, and its findings would be of greater value to the human community at large.

Meanwhile, back at the university, academic anthropology was undergoing a shift similar to that in archaeology, with anthropologists moving on from descriptive to problem-oriented studies. This was most obvious in ethno-

The People as Colleagues

Rosalie and Murray Wax came out of the University of Chicago, where they were influenced by Sol Tax. They made many contributions to American Indian education reform during their careers. In the following passage, the late Rosalie Wax emphasizes a key principle in action anthropology—training the people to do the work themselves.

If we had hired white research assistants, we might also have avoided trouble, simply because we would probably never have become so deeply and personally involved in the life of the community. The practice of working with members of a host people as colleagues rather than "informants" is well established among sociologists, but at this time (1962) it had seldom been attempted by anthropologists. We wanted to hire young Indians as apprentices rather than as helpers, because we knew that this kind of experience, in which an intelligent and perceptive younger person watches a professional work, plan, flounder, and (sometimes) succeed, is one of the most efficient means of education. We thought that if a couple of young and educated Indians were given a fair notion of how to go about studying a community—if they actually saw it done before their eyes—they might, in the long run, help their people more than would any number of reports written by outsiders. (Wax 1971, 181)

graphic work, where the traditional holistic ethnography gave way to specialized studies focused on specific aspects of a culture. Although these "new ethnography" studies were enlightening, the field has suffered because we lack basic ethnographic information about many groups during the 1960 and 1970s, a period of dynamic cultural change.

Another development at the university was the formation of Native American/ American Indian studies programs, which began to appear in the 1960s and 1970s (Heidenreich 1991). These programs were conceived to have the potential to better educate and sensitize others to American Indians and their unique issues (Medicine 1971). The establishment of a Native American Studies program at the University of California at Berkeley in 1969 was only one of these. American Indians increasingly became more vocal in the 1970s toward "their frustration at the insensitivity of a larger society to their cultural heritage and religious practices" (Laidlaw 1990, 238).

As a sidenote, many times these days we hear how American Indians are thankful for the work of an-

The Anthropology of Robert K. Thomas

Robert K. Thomas (1925–1991) was a Cherokee Nationalist, social scientist, anthropologist, philosopher, teacher, activist, and spiritual leader. Steve Pavlik, one of Thomas's students at the University of Arizona, described some of his professor's accomplishments.

From 1957 through 1967, for example, [Bob Thomas] helped organize, teach, and often direct a series of summer workshops on American Indian affairs which were held annually in Colorado. These workshops were designed to give American Indian college students a chance to learn about the issues that were currently affecting tribal people. They proved to be so successful that Thomas would later organize a series of similar gatherings throughout Canada. In 1961 he also played an instrumental role in helping to organize the historic American Indian Chicago Conference, a watershed event that brought Indian leaders and non-Indian academics together for the purpose of finding common ground, to review past federal Indian policy and to make recommendations for future policy changes. It would be impossible to overstate the importance of the summer workshops and the Chicago conference, and the role played by Bob Thomas in making these things happen. These activities served to educate, organize, and focus Indian people toward addressing many of the problems and injustices that had long plagued Indian country. Most importantly, these events were key to developing the leadership potential of young Indians and mobilizing them to action. In a very real sense this was the beginning of an American Indian reform movement that continues even today. (Pavlik 1998, xv–xvi)

45

thropologists who recorded tribal practices, stories, and languages long ago. As the stories go, the anthropological works are the tribe's only source for this information because the elders are gone and no one in the tribe retains this knowledge. These stories may be true, and it is good to see that some good came out of this work, but it needs to be pointed out that documenting information so tribes could have it was not the reason the studies were conducted.

Archaeologists, Anthropologists, and the Resurgence of American Indians

Action anthropology notwithstanding, American anthropology remained a largely inwardly focused research-oriented field during the 1960s and 1970s. The majority of work focused *on* American Indians, with little anthropology done *for* American Indians. This point would be made quite clear by Vine Deloria in his hard-hitting book *Custer Died for Your Sins* (1969). Deloria wrote, "Indians have been cursed above all other people in history. Indians have anthropologists. . . . The fundamental thesis of the anthropologist is that people are objects for observation, people are then considered objects for experimentation, for manipulation, and for eventual extinction" (Deloria 1969, 81).

Others soon joined in. One writer, for example, suggested Indian people organize themselves as the American Indian Association to obtain the necessary funding to begin studying anthropologists (Martin 1971, 66). Ortiz (1971) published an article titled, "An Indian Anthropologist's Perspective on Anthropology."

While Deloria clearly ignored the honorable efforts of the many action and applied anthropologists who were trying to help American Indians in their anthropological work, it is hard to refute his general characterization of the broader field of anthropology. Some anthropologists did not take Deloria's words lightly, even if they disagreed, and attempted to improve the situation. One notable gathering at an annual conference resulted in a volume entitled, *Anthropology and the American Indian*, with papers and comments by a veritable who's who in American anthropology at the time, including Nancy Lurie, Margaret Mead, Bea Medicine, Phileo Nash, and Omer C. Stewart (Officer 1973).

Another example of anthropologists using their skills and knowledge

Good Medicine

American Indian anthropologist Bea Medicine recalled a 1970 session at the American Anthropological Meetings and commented on its significance in her new book, Learning to Be an Anthropologist and Remaining "Native."

Some anthropology programs [at conferences] have included Native participants. In [1970] the annual "tribal rites" of the American Anthropological Association featured a symposium on "Anthropology and the American Indian," which subsequently was published in [1973] by the now-defunct Indian Historian Press. It included such persons as Al Ortiz, Roger Buffalohead, Ken Martin, me, and the adversarial Vine Deloria, Jr. The house was packed. The symposium might be viewed as a nod in the direction of ethnic studies, which grew out of the 1960s' protests and housed many American Indian programs. The most memorable event, however, was the "takeover" of the AAA executive suite for an evening party. (Medicine 2001, 327)

to help Indians came from the Pacific Northwest. Beginning in the mid-1960s, Roderick Sprague, Deward E. Walker, Jr., and others cooperatively undertook numerous projects with the Lummi, Colville, Kalispel, Kootenai of Idaho, Coeur d'Alene, Spokane, Yakima, Umatilla, and Nez Perce tribes to assist with the increasing number of human burials being unearthed during construction and other development efforts. Sprague and Walker respected tribal wishes to rebury human remains, something that was heretical to most in archaeology and physical anthropology at the time (Sprague 1974).

In 1967, they arranged an agreement between the university and the Nez Perce Tribe of Idaho. This agreement gave the university the responsibility of conducting investigations of all disturbed or potentially disturbed graves, with stipulations by the Nez Perce Tribe (Karklins 2000, 3). Walker and Sprague also agreed that the University of Idaho would not maintain a collection of American Indian skeletal material. Similar agreements were eventually developed by other Plateau tribal groups in the area.

In addition to establishing these kinds of agreements, in cooperation with the affected tribe or tribes, the University of Idaho anthropology program, early on, advocated for: (1) consulting with tribes prior to working on aboriginal sites; (2) providing copies of all written reports and published works to tribes for their archives; and (3) hiring of tribal members, to the greatest extent possible (Sprague 1974, 1).

Despite objections by American Indians such as Vine Deloria, Jr., anthropologists never did stop coming to the reservation. New federal legislation required more anthropology, not less. For example, the American Indian Religious Freedom Act of 1978 required agencies to understand better the places that were important to American Indians. Furthermore, the concept of traditional cultural places was emerging and being incorporated into cultural resource management efforts, even though the concept would not be formalized until 1990.

In response to this newfound demand, cultural resource management witnessed the introduction of contract anthropology and "ethnographic contract archaeology" (Hardesty, Green, and Lindsay 1986). In a pattern similar to that of contract archaeology, agencies awarded contracts to anthropologists to identify and document nonarchaeological cultural resources and places important to specific ethnic groups. This new need for project-assessment ethnographic studies would pave the way for starting active "consultations" with interested and concerned Indian tribes and planted the seeds for development of tribal programs (Cushman 1993).

Was this increased activity the precursor to "Cultural Resource Management, of the People, by the People, and for the People" as outlined by Katz (1979)? Not really. The fact is, there were few Indians, or tribes, being consulted, or included, in the cultural resource management of the 1970s and 1980s. What was happening was very intense energy development on federal lands, where irreplaceable, nonrenewable, ethnically significant, Indian-related cultural resources were being lost without consulting concerned Indian tribes. Note that while tribes were certainly concerned about preserving historic properties and other cultural resources on reservation lands, they were often equally or even more concerned about preserving ancestral sites and traditional use areas on lands they no longer controlled, whether those lands were now under local, state, or federal control or private ownership. Times were changing, but not that fast.

Relationships between American Indians and Archaeologists

Despite the efforts of some pioneering archaeologists and anthropologists, relationships between American Indians and archaeologists improved only slightly during the 1960s and 1970s. There may have been more archaeologists asking Indians how they did things, or why they did them, but there were fewer opportunities for American Indians in the field, and still fewer professionals were asking the Indians what they thought needed to be done. There still was a total lack of regard for human burials by most archaeologists, and virtually no archaeologist ever thought to ask a tribal representative whether it was appropriate to excavate a site, what to do with the artifacts, or whether any special precautions should be taken. Many sites were never even backfilled after the excavations were completed. The fact that no one even thought about the need to do these things or to consult with the descendants of the sites they investigated speaks volumes about this time period. Clearly, archaeologists saw no relationship between the site and materials they investigated and the people who still had spiritual and cultural ties to these sites and materials. This would soon change.

Many events started to wake archaeologists up to the idea that their work was impinging on the rights of American Indians. The disrespect shown to burials in museums, roadside attractions, archaeological excavations, and elsewhere certainly was a catalyst for change (Echo-Hawk and Echo-Hawk 1994). Concern over even routine archaeological excavations started to be expressed, as it was for the protection of spiritual places such as Devils Tower, Wyoming, and Bear Butte, South Dakota. These issues were all ripe for attention by the Red Power movement in the 1970s.

Interestingly, as early as 1968 the Society of American Archaeology had attempted to foster greater respect for native peoples by archaeologists. Soon thereafter the Society recognized that the relationship between archaeologists and Indians needed improvement. American Indian concerns were deemed legitimate and the Society recommended that archaeologists communicate more effectively with American Indians and find ways to increase their participation in archaeological research (Ferguson 1996). But implementation of these ideas lagged.

In the early 1970s, Elden Johnson (1973) asked in the pages of the Society for American Archaeology's *American Antiquity*, "Do we as archaeologists need to consult with American Indians who are the cultural and biological descendants, particular or general, of the past residents of the sites we excavate?" The piece, entitled "Professional Responsibilities and the American Indian," shows that some archaeologists were beginning to recognize that American Indians had a role to play in archaeology beyond simply being a source for data or information.

Then, in 1974 Roderick Sprague wrote the lead editorial for *American Antiquity*, entitled "American Indians and American Archaeology," in which he compassionately laid out proper codes of behavior for archaeologists to follow in working with indigenous human remains. For Sprague, the issue was one of simple respect for people who cared about the remains of their ancestors. By what right could archaeologists supersede the rights of a people to their ancestors, and why would they anyway? Times were changing.

The Emergence of Tribal CRM

American Indians' initial interest in cultural resource management was adversarial. One gentleman, an American Indian Movement leader from the California Bay area, warned the participants at the 1976 Annual Meeting of the Society for California Archaeology "that Indians would 'shut archaeology down' if [archaeologists] continued to ignore Native American heritage rights" (Winter 1980).

This was a time when American Indians began to increasingly protest archaeological research, particularly when this disturbed human remains. Likewise, native groups in British Columbia were also becoming increasingly concerned. Indians saw archaeology as a continuation of the centuries-long disrespect for their sites and ancestors. To them, Europeans had been disturbing Indian grave sites since the Pilgrims landed at Plymouth Rock in 1620 (Trope and Echo-Hawk 1992, 40). There certainly was truth to this notion. The first "archaeological excavations" in the Pacific Northwest involved three ethnographic grave-robbing incidents at the mouth of the Columbia River between 1811 and 1835 (Sprague 1973, 253). Without question, archaeology has been a highly destructive method of "preserving" cultural resources—being rooted in the national perception that America's native peoples were a vanished race. Archaeology provided the only mechanism to document that history.

Generally, there were few Indian tribes, or tribal members, involved with cultural resource management during the 1960s and 1970s, but slowly, tribes did start to get involved. Some of the tribes that were active in contract archaeology during the early 1970s included the Sisseton-Wahpeton Sioux Tribe, the Inuit Alaskan Community, the Confederated Tribes of the Colville Reservation, the Pueblo of Zuni, the Navajo Nation, and the Southern Paiute people at Pahrump, Mojave Desert area of California.

The Colville, for example, began consulting with the U.S. Army Corps of Engineers, Seattle District, on projects in 1974. Their collaboration continued in 1976 when the Chief Joseph Dam Survey Project began. The tribe's History/Archaeology Department was created in 1978, about the time fieldwork began on the Chief Joseph Dam project. In turn, the Chief Joseph Dam project established a Tribal Trainee Program to teach field archaeology and laboratory analysis to members of the Colville Confederated Tribes. Consequently, tribal members were present throughout the fieldwork.

The Pueblo of Zuni of Arizona and New Mexico also became active in contract archaeology during the early 1970s. In 1975 the Zuni Tribe began its own Zuni Archaeological Conservation Team (ZACT), providing a year of formal classroom instruction to tribal members in archaeology. This training "stressed the vocabulary and concepts needed to communicate with non-Zuni professional archaeologists" (Anyon and Ferguson 1995, 915). ZACT was replaced in 1976 with the Zuni Archaeological Enterprise (ZAE; Anyon and Ferguson 1995, 916). The ZAE was soon abolished, being replaced in 1978 by the Zuni Archaeology Program (ZAP), administered by the tribal government.

The Navajo were another early participant. Martin (1997, 128), discussing cultural resource management for the Navajo Nation, writes, "The Navajo Nation has been named repeatedly as one of the front-runners of tribes who are 'managing their own cultural resources.'" The Navajo Nation Tribal Council passed an antiquities preservation law in January 1972, and their program has been in existence since 1977. In 1975, the Navajo Nation Museum hosted the Southwest Region Cultural Resource Management Seminar, drawing approximately one hundred attendees, many of them Indians. The success of this conference reflected the growing awareness and concern many tribes had regarding their lands and culture.

As we will see in the next chapter, future tribal interest in cultural resource management built upon this foundation of tribal programs from the 1970s and grew rapidly.

CHAPTER FOUR

ARCHAEOLOGY, ANTHROPOLOGY, AND AMERICAN INDIANS, THE 1980s AND 1990s

> There has to be an outreach from the Native American community as
> well as from the archaeological community in order to share perspec-
> tives. We are all a part of our own culture; my culture places a strong em-
> phasis on scientific research and data. Native American culture places a
> great emphasis on oral histories and traditional beliefs. Neither is wrong.
> (Kluth 1996, 30)

If a pro-tribal person were to write a script for what he or she wanted to
see happen in the 1980s and 1990s for tribes in cultural resource management, it would probably have been similar to the script that actually got
written. To put it briefly, things went about as well as we could have expected. T. J. Ferguson reported in his 1997 paper, given at the 62nd Annual Meeting of the Society for American Archaeology, that fifty-seven
tribes "are actively involved in tribally based archaeological research and
historic preservation programs" (Walker and Jones 2000, 68). In this
chapter we will review the legislative changes that facilitated tribal involvement, briefly review what was going on in archaeology and anthropology, and conclude with the accomplishments that tribes made during
this period. Key events during this period are identified in table 4.1.

Cultural Resource Management Matures

By the 1980s, cultural resource management was well on its way to becoming the profession it is today. Federal land-managing agencies were
staffed with archaeologists learning how to be cultural resource managers,
106 reviews and mitigation were commonplace, the Advisory Council on
Historic Preservation and state historic preservation officers and their
staffs were functioning, contractors were getting contracts, and the Na-

52

tional Park Service was developing its role as facilitator. Universities even began offering courses as part of their curriculum, and training courses appeared across the land.

The National Historic Preservation Act continued to strengthen through implementing regulations, amendments, and simple use. For our purposes, we focus on the implementing regulations that were issued in 1979; the 1980 amendments, which produced Section 110 and provided for grants to Indian tribes; and the 1992 amendments, which strengthened consultation requirements and created the Tribal Historic Preservation Office program. These changes really propped open the door for tribes that the National Environmental Policy Act (NEPA) initially opened. For some reason, Section 106 undertakings seem to be more frequent and to require more meaningful consultations than do NEPA actions, except for full-blown environmental impact statements. We'll come back to this in the section on tribal cultural resource management.

Other legislation strengthened the cultural resource management movement in general. The American Indian Religious Freedom Act was passed in 1978, which generally acknowledged that there were places important to tribes that needed to be protected and that tribes need to be able to access. The Archaeological Resource Protection Act of 1979 established penalties for looters, it required archaeologists to obtain a permit to conduct work on federal lands, and it required the agency to consult with tribes about the proposed work when sacred Indian resources were involved.

The 1980s were a relatively quiet period, as the Reagan administration generally put the cultural resource community under threat of elimination. The field survived, however, and by the end of the decade, the trend toward greater involvement for American Indians continued. Most significant in 1990 was the passage of the Native American Graves and Repatriation Act (commonly known as NAGPRA). This act was quite specific about the need for agencies to inventory their collections by certain dates and consult with tribal representatives concerning a future course of action. The Act was also quite specific about inadvertent discoveries of human remains and the actions that agencies had to take in consulting with tribes about disposition.

Also in 1990 came the National Park Service publication on traditional cultural properties (Parker and King 1990). *National Register Bulletin 38*

Table 4.1 National, Native American, Archaeological, Anthropological, and Cultural Resource Management Events, 1980–2000

Year	National/ International Events	Native American Events	Anthropological Events	Archaeological Events	Cultural Resource Management Events
1980		Sioux Nation wins Supreme Court case over Black Hills			NHPA Amendments, Section 110, 101 issued
1981	Personal computer introduced				
1983					Standards and Guidelines for Archaeology and Historic Preservation issued
1985			American Anthropological Association (AAA) reorganized	Society for American Archaeology splits from AAA	
1986					36CFR800 significantly revised
1987					Abandoned Shipwreck Act enacted
1988					ARPA amendments strengthen protection
1989	Berlin Wall falls	National Museum of the American Indian Act enacted		Dillehay publishes report on Monte Verde site in Chile	

Year				
1990	Operation Desert Storm; Nelson Mandela freed	Native American Graves Protection and Repatriation Act enacted	American Anthropological Association issues statement on race	36CFR79 published
1991	Collapse of Soviet Union			
1992	Official end of Cold War			
1993	Internet takes off	Ada Deer becomes first American Indian to head Bureau of Indian Affairs		NHPA Amendments
1994		Executive Order 12898 issued "Environmental Justice"		
1995		Tribal Historic Preservation Offices authorized		
1996		Executive Order 13007 issued "Indian Sacred Sites"	SAA Native American Committee formed; Ethics Report issued; Kennewick Man discovered	
2001				Advisory Council revises Section 106 regulations

changed people's perception of cultural resources from places containing "things" to places that were important in their own right. "The land itself is an important element in native religion and may have no visible indication of being sacred to non-Indians" (Eiselein 1993, 47). For example, locations where Sun Dances were held are considered sacred, and yet there may be little to distinguish them from the surrounding countryside, particularly if the arbor or other nearby temporary brush-like structures are no longer visible. The area where an intertribal Sun Dance was held in late August of 1843, near present-day Fort Lupton (formerly Fort Lancaster), Colorado, by Arapahos, Cheyennes, Sioux, Comanches, Blackfeet, and Arikaras (estimated to be about 1,000 lodges) may not be a traditional cultural property, as defined in *Bulletin 38*, but it is a holy site, even today.

Formally recording traditional cultural places can be a useful approach, at times, to identify and protect a special place, but not always (Hadley 1993). To be eligible for inclusion on the National Register of Historic Places, the traditional cultural property must be associated with cultural practices and beliefs that are (1) rooted in the history of a community, and (2) are important to maintaining the continuity of that community's traditional beliefs and practices (Parker and King 1990). Moreover, to formally nominate a property, the keeper of the National Register wants proof and well-defined boundaries. For many, it is just not worth revealing so much information, when the perceived benefit is minimal.

An example of a "place" possibly significant to tribes, but lacking archaeological evidence, is near Estes Park, Colorado. The Arapaho name for Old Man Mountain was known as "*hinantoXthaoXut*," or Sitting Man, where "Indians often fasted on the top of this hill" (Toll 1913). Toll also made mention of a small round hill east of the Stanley Hotel (remember the movie *The Shining*?) where the Arapaho conducted their "Sage Chicken Dance." Toll explained, "This ceremony consisted of a fast during the day, and a big sage chicken dinner at night, after which they gave this special dance."

As it evolved, agency cultural resource management programs moved from doing archaeological surveys (often called inventories) and historical and archaeological overviews to creating established programs. The principal drivers for these programs were the Section 106 project reviews, but in order to conduct Section 106 reviews, agency archaeologists needed to build a basic understanding of the lands they were managing. This meant knowing what had happened there, what types of resources were there, their significance, which lands had been surveyed, and the threats facing the resources. Funding was almost always a problem, but when possible, funds were obtained to continue surveying lands, monitoring sites to check their condition, sharing information with the public, and occasionally restoring sites and historic buildings.

Archaeology in the 1980s and 1990s

In the archaeological profession, the 1980s and 1990s were a period of yet another shift in theoretical orientation. The New Archaeology of the 1960s and 1970s lingered on, but a new era commonly called Post-Processual emerged. In contrast to the scientific New Archaeology, the Post-Processualists sought alternative ways of knowing, alternative approaches to interpreting archaeological data. We are not the ones to attempt to explain Post-Processualism, except to say that its proponents would seem to be more open to tribal perspectives and involvement than are the scientifically minded archaeologists.

While the academic community does not seem

Personal Reflections on CRM: Part II

Evan DeBloois continues his personal reflections on his U.S. Forest Service career. Here he notes the evolution of cultural resource management in his own agency and captures the complexity that agency professionals face in protecting cultural resources.

In spite of efforts to the contrary, by the early 1990s, "cultural resource management" in the Forest Service came to mean Section 106 compliance and "salvage archaeology." In an effort to break this unfortunate and limited stereotype, the Forest Service changed its cultural resource management program to the "heritage resource management program," and produced a program definition that attempted, not only to broaden the view of what the program was about, but also to broaden the scope of responsibility for that program.

Much of the recent discussion among cultural resource management professionals reflects the nature of the problem that led to the program name change in the Forest Service. There is not a simple dichotomy in the CRM field today of "academic" vs. "contract archaeology." It is more complicated than that. In addition to academic archaeology and contract archaeology, we have to add the regulatory and land management roles.

to have picked up much on the rising trend toward tribal cultural resource management, the Society for American Archaeology did. For example, in 1990 the SAA established a task force to advise the society on how to develop a better relationship with Native Americans. This task force was changed to a standing committee in 1995 and continues to advise regarding the relationship between the archaeological community and Native Americans. One outgrowth of this was a Native American scholarship fund for Native Americans who want to pursue archaeology degrees. Native Americans have been accepted into the Society for American Archaeology annual meeting,

(Continued)
There is a vast difference between the agency missions of the Forest Service and Bureau of Land Management on one hand and that of the Federal Energy Regulatory Commission and Housing and Urban Development on the other. Where regulatory agencies have a relative narrow responsibility under Section 106 when they are issuing permits or licenses, land management agencies have a broad responsibility for cultural resources even when there is no threat of impact from a project. It is this latter responsibility that, I believe, most closely approaches a definition of "cultural resource management." Agencies that really manage cultural resources regulate uses, license projects, and fund activities, requiring the execution of the role of a "cultural resource regulator," as well as carrying out or overseeing "contract archaeology." They also issue permits for "academic archaeology" and play a role in assuring that consumptive uses of the resource comply with some measure of best practice and current technology in order to maximize the information obtained and minimize the information lost.

where attendance and papers by Native Americans have steadily increased. One session with Native Americans was jointly published by the Society for American Archaeology (Swidler, Dongoske, Anyon, and Downer 1997), with proceeds going to the scholarship fund. Many collaborative projects are described in the publication *Working Together: Native Americans and Archaeologists* (Dongoske, Aldenderfer, and Doebner 2000).

Few archaeology students from undergraduate to graduate school ever worked with Indians on or off an Indian reservation (Downer 1997, 29). As noted by Stapp (2000, 73), university education and training in archaeology do not really address these kinds of intercultural interactions or the claims of American Indians to their own cultural resources. Consequently, most of the cultural resource management practitioners in the late 1970s and early 1980s had little to no experience with native peoples outside the university; and there were few Indian anthropology and archaeology students to learn from. This was a time of big money: contract archaeology without Indians, a cultural vacuum where huge sums of money were generated from aboriginal lands and resources, with no economic benefits to tribes.

A recent volume devoted to Deloria and his critique of anthropology is *Indians and Anthropologists* (Biolsi and Zimmerman 1997). A series of articles presents the reader with a host of views on archaeology and Indians and is well worth reading. Deloria contributes the conclusion, entitled "Anthros, Indians, and Planetary Reality" (Biolsi and Zimmerman 1997, 209–21). Deloria acknowledges the contributions archaeologists and anthropologists have made to Native Americans, citing Dr. Deward Walker, Jr., as an example. Deloria writes, "Scholars better understand their skills and the degree to which they can assist Indians, and Indians have come to rely on anthropologists once they are satisfied that the individual is competent and understands the nature of what they are trying to do."

The Emergence of Tribal Cultural Resource Management

When this period started, Bruce Trigger (1980, 670) wrote "relations between archaeology and native peoples are not good. . . . [archaeologists] have not begun seriously to assess archaeology's moral and intellectual responsibility to native people." This characterization is not surprising, in that, as noted previously, few tribes or tribal members were participating in any kind of archaeological work. What was the ratio of dollars between nonnative and native contract personnel in all the United States in the 1970s, for example, working on tribal resources? Maybe one hundred to one?

As noted by a western shore Puget Sound tribal member from the Pacific Northwest, "In the case of the Suquamish . . . archaeological sites may be the only pristine resource remaining from the aboriginal world that has not been encroached upon by non-Indians. Therefore, Indians see archaeology as a 'last stand' in their struggle to maintain their land base, identity, and sovereignty" (Forsman 1997, 109). Tribes now define cultural resources according to their beliefs (i.e., ethnic significance) (Doyel 1982), make decisions about cultural resources according to their values, and deal with nontribal outside parties on their own terms.

A late-1970s project sponsored by the Lewis and Clark National Forest, working with the Blackfeet Tribe of Montana and "gathering data pertaining to traditional Blackfeet Indian religious activities on the Forest with special emphasis on the Rocky Mountain Front south of Glacier National Park," was uncommon for its time (Knight 1979, 22). Other notable exceptions, including consultations with Indians, were the U.S. Army, Fort Carson Piñon Cañyon Maneuver Area, in southeastern Colorado (Stoffle 1983; Stoffle, Dobyns, Evans, and Stewart 1984) and consultations with Great Basin tribes regarding an electric transmission line (Stoffle and Dobyns 1983; Stoffle, Dobyns, and Evans 1983). A Nevada publication from the mid-1980s (Aikens 1986) contained several articles on the status of tribes and cultural resource management in the Great Basin, including California, Idaho, Nevada, Oregon, and Utah.

In the mid-1980s, Green (1986, 128) was of the opinion that "For archaeologists working in Idaho communication with Native American peoples has become an operational necessity." He also made an invitation to representatives from Idaho's federally recognized Indian tribes to attend the semiannual meetings of the Idaho Advisory Council of Professional Archaeologists. As for Nevada, Becker (1986, 25) notes for the Bureau of Land Management that "Native American groups have not routinely been notified of archeological work." However, formal consultation with tribes is requested for the larger projects like transmission lines and land withdrawals. This lack of consultation was a major factor in the recent ruling on the repatriation of Spirit Cave Man by the NAGPRA Review Committee, favoring the Fallon Paiute Shoshone Tribe. A model for consultation by a federal agency is found at the Nevada Test Site (Stoffle, Zedeño, and Halmo 2001).

Focusing primarily on Native American burials in Oregon, Gilsen (1986, 112) optimistically noted that the May 1986 conference on American Indian cultural resources held at the University of Oregon, "which attracted many Native Americans and archaeologists, was highly successful in furthering communication between the two groups and focusing attention on the importance of further fostering mutually beneficial interactions." Finally, Dykman (1986, 142) reported that Utah had an Office of

Indian Affairs that served as a point of contact with Native Americans in cultural resource management matters (e.g., the Paiute, Ute, and Gosiute tribes). He also reports that the Utah Department of Transportation involves Indians in its projects "through consultation and employment of tribal members on field crews."

The issue of burials treated as archaeological remains is a long-standing one. It reached a head in the late 1970s when the Archaeological Resource Protection Act was in preparation. Here, in black and white, human remains and grave goods were defined as archaeological resources. Tribes took a stand and were adamant that human remains, burials, and cemeteries were not archaeological sites, artifacts, or cultural resources. They are human remains in a special category outside of cultural resources, Indian burials and cemeteries of "those who came before." Other sacred sites, such as spirit questing locations, may be cultural resources for state and federal administrative purposes but not for tribes. They are sacred remains not to be subjected to research without explicit tribal authorization. These kinds of sacred and sensitive native places are treated much differently by nonnatives, oftentimes in ways incompatible with native worldviews. Clearly, human remains located on an Indian reservation would be best dealt with by the Indian people themselves, unless they chose otherwise.

As outlined previously, the pendulum started reversing direction toward the end of the 1980s. The addition of traditional cultural properties as cultural resources was a major breakthrough. Performing a cultural resource inventory by itself was no longer necessarily sufficient. As noted earlier, archaeological remains may, or may not, have anything to do with a traditional cultural property. Many, if not most, native traditional cultural properties do not have associated material culture. Rather, the traditional cultural property is simply a place on the landscape, but a place identified in a unique way by the native culture (Cushman 1993; Othole and Anyon 1993; Sebastian 1993). Thus, to adequately survey an area to fulfill cultural resource requirements, tribes had to be contacted to determine if any traditional cultural properties existed.

Another major breakthrough came in the 1992 amendments to NHPA. Section 101(d)2 of the National Historic Preservation Act provides that "A tribe may assume all or any part of the functions of a State Historic Preservation Officer." By July 1996, twelve tribes had been certified by the National Park Service historic preservation program as Tribal Historic Preservation Offices; they, in turn, make up the National Association of Tribal Historic Preservation Officers. The counterparts to the Tribal Historic Preservation Offices are the State Historic Preservation Offices, which comprise the National Conference of State Historic Preservation Offices. The *Keepers of the Treasures* is an intertribal counterpart to the National Conference of State Historic Preservation Offices. By 2002, that number had been increased to about *30* federally recognized Indian tribes certified by the National Park Service to Tribal Historic Preservation Office status (Salazar and Barrow 2000, 3).

Having more than 30 tribes certified as Tribal Historic Preservation Offices out of a total of 562 federally recognized Indian tribes may not seem significant, but it is. Only a few years ago, no tribes had achieved this status. The number of certified tribes will only increase in membership, providing for a stronger and more influential national organization. The National Association of Tribal Historic Preservation Offices typically meets twice yearly for two national conferences. The Tribal Historic Preservation Offices are identified in the appendix.

For tribes just starting in cultural resource management, a visit to a tribe with an established program is well worthwhile. The visitors can meet with tribal staff, tour their tribal facilities, and shadow staff members as part of their introduction to an up-and-running program. Literature, contacts, expertise, possible solutions to common problems, bibliographies, language programs, oral history programs of working with elders, tribal museums, and much more can be shared.

The Pueblo of Zuni Approach

The Pueblo of Zuni in New Mexico began its cultural resource and archaeology program in 1973. The goals of that program, known as the Zuni Archaeology Program, illustrate well what was important to the Zuni people:

1. To provide tribal members with increased employment and career opportunities;
2. To enhance archaeological and historic research by involving tribal members in the design, implementation, and dissemination of that research;
3. To facilitate the development of the Reservation with a locally based professional archaeological organization; and
4. To implement CRM policies that respect Zuni values and beliefs.

(Continued)
Today, the Zuni heritage management program has two components: the Zuni Heritage and Historic Preservation Office, authorized by the National Park Service in 1973, and the Zuni Cultural Resources Enterprise. The functions of the Preservation Office are:

1. To promote the protection and conservation of cultural resources significant to the Zuni Tribe on and off the Reservation;
2. To be the point of contact for the Zuni Tribe in its national and international repatriation efforts;
3. To represent the Tribe and negotiate agreements regarding cultural resources with federal, state, and private agencies;
4. To perform Zuni traditional cultural property consultations; and
5. To assume the responsibilities of the State Historic Preservation Offices on Zuni lands in New Mexico and Arizona.

The other component, Zuni Cultural Resources Enterprise, started in 1982 to provide cultural resource services on and off the Zuni Reservation. Over twenty full-time positions exist, most of whom are Native Americans, with many more hired on a temporary basis when needed. The Pueblo of Zuni is a good example of how a tribe can become active in cultural resource management and incorporate its own values when developing its historic preservation program (Anyon and Ferguson 1995).

Being a Tribal Historic Preservation Office brings with it several advantages. First, it enables tribes to take over responsibilities on their reservation that previously had been relegated to a state agency (the State Historic Preservation Office). It also provides funds to develop capabilities, conduct work on the reservation, and receive training and provides opportunities to interact with other tribes on common issues through the national organization of the Tribal Historic Preservation Offices.

Not all tribes see the advantage of developing a Tribal Historic Preservation Office. There could be many reasons why, but a major reason certainly is the need to adhere to National Park Service rules, as well as to disclose information the tribe may not want to share. Many tribes, such as the Yakama Nation in Washington State and others, are fully functioning without this formal status, so becoming a Tribal Historic Preservation Office is by no means a prerequisite for a tribe to develop its cultural resource program.

Several examples of tribes with archaeology or historic preservation programs are the Gila River Indian Community; the Hopi Tribe, Cultural Preservation Office in operation since about 1988 (Adams 1984; Ferguson, Dongoske, Jenkins, Yeatts, and Polingyouma 1994; Ferguson, Dongoske, Yeatts, and Jenkins 1995); the Klamath, Modoc, and Yaahooskin Tribes; the Mashantucket Pequot of Connecticut (since 1980; McBride 1995); the MeWuk of California; the Mohegan Nation; the Yakama Indian Nation; and the Pueblo of Zuni (Hart 1991, 1993). These tribes will undoubtedly continue to participate in the cultural resource management of their reservations, ceded lands, and aboriginal lands, making additional contributions to native anthropology and archaeology.

The Hualapai Tribe (traditionally composed of fourteen bands) cultural resources program and Sierran Me-Wuk of Central California's Cultural and Historic Preservation Committee were started in 1991 (Fuller 1997a, 1997b; Jackson and Stevens 1997). The Seminole Tribe began its historic preservation program in 1992 with a project called the Seminole Heritage Survey (Cypress 1997); and in 1994 the Caddo, Cherokees, Chickasaw, Creek, Osage, and Wichita Tribes participated in a cultural workshop administered by the U.S. Forest Service to train Bureau of Indian Affairs and tribal members in cultural resource management. The Oklahoma Archaeological Survey assisted (Brooks 1997, 212). The Leech Lake Heritage Sites Program is a part of the Division of Resource Management of Leech Lake Reservation in north-central Minnesota. "The objective of our program is to provide cultural resource management services from a Native American perspective" (Kluth 1996, 28). Tribal members are hired and provided training, supplemented with on-the-job education (Kluth and Munnell 1997).

Tribes that have successfully collaborated with archaeologists to co-manage cultural resources or participate in archaeological projects include the Blackfeet of Montana; the Catawba; the Chugach; the Chumash of California; the Cocopah; the Quechan; the Cree; the Crow Tribe of Montana; the Inuit of Alaska; the Iroquois; the Kodiak Area Native Association and other Native corporations in Alaska; the Makah of Washington; the Mashantucket Pequot; the Mescalero Apache Tribe; the Micmac of New Brunswick, Canada; the Mountain Dene; the Northern Cheyenne Tribe of Montana; the Pawnee of Oklahoma; the Sechelt Indians of Canada; the Seminole Tribe of Florida; the Seneca Nation of Indians; the Shoshone-Bannock; the Shuswap; the Sioux; the Confederated Tribes of

Siletz Indians of Oregon; the Tungatsivvik; the Wampanoag Tribe of Gay Head; and the Wanapum Band of Indians, Priest Rapids, Washington.

The Participants in Cultural Resource Management at the Start of the Century

Anyone working in cultural resource management at the start of the twenty-first century found that his or her work involved many individuals and organizations. Success to a large degree depended on the ability to work with others in a cooperative and productive manner. To conclude this overview of the roots of tribal cultural resource management, we will describe the major players in cultural resource management and some of the issues confronting them at the end of the century. The participants we describe are federal land-managing agencies, tribes, cultural resource regulators, the public, and archaeologists and anthropologists.

Federal Land-Managing Agencies

We begin with federal land-managing agencies because they control a great deal of sensitive acreage, particularly in the American West, where many tribes are located. By *federal land-managing agency*, we mean the field office, not agency headquarters in Washington, D.C. Examples include national forests, wildlife refuges, Department of Defense installations, and Department of Energy facilities. These offices have several things in common:

- They are responsible for managing large areas, typically hundreds of square miles, which often contain significant cultural landscapes, or portions thereof.

- They are able to budget the activities that need to be performed from year to year. These activities include planning for and maintaining a cultural resource program.

- They are responsible for complying with the many historic preservation regulations referenced in earlier chapters and, in so doing, will be interacting with the state and tribal historic preservation officers, the Advisory Council on Historic Preservation, the Keeper of the National Register, tribes, and interested parties.

65

- Many offices retain a cultural resource professional to coordinate the work and advise the facility manager on actions needing consideration. These individuals, and their staff, will be familiar with the culture history, the physical manifestations, and threats facing the resources. This knowledge enables them to serve as intermediaries between the facility managers, or their designates, and the regulators, tribes, interested parties, and public.

- Other facilities perform most of their cultural resource work through annual contracts. The main disadvantages of such contracting strategies are that agencies consistently award contracts to the low bidder, which oftentimes compromises the quality of work performed; they typically award contracts to *different* contractors, eliminating continuity in work performed from year to year; and revolving contracts inhibit relationship-building among the parties because there are always new people doing the work.

Few agencies have accomplished their initial goals of inventorying all their lands and evaluating all their sites for eligibility determinations. More encouraging is the trend for agencies to begin long-term monitoring of resources and implementing protective measures to threatened and damaged places.

One area of concern is a possible national trend to reduce the number of cultural resource managers employed by federal agencies. If this trend is real, and agencies start relying on short-term contracting as they did in the past, resources and all the people who depend on them would suffer for reasons cited previously. Tribes and stakeholders need to stay involved with the agencies and provide input to ensure that agencies do not abandon their cultural resource programs.

American Indians

Projects located in areas near where American Indians reside are increasingly likely to require tribal consultations and involvement of tribal members. This is especially true on lands ceded to the U.S. government in exchange for certain promises and on lands for which tribes have historic and cultural ties. In these situations, tribes are often able to exert their influence and affect the way resources are managed. If projects are located on a reservation, then consultation may be through the tribal historic preservation office, if there is one.

Across the continent, the degree and nature of tribal consultation can vary considerably. There may be no consultation because the agency has never recognized that a tribe has an interest in its activities. Sometimes letters are sent to inform a tribe about a project; if the tribe responds with questions or concerns, there may be additional letters and meetings. Depending on the circumstances, formal agreements may result from the consultations.

The interactions between a tribe and others can be complex, due to the cultural differences and lack of familiarity with one another. Further complicating matters for everyone is the fact that usually more than one tribe will be involved, due to the overlapping aboriginal territories and historical movements of different groups. Each tribe may have different interests and ways of consulting, and sometimes intertribal relations are not good. In general, it is probably safe to say that no two situations are alike.

Consultations can be effective for helping projects proceed in a cooperative manner. Occasionally, impasses occur, and a process will be followed to resolve the conflict. Exactly how depends on whether the efforts are being conducted under the National Environmental Policy Act, the National Historic Preservation Act, or some other statute. Occasionally, it will be necessary to go to court, as was done in the Enola Hill case in Oregon (Occhipinti 2002).

Just as the consultation varies, so, too, do the degree and nature of tribal involvement. In some situations, tribal involvement may mean tribal monitors throughout the project. Other situations may require tribal technicians to be part of the cultural resource survey and excavation teams. In other cases, tribal elders may be involved. In yet other cases, tribes may have no interest in actually being involved in the work.

Local Governments

Increasingly, states and counties, and even municipalities (usually cities), are hiring staff to handle cultural resource issues. The need for staff is driven by county planning ordinances, state planning requirements, and other locality-specific requirements. These requirements, of course, did not appear out of nowhere; they are typically the result of concern expressed by local tribes, special interest groups, and the public. While requirements are generally less restrictive than federal requirements, they do provide for some measure of review before permits are granted and construction begins. The trend appears to be for more county and local cultural resource requirements, but we've not seen any statistics to confirm this trend.

Cultural Resource Regulatory Bodies

Cultural resource regulatory bodies include the offices of the individual state and tribal historic preservation offices, the Advisory Council on Historic Preservation, and certain offices within the National Park Service (e.g., Native American Graves and Repatriation Act Committee and Consulting Archaeologist, Keeper of the National Register). The respective state and tribal historic preservation office and Advisory Council on Historic Preservation responsibilities are the strongest and most clearly defined within the Section 106 process. For other types of activities related to Section 110, the Archaeological Resource Protection Act, or the Native American Graves Protection and Repatriation Act, the regulators may serve more in an advisory capacity, as a facilitator, or as an interested party. Federal agencies, for example, will typically forward site forms, survey reports, and management plans to the state historic preservation office for comment, whether they are absolutely required to or not. As King (1998) points out, there is considerable variation in how different state historic preservation offices approach their responsibilities. This may also be true for tribal historic preservation offices.

These regulatory organizations are important because they provide regulatory support to tribes and agency cultural resource staff. Whereas an agency manager may not pay attention to the recommendations of his or her own cultural resource staff, the manager will generally pay attention to the state or tribal historic preservation office or the Advisory Council on Historic Preservation. With this help, the agencies can achieve more complete compliance.

The regulatory agencies play another important role at levels above a specific landscape. State historic preservation officers, for example, are stewards for their respective states and, as such, can work to obtain consistency across the state. The state historic preservation office is the only organization that centralizes the cultural resource information for the state and, in turn, makes that information available to others working in the profession. The tribal historic preservation offices centralize the information for their respective reservations, ceded lands, and aboriginal territories. The Advisory Council on Historic Preservation and the National Park Service serve the same function, but more at the national level. These regulatory agencies, especially the National Park Service, provide a wealth of support services to agencies and facilities. Services include providing guidelines, technical bulletins, and training. These organizations, especially tribes, have shown that they are open to, if not encouraging of, the cultural landscape approach, discussed in chapter 8.

Interested Parties and the Public

Interested parties and the public can provide an active voice in how those resources should be managed at a given place. How do these groups get involved? Under the National Historic Preservation Act, any group can contact an agency and apply to be an interested party. If the agency designates the group as such, it will receive information about projects and be provided with the opportunity to comment. Under the National Environmental Policy Act, anyone can provide public comment during the decision-making process.

Although agencies should identify local groups that have an interest in the resources they manage, this is not always the case. The National Park Service's Applied Ethnography Program is an example of an approach to locate groups that are historically connected to cultural landscapes and resources or that otherwise have an interest in agency lands. Other kinds of efforts to connect with local groups are also common. Each federal agency is responsible for locating and notifying groups that requested to be consulted on environmental and cultural issues. When this does not happen, groups need to make themselves part of the process. While agencies may be required to consult, every group needs to take responsibility to work with an agency to ensure that its preferred alternative of preservation, protection, and accessibility is registered.

Cultural Resource Contractors

A substantial amount of the cultural resource work done in North American is accomplished by cultural resource contractors. Unless an agency or company can do the work in-house, it will need to contract out the work to some type of archaeological contracting firm. Most of these kinds of services are provided by private sector firms. Many are small businesses, but over the years, large environmental and engineering firms have become increasingly popular because of the full range of services they provide. Universities may also provide services, either by contracting directly with a professor or through a small business unit established to contract out services. Some federal agencies, most notably the Army Corps of Engineers, also provide some cultural resource services.

Most contracts issued are relatively small (under $100,000) and of short duration (one to two years). Scopes are well-defined and the bidding competitive. Project examples include an inventory of 50,000 acres, archaeological testing of ten sites for National Register of Historic Places eligibility recommendations, curating a collection of artifacts, or mitigating a site to be impacted by highway construction. Occasionally, contracts are issued for services over a longer period of time (e.g., renewable indefinite quantity contracts). Providing long-term curation of a facility's collections and providing cultural resource services for a large federal facility such as an Air Force base are just two examples.

Typically, those providing contracting services don't work in any one area long enough to fully understand the importance of cultural resources to local tribes and communities. They accomplish the work and move on to their next contract. At a national level, contractors have formed the American Cultural Resources Association, to provide lobbying and other support services.

University Archaeologists and Anthropologists

Most archaeologists and anthropologists in the United States work in universities, where teaching and research are the primary responsibilities. These professionals have methods and knowledge that can be useful in helping to identify and protect cultural landscapes. They also have a certain amount of status and credibility among the public and the politicians, which can be useful when new legislation is needed.

Archaeologists may be just another interested party when it comes to commenting on a particular cultural resource situation, but they are an important one. Archaeologists were helpful in developing the cultural resource management profession and still control many parts of it. Also, university archaeologists train the vast majority of archaeological students, who then pursue cultural resource management.

Summary

More than ever, American archaeology is being influenced by native peoples from all different walks of life across North America. University researchers, state and federal agencies, and industry-wide cultural resource management specialists are cooperating with American Indians to better ensure the protection and long-term management these resources deserve.

The thirty-plus Tribal Historic Preservation Offices, and some of the many other tribes with historic preservation capabilities, have come to realize the benefits of actively participating in cultural resource management. Other tribes aspire to do the same. The bottom line is, tribal cultural resource management can bring dollars to the reservation! Those dollars can be used for the protection of ancestral resources, while providing education, training, and employment for tribal members. Unlike most of the work done in the past, this strategy stresses anthropology and archaeology helping tribes and their cultural protection needs.

CASE STUDY: THE CULTURAL RESOURCE PROTECTION PROGRAM OF THE CONFEDERATED TRIBES OF THE UMATILLA INDIAN RESERVATION

I n this chapter we present a case study from a setting with which we are most familiar: the Confederated Tribes of the Umatilla Indian Reservation (CTUIR) Cultural Resource Protection Program. The purpose of this chapter is twofold. First, we use the CTUIR example to illustrate how many of the events mentioned in the previous chapters unfolded in a real-life setting. Second, we use it to illustrate many of the issues that we discuss in the next chapters.

The Confederated Tribes of the Umatilla Indian Reservation

The federally recognized, and sovereign, Confederated Tribes of the Umatilla Indian Reservation (the Umatilla [Imatallum], Cayuse [Wáylat-pam], and Walla Walla [Walúulapam] tribes, hereafter referred to as the CTUIR) live in northeastern Oregon, with ceded lands extending far beyond their reservation boundaries into central Oregon and southeastern Washington (figure 5.1). They were semisedentary, wintering along the Columbia River and smaller tributaries. Their nonwinter camps were mobile, moving as the different natural resources became available during the spring, summer, and fall seasons. Salmon was (and still is) a major resource for all of the Columbia River bands and tribes.

The CTUIR are a treaty tribe, and the Treaty of June 9, 1855 (ratified by Congress on March 8, 1859), is an extremely important component in the tribe's protection of its aboriginal homeland. This initial reservation

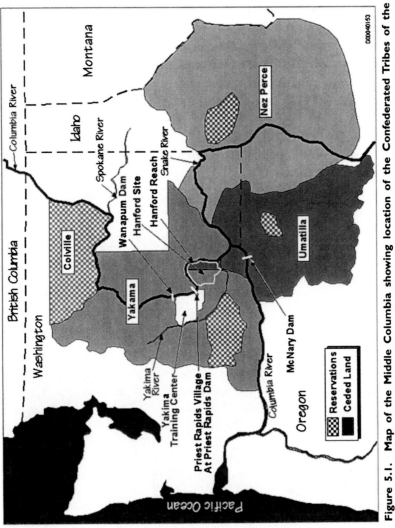

Figure 5.1. Map of the Middle Columbia showing location of the Confederated Tribes of the Umatilla Indian Reservation, other tribes in the regions, and other places mentioned in the text.

encompassed about 245,700 acres, but was later reduced when reservation lands were made available to white settlers through the allotment process. On December 4, 1888, the boundaries of the diminished Umatilla Indian Reservation were fixed to about 157,982 acres. In the 1855 treaty 6.5 million acres were ceded to the U.S. government, but the people retained the right to fish, hunt, graze cattle, and gather traditional foods and medicines at customary sites, many of which were outside the reservation. Today, through recent tribal purchases, the reservation consists of about 172,000 acres, of which over 18,000 acres are actually deeded to the tribe (see figure 5.1). Overviews of the prehistory, environment, and ethnohistory are found in Walker (1998).

CTUIR Cultural Resource Protection Program Overview

The CTUIR Cultural Resource Protection Program began in 1987 with the "three amigos": Paul Minthorn and Jeff Van Pelt (Nez Perce and CTUIR tribal members, respectively) and Michael S. Burney, a *Siyapo* (nonnative) from Boulder, Colorado. Michael's involvement came through a subcontract with the Council for Energy Research Tribes under the auspices of Dr. Deward Walker, Jr., an anthropologist from the University of Colorado, Boulder. Moneys came from the U.S. Department of Energy, which had identified

Today's Confederated Tribes of the Umatilla Indian Reservation

The Confederated Tribes of the Umatilla Indian Reservation's homeland once encompassed 6.4 million acres in northeastern Oregon and southeastern Washington. As a result of the 1855 Treaty with the U.S. government and subsequent federal legislation, the present-day reservation consists of 172,000 acres. Despite ceding millions of acres, CTUIR reserved their sovereign authority and *"the right to govern, to determine our destiny, and to control all persons, land, water, resources and activities, free of all outside interference throughout our homeland."*

They also reserved rights to harvest fish, wildlife, and other natural resources in their traditional homeland.

Once numbering over 8,000 strong (prior to European contact), the Confederated Tribes of the Umatilla Indian Reservation (CTUIR) now have 2,314 enrolled members, of which two-thirds live on or near the Umatilla Reservation. Located just outside of Pendleton, Oregon, the reservation is also home to another 1,000 Indians from other

(Continued) tribes such as the Yakama, Warm Springs, and Nez Perce, as well as to nearly 1,700 non-Indians. We adopted our modern-day Constitution and By-Laws in 1949. As a sovereign government, tribal affairs are governed by a nine-member Board of Trustees. The Board is elected by the General Council that consists of all tribal members age 18 and older. The General Council also elects its own officers and its Chairman serves to represent the General Council on the Board.

The day-to-day operation of the tribal government is carried out by a staff of more than 600 employees and includes departments such as administration, tribal court, economic and community development, education, enrollment, finance, fire protection, health and human services, housing, natural resources, personnel, planning, public works, police, and recreation.

After years of struggle and limited opportunity, CTUIR today are rapidly moving toward economic self-sufficiency by diversifying their Reservation economy. An economy once based strongly on agriculture and natural resources has grown to include commercial development such as a trailer court, grain elevator, and the Wildhorse Casino Resort, which includes a casino, hotel, RV park, golf course, and the Tamástslikt Cultural Institute. About 382 individuals are employed at the Casino.

Based on the number of employees (including our tribal government and our Wildhorse Casino Resort—1,100) we are the second largest employer in Umatilla County, following behind the state of Oregon agencies and institutions.

(Reproduced with permission from the CTUIR website <www.umatilla.nsn.us/today.html>)

the CTUIR as an "affected tribe" under the Nuclear Waste Policy Act of 1982. Plans for a high-level nuclear repository at the Hanford Nuclear Reservation, located about seventy-five miles north of the Umatilla Indian Reservation, required involvement of affected tribes in Hanford planning and implementation. The trio started working with one major goal in mind: to establish a self-sustaining cultural resource protection program (Van Pelt, Burney, and Bailor 1997).

The founding concept for the new program was to empower tribal members to proactively manage their cultural resources through education, training, and employment. The context for the Tribal CRM program would be "to develop and manage a tribal program specifically driven by the Indian worldview of the Earth and all the resources on earth, natural and cultural alike" (Longenecker and Van Pelt 2000, 90). In the very early years of the CTUIR's Cultural

Resource Protection Program, Michael and Jeff spent many days together in the field doing cultural resource inventories for the Umatilla National Forest, practicing their anthropology, and "walking in two worlds."

A main interest of the program was to combat the ongoing degradation of tribal resources through vandalism, theft, illegal trafficking, collecting, excavating, and development. As early as 1971, the Board of Trustees had passed Resolution 71–42, stating, in part, "The CTUIR did not feel it was in the best interest of the Indian community to authorize archaeological studies, treasure hunts, coin hunts, artifact searches, or any like investigation or collection efforts be allowed within or outside the boundaries of the Umatilla Indian Reservation without the specific authorization and direction of the CTUIR Board of Trustees."

For example, in 1987, while just beginning the CTUIR's program, several tribal members discovered a large number of tribal records and reel-to-reel tapes of past Board of Trustees' meetings from the 1950s–1960s, stored in the basement of a tribal building built in 1906. The building was originally used as the

Full-Circle Archaeology on the Umatilla Indian Reservation

Starting a new job on an Indian reservation is much like starting a new job anywhere. There is the usual curiosity about the new environment, co-workers, and anxiety over job performance. Clearly, however, beginning a new job on "the rez" will usually provide unforgettable experiences, even if some of them are rougher than others, as Michael Burney recalls of his years with the CTUIR.

It's an understatement to say I had no idea what to expect upon leaving for the Umatilla Reservation. I knew the experience would change me forever, and it did. And I believe the experience changed the Umatilla. The persistence and success of their cultural resource protection program over the past fourteen years is ample testimony. Finding myself on the reservation meant archaeology, at least for me, was going full circle; that is, I was, in a sense, coming home. Archaeology had always been enjoyable for me, but the real excitement came when I was given the opportunity to share my anthropological and archaeological education with my tribal students.

My initial time on the Umatilla Reservation was not without its challenges and problems, including being fired and rehired within a month's time. And I've since been fired from another reservation, too. Indians can make you cry, but as the years go by I've come to accept much of my experiences in Indian Country as just part of the cultural interchange necessary in the two-way learning process (adapted from Burney 2000).

school laundry and from 1923 to 1950 as classrooms for the Umatilla County District Number 44 Public School. In 1966 it was used for the Tribal Business Office and Board of Trustees' meeting hall. Unfortunately, a hot water heater had rusted through, leaking a considerable amount of water onto the basement floor and partially soaking the cardboard boxes storing the files. The boxes were immediately removed and placed in temporary storage on the second floor of the Administration Building, another historic tribal building.

A cursory examination of this material indicated a tremendously valuable collection of data, records, past studies, reports, and audio tapes pertaining to the recent history of the CTUIR. Unfortunately, without adequate funding, this database had not been properly restored, catalogued, and archived for use by tribal researchers. The lack of building space suitable for housing the tribe's archives was problematic. Many of the historic buildings still being used on Indian reservations do not meet today's standards for fire protection, security, climate control, or other amenities ideally sought for library and research facilities. Consequently, archival and research materials may be more often found in cardboard boxes in an obscure basement of a little-used tribal building.

In addition to quickly gathering as much cultural resource management information as possible, the CTUIR staff began developing partnerships with key regulatory organizations, including the U.S. Department of Energy; the Oregon and Washington State Historic Preservation Offices; the Advisory Council on Historic Preservation, Western Divisional Office; the Bureau of Land Management; the U.S. Forest Service; the Bureau of Reclamation; the Bonneville Power Administration; the U.S. Army Corps of Engineers; the National Park Service; and the Bureau of Indian Affairs, to name a few. Staff also began attending local, state, regional, and national professional archaeological and anthropological conferences to gain support and lobby for the newly formed tribal program.

The CTUIR were eager to work not only with the non-Indian archaeological community, but with other Indian bands and tribes that have traditionally used the Mid-Columbia River as well. Early in the development of the CTUIR cultural resource protection program, the staff had the opportunity of working with the Nez Perce Tribe of Idaho, the Confederated Tribes of the Warm Springs Indian Reservation, the Yakama Indian Nation, the Confederated Tribes of the Colville Reservation of Washington, and the Wanapum Band, also of Washington. CTUIR staff has also consulted with the Klamath Tribe, Chiloquin, Oregon; and the Confederated Tribes of the Siletz Indians, Siletz, Oregon. During 1992, the CTUIR engaged in a joint cultural resource management project with the Nez Perce Tribe to provide the Bonneville Power Administration with inventories, limited testing, and oral histories. The CTUIR continue to partner with tribes in their quest to keep the tribal cultural resource protection movement growing.

There are many good reasons to partner with these agencies and others (e.g., private clients), when a tribe begins building alliances to support its tribal program. The Umatilla and Wallowa Whitman national forests in northeastern Oregon made significant efforts in involving regional Indian tribes in cultural resource management. For example, the Forest Service, Pacific Northwest Region, was generous enough to provide financial support for four CTUIR tribal members to attend the Forest Service Paraprofessional Rec-7 Cultural Resource Management Training Program at Otter Rock, Oregon, and Fort Worden State Park, Washington. These one-week training sessions were just introductions but perfect for tribal staff members as part of their education and training.

Hey, Jeff, Is It a Sign if the Tent Collapses?

Establishing and maintaining a tribal cultural resource management program can be elusive and difficult, at best. More often than not, it's an uphill battle requiring vision and years of commitment. That commitment and vision were a vital part of one dark and lonely night in the Blue Mountains of northeastern Oregon, as Michael Burney again recalls.

Jeff and I spent most of the night hugging our center tent pole, trying to survive a bad high-country storm of rain, sleet, snow, hail, and high winds in the Blue Mountains of northeastern Oregon. It was a dark and lonely, dismal night, but we told stories and laughed our way through it. I had finally found the "action anthropology" missing during my previous years in CRM. In those early years of the program, Jeff and I spent a lot of nights in the bush, or on the road in some motel, but we were doing what we believed in. Back then, we *were* the Umatilla's cultural resource protection program. Since that humble beginning over a decade ago, the Umatilla Tribal CRM program has persevered to become one of the major tribal CRM programs in North America—the result of many natives and nonnatives working together (adapted from Burney 2000).

By 1990, the CTUIR program, only about three years old, had several achievements, which included: (1) the establishment of a tribal cultural resource archives; (2) providing education, training, and employment for tribal members; (3) preparation of a Tribal Cultural Resources Protection Act; (4) undertaking oral and written consultations with state and federal agencies, including the Idaho, Oregon, and Washington archaeological communities; (5) undertaking cultural resource inventories on the Umatilla Indian Reservation; (6) assisting with reburial of human remains; (7) participating with the Forest Service on the Columbia River Gorge Project; (8) participating with the U.S. Department of Energy in the Nuclear Waste Study Program; (9) working with other CTUIR departments to further awareness of having a tribal cultural resource program; (10) and preparing tribal cultural resource classes for federal management personnel such as the Forest Service.

The CTUIR obtained their tribal historic preservation office certification from the National Park Service in 1996. Michael S. Burney was their first tribal historic preservation officer from 1996 to 1998. Manfred E. W. (Fred) Jaehnig is presently in that position. In the early part of 2002, the CTUIR Cultural Resource Protection Program employed nearly thirty staff members—primarily tribal members, and non-Indian archaeologists based out of Mission, Oregon, and Richland, Washington. Jeff Van Pelt, an enrolled CTUIR tribal member and one of the "three amigos," manages the program.

The Bureau of Indian Affairs as a Catalyst

In 1987 and 1988, the Bureau of Indian Affairs had been less than enthusiastic about the CTUIR's new cultural resource program. The program had opposed efforts by the Bureau of Indian Affairs to demolish one of the twelve remaining Edwardian vernacular historic buildings comprising the Mission Campus on the reservation. These twelve buildings, dating between 1890 and 1940, represented about half of the total number of structures that once existed. The building scheduled for demolition in 1991 was the most imposing one left on the grounds. Once known as the Old School, it's now referred to as the Administration Building. It is a two-story brick building with a full basement, constructed sometime before 1910. The classrooms of the Umatilla Boarding School were housed on the first floor, and the auditorium and chapel were on the second floor.

In 1987, in response to the issues brought up through the Mission Campus, the CTUIR Board of Trustees had passed Resolution 88–17:

> It is a concern with the Board of Trustees that steps are taken promptly to protect the historic properties on the reservation from damage, destruction, or alteration and that the Board of Trustees requests the Bureau of Indian Affairs to initiate the Section 106 Review process of the National Historic Preservation Act to identify and protect historic buildings on the Umatilla Indian Reservation.

The tribal staff was eager to consult with the Bureau of Indian Affairs as co-managers in the treatment of prehistoric and historic cultural resources on the reservation. Despite repeated attempts to engage the Bureau of Indian Affairs in consultation, however, there was little response. To encourage action, the tribal staff made the following five recommendations to the Bureau of Indian Affairs:

1. That tribal staff be engaged in meaningful consultation on all cultural resource issues undertaken where the Bureau of Indian Affairs has a role;

2. That the Bureau of Indian Affairs consult specifically with the tribal staff regarding their thinking pertaining to the National Register eligibility of the Campus as a traditional cultural property;

3. That the Bureau of Indian Affairs consult the tribal staff in developing a long-term strategy for the preservation, conservation, and enhancement of the historic buildings comprising the Campus;

4. That the Bureau of Indian Affairs consult the tribal staff in developing a close working relationship in the co-management of the tribe's prehistoric and historic cultural resources; and

5. That the Bureau of Indian Affairs provide tribal staff access to data that would assist the tribes in better understanding the last 136 years of history on the Umatilla reservation (Burney 1991).

Prior to about 1988, the Bureau of Indian Affairs, its contractors, or other non-Indian groups undertook archaeological projects on the Umatilla Indian Reservation. With the inception of the CTUIR's cultural resource capability, it no longer made sense for the Bureau of Indian Affairs archaeologist to travel from Portland to undertake small cultural resource inventories. These kinds of on-reservation projects provided the funding and education, training, and employment of tribal members to assist with the archival research and on through draft and final report preparation. The CTUIR could now co-partner with archaeologists and work cooperatively on a contractual basis.

Achieving Recognition

A particular challenge revolved around the CTUIR's Cultural Resource Protection Program being accepted by state and federal agencies, as well as by the private sector, as capable of providing professional cultural resource services. With the exception of the initial Hanford project, described further on, the CTUIR's program had no experience, no track record in the cultural resource management business. The tribal staff, however, was eager to begin establishing its tribal program by obtaining and participating in any project, no matter how large or small, on or off the reservation.

When the CTUIR first began photocopying site forms and replicating inventory and site location data on U.S. Geological Society maps on file with Oregon and Washington State Historic Preservation Offices, the regional archaeologist for the Pacific Northwest Region of the U.S. Forest Service objected. He felt it inappropriate to release this site-sensitive data, especially if the information had been derived from lands administered by the U.S. Forest Service. Both state historic preservation offices released the information anyway, and the database became the beginning of the CTUIR archives.

Because of the Nuclear Waste Policy Act of 1982, the CTUIR, along with the Yakama Nation in Washington and the Nez Perce Tribe in Idaho were granted the status of "Affected Indian Tribes" by the U.S. Department of Energy and were provided with funding for their Nuclear Waste Study Programs. The Hanford Site in southeastern Washington was being considered for the storage of nuclear waste.

Both the CTUIR and the Yakama Nation have treaty-ceded lands within Hanford's 560 square miles. The initial funding to start the CTUIR's tribal program came from the U.S. Department of Energy through the Council of Energy Resource Tribes in the mid-1980s. As early as January 1988, the CTUIR submitted a proposal to the Hanford Site, titled "Tribal Participation in Cultural Resource Management at the Hanford Nuclear Reservation." This was a bold effort, considering that the CTUIR's program was in its infancy.

The Hanford funding, however, quickly disappeared in the winter of 1989, with the Hanford Site's elimination as a potential nuclear waste repository. This loss of funding eliminated the Nuclear Waste Study Program, the newly hired archaeologist, three tribal archaeological technicians, and their supervisor. The building and offices disappeared, and the program's office was relocated in the tribal administration building. The new office was so small that one of the three staff members had to step into the hallway to open the one, very worn, file cabinet.

The loss of U.S. Department of Energy funding did bring an abrupt, though temporary, halt to the CTUIR's hopes for a cultural resource protection program. Nevertheless, the founding concept of empowering tribal members to actively manage their cultural resources continued to be pursued by the "three amigos" on a volunteer basis. The idea was to keep talking to one another, thereby continuing the dialogue and keeping the cultural resource protection program alive until Hanford's funding might reappear or alternative funding could be identified.

After the loss of the Hanford funding, alternative sources of moneys were obtained by the CTUIR contracting out their cultural resource management services. This idea was new, however, and required considerable effort to gain tribal support and approval. And equally important was establishing the procedures needed when employing tribal accounting practices. Tribal government can be very sensitive to the potential for mismanagement and contractual difficulties, resulting in a financial liability to the tribe. Convincing the tribal government of the need for a tribal program was one thing, but selling the program as self-supportive through its own contractual funding was another. The CTUIR contracting business slowly expanded. Contracts were awarded by the Bonneville Power Administration, the Bureau of Reclamation, the Forest Service, the Bureau of Indian Affairs, and various private companies and local governments. The Hanford funding eventually returned as well.

The U.S. Department of Energy's early funding, however, allowed the CTUIR to begin advertising their new tribal program by publishing and preparing cultural resource reports; establishing their archives, the foundation to any tribal program; and developing valuable professional relationships between tribal members and state and federal cultural resource management personnel. Between 1988 and 2001, the CTUIR routinely gave at least one paper, and oftentimes more, at the Northwest Anthropological Conference held annually in the Pacific Northwest. *Northwest Anthropological Research Notes*, Moscow, Idaho, has published each paper's abstract.

All of the CTUIR professional papers presented at conferences from 1988 to 1999 can be found in a special issue of the *Journal of Northwest Anthropology* (formerly *Northwest Anthropological Research Notes*; Burney and Van Pelt 2002). Topics covered include why Native Americans should be involved with cultural resource management; expectations that Native Americans had from society, agencies, anthropologists, archaeologists, and other cultural resource personnel; the need to consider other types of resources as cultural resources (which eventually became traditional cultural properties); and managing these resources holistically (which eventually became ecosystem management and, more currently, stewardship).

The CTUIR Approach to Protecting Cultural Resources

The CTUIR program emphasizes that tribal members work directly with elders in the field to provide day-to-day historical information to younger tribal members. This traditional method of teaching provides tribal youth with knowledge that is unique to elders. By adhering to this oral tradition of teaching and learning, the program supports the native system in which tribal members live.

The CTUIR program oftentimes required an oral history component as part of the Class I file and literature search and cultural resource inventory. Information was obtained from elders and other tribal members about different places on and off the reservation that would otherwise be unavailable in the background research and archaeological record. Since the late 1980s the CTUIR have accumulated a significant number of oral histories, some recorded on tape and film.

The CTUIR worldview embraces Mother Earth as sacred, so it is not surprising that the CTUIR see their aboriginal territory as abundant with resources. The CTUIR program recognizes the same kinds of prehistoric and historic resources that non-Indian cultural resource programs do, ranging from Columbia River fishing sites to chipped stone scatters in the Blue Mountains to historic buildings on the reservation. In addition to working with artifacts and features, they broadly identify a wide range of cultural resources.

Resources significant to the CTUIR include such things as the Indian people themselves, their communities, and their way of life; and Indian elders, with their unique information regarding their personal histories as well as tribal histories. Places sacred to CTUIR tribal members can include dance grounds and associated lodges; vision questing sites; sweat bath sites; monumental geological features; ritually modified areas or rock art sites; burial areas and cemeteries; boundaries between cultural, life, and geological zones; mountain passes; headwaters of streams and rivers; confluences of rivers; cascades, waterfalls, rapids, hot and cold springs; caves; gathering areas where sacred plants, stones, and other cultural materials are available; sites of historical significance; hills; lakes, such as Wallowa Lake in northeastern Oregon; rivers; islands; cairns; and other rock alignments.

Where Does the Passion for Protection Come From?

Prior to European contact, the Indian people had effectively managed their resources, including the sacred areas of their ancestors. Since their treaty with the United States government of June 9, 1855, the Umatilla, Walla Walla, and Cayuse relinquished management of their aboriginal lands and abundant natural and cultural resources. Many Indian lands and resources are now government property, state property, or private property. Deward Walker Jr. (1991, 101) has noted, "Clearly sacred geography is a universal and essential feature of the practice of American Indian religions. Without continuing access to many sacred sites that maintain their physical integrity, most practitioners of traditional American Indian religions will be denied the opportunity to practice many vital ceremonies."

Soon after contact, however, the people lost most of their aboriginal homeland and resources that were needed to sustain a traditional way of life: water for a clean environment, where the salmon and other fish, eels, and riverine resources so highly prized by the people for their way of life and subsistence can be found; the elk, deer, and other forest animals; the root grounds scattered throughout the Blue Mountains, which provide a multitude of edible roots traditional to the people for their everyday dietary needs; and the berry patches, especially huckleberries, likewise scattered throughout the Blue Mountains. The huckleberry and other edible berries are an important food crop that is traditional to the people. The woods and prairies traditionally used by the people are themselves a cultural resource for many reasons. The younger tribal members are being taught the importance of protecting these sacred areas on their reservations and ceded lands.

Indian elders, and others, are concerned about future activities in their traditional use areas because of the burial sites scattered throughout. In the past, tribal members were able to travel at will throughout the Umatilla National Forest for subsistence and religious uses of the land. This traditional use pattern is not a reality today. Tribal members are restricted, due to increased road development, logging activity, utilization of the natural resources by non-Indians, and increasing private land ownership.

Ethnographic resources refer to those resources associated with traditional subsistence or with sacred ceremonial, religious, or other cultural meaning for native peoples. The Hanford Reach of the Columbia River is perhaps the most striking ethnographic resource that is significant to the Umatilla, Walla Walla, Cayuse, Wanapum, Yakama, Palus, and other tribes. Not only is the history of Indian use of the Hanford Reach well documented, Indian people today continue to focus much of their attention on the river and its resources, principally fish.

These various tribes, having used the Hanford Reach for thousands of years, advocate for resource protection, while maintaining a constant vigil to protect their environment, natural resources, and cultural history. Fishing stations along the banks of the Columbia River are good examples of contemporary use areas, and they may have an archaeological component as well. The CTUIR have even suggested that the Hanford Reach itself be regarded a traditional cultural property. As noted by one researcher:

> Indian people today continue to focus attention on their ancestral usual and accustomed places at Hanford and the Reach. The People came, lived, and died there representing a continuity important to middle

Columbia native peoples. The entire landscape that comprises the Hanford Site possesses considerable cultural and religious value for Indian people. (Nickens 1998, 1)

Developing a Contracting Program

The CTUIR's position is that any project requiring cultural resources undertaken on their reservation, or ceded lands, be accomplished through their tribal program. Early on, the program was awarded several contracts, primarily inventories, through the Umatilla National Forest, providing additional education, training, and employment for tribal members. The CTUIR undertook several contracts with the U.S Forest Service in relation to cultural studies for the Columbia River Gorge National Scenic Area and the Malheur National Forest.

Likewise, the CTUIR secured a large contract with the Bonneville Power Administration to undertake inventories and testing of twenty-one fishery-enhancement locations. Additional contracts for archaeological services came from the Bureau of Reclamation, Pacific Northwest Region; the Bureau of Indian Affairs-Umatilla Agency; and the Oregon Department of Transportation. The work undertaken for these agencies was on the Umatilla Indian Reservation or on treaty-ceded lands. Projects included everything from conducting Class I file and literature searches, monitoring, Class II (sample) nondisturbing pedestrian inventories, Class III (100 percent) intensive nondisturbing pedestrian inventories, testing, oral histories, and report preparation.

Most of these projects also have an oral history report prepared to supplement the archival and archaeological field data. This aspect of tribal CRM may, more than others, actively involve older tribal members, or elders. This is, of course, a very good thing. Many elders enjoy being consulted regarding cultural and archaeological issues and appreciate the opportunity to participate. Other guidance to the program comes from the CTUIR Cultural Resource Commission.

Finding and Training a Staff to Be Self-Sustaining

The CTUIR Cultural Resource Protection Program uses a combination of tribal and nontribal members to staff the program. Nontribal members typically have degrees in anthropology and experience in archaeology and cultural resource management. They provide the expertise required by agencies, which needs to conform to the Secretary of Interior's qualification standards. Tribal members typically staff the manager position and administrative, cultural resource crew chief, and technician positions. They provide the tribal perspective and heart needed to keep it a tribal program.

In time, the expectation is that tribal members will gain education and experience and gradually take on positions with increasing authority. While the CTUIR are open to the idea of tribal members earning degrees in anthropology with emphasis in archaeology, it is not required. If the CTUIR must continue to rely on the non-Indian community for archaeological expertise, so be it. The idea is not to turn tribal members into archaeologists, but rather to develop a cultural resource protection program that incorporates tribal values and expertise from wherever it comes.

In the beginning, few tribal members had any cultural resource experience. One of the first remedies was to send promising tribal members to a Paraprofessional Cultural Resource Management Training Program offered by the U.S. Forest Service. Afterward, they worked as summer employees in cultural resources with the Umatilla and Wallowa Whitman National Forests, thereby increasing their on-the-job cultural resource management experience without having to travel great distances from the reservation. The sensitivity of the Umatilla and Wallowa Whitman National Forests to local Indian concerns for the co-management of Indian cultural resources exemplifies a spirit of cooperation for other federal land-managing agencies.

In 1995, the CTUIR initiated the Indian Lake (Lake Humtepin) Aboriginal Lifeways, Prehistoric Artifact Recognition and Documentation Training, primarily for tribal youth (Burney, Van Pelt, and Bailor 1998). This forty-hour outdoor cultural resource certification course on the Umatilla Indian Reservation emphasized the importance of documenting prehistoric archaeological sites and the technologies utilized by peoples in the prehistoric past. Another forty hours of on-the-job training were received after completion of the outdoor session. This tribally designed course used both native and nonnative instructors and ways of teaching. Included were tribal elders; tribal staff; academics in their respective fields of anthropology, archaeology, or one of the many subdisciplines; state and federal historic preservation personnel; cultural resource management practitioners; and experts in aboriginal tool replication. A video, *Not Just Stones and Bones*, was produced and is now distributed worldwide through the Archaeology Channel (<www.archaeology channel.org>).

Training Non-Indians about Tribal Perspectives

The CTUIR Program provides three various cultural resource protection–related training sessions for other tribes and state and federal agencies. One example, initiated in 1998, is the Archaeological Resource Protection Act Training for Law Enforcement (Longenecker and Van Pelt 1999), designed to teach officers how

The Grass Roots of Tribal CRM

The courage taken by one tribal member to step forward and take on something new is well illustrated in this moving testimony by Lloyd Barkley, an employee of the CTUIR Cultural Resource Protection Program. This "beginner" to cultural resource protection is now one of the senior personnel.

My name is Lloyd Barkley. I am a Yakama Nation tribal member[,] born and raised on the Umatilla Indian Reservation. I have been working in CRM for the Umatilla for about eight and one-half years. When I first started[,] the Chevron Pipeline Company was replacing valves on an existing pipeline on both sides of the Umatilla River. Paul and Randy Minthorn happened to drive by and ended up negotiating on the hood of a Chevron vehicle for a tribal monitor to address cultural resources. I was sought out because the qualifications were having a driver's license and an insured vehicle. Paul briefed me about what to look for as far as artifacts and human remains were concerned. So I found myself monitoring this project with a camera around my neck I didn't know how to use, a notebook without knowing what kinds of notes were expected of me, and still not sure what I was looking for. This is why we train our staff so extensively (Barkley 1998).

to catch and convict archaeological looters. The CTUIR staff found that other training—for example, courses offered by the Federal Law Enforcement Training Center—failed to provide an adequate tribal perspective. The CTUIR designed a two-day course that included lectures by tribal managers and tribal elders, as well as an intensive in-field component using simulated looted sites. By focusing on the harm done to Native Americans by looters, law enforcement officials lost their preconceived idea that looting was a "victimless crime" and left with a newfound commitment to stop looting.

Figure 5.2. Lloyd Barkley reviewing notes of a student in the CTUIR cultural resources technician training program.

Building on the success of the Archaeological Resource Protection Act training, the CTUIR have designed training programs for other tribes, tribal judges, and Oregon State officials. For example, the State and Tribal Summit for Oregon workshop provides training by, and for, Oregon agencies and tribes to address culture-specific concerns, beliefs, issues, ideas, and the protection and preservation of cultural resources (Longenecker and Van Pelt 2000).

Summary

Today, the CTUIR Cultural Resource Protection Program routinely undertakes all phases of cultural resource management, both on and off the reservation. Activities include everyday Section 106 compliance activities, administering of the program, conducting file and literature searches, recording oral histories, monitoring, undertaking inventories, testing and evaluating sites, responding to inadvertent discoveries of human remains, training, sharing experiences with other tribes, interacting with agencies and universities, preparing professional papers and attending archaeological and anthropological conferences, preparing technical reports, and publishing in journals.

As the CTUIR's program grows, maintaining adequate space for tribal staff and archives is a constant challenge. Moneys are needed for curating the oral history tapes and videos, photographs, maps, and voluminous written material pertaining to the CTUIR's prehistory and history. The collection is already of amazing proportions when we consider that it didn't exist in 1987. At that time, tribal records (paper and audio tape) were scattered and in danger of being destroyed through water damage, fire, and neglect. An exciting new facility on the Umatilla Indian Reservation is the Tamástslikt Cultural Institute. Tamástslikt is an interpretive facility that houses a large variety of items, including old tribal newspapers, records, and historical photographs. Photographs from the famous Major Moorhouse collection are included. Tamástslikt is the only Oregon Trail Interpretive Center located on an Indian reservation.

As a result of the CTUIR efforts over the last fifteen years, the CTUIR Cultural Resource Protection Program is one of the larger and most effective native cultural resource management organizations in the nation. A large portion of the CTUIR's Cultural Resource Protection Program's success has been due to support from within the tribe's governing body, through the Board of Trustees, Cultural Resource Commission, elders, and leaders. Tribal members are encouraged to participate actively in the program. Sensitive issues addressed, in part, through anthropology, archaeology, oral history, and archival research are given attention by tribal teachers and elders. Tribal cultural resource management on the Umatilla Reservation demonstrates that cultural resource management can go beyond rote compliance with federal cultural resource legislation and be a true community effort.

Part II
IMPLEMENTING A TRIBAL CULTURAL RESOURCE MANAGEMENT AGENDA

Tribal cultural resource management is still evolving. Today, for example, some tribes have full-fledged programs, working daily with agencies to protect resources, while other tribes, with federal agencies located on their native lands, have virtually no involvement in agency efforts and no idea how to get started. Many honest and sincere cultural resource professionals are working with tribes to protect resources in a spirit of cooperative management; but there are also others who still believe Indians should not be involved in cultural resource management—at least, in any decision-making capacity—and do little, if anything, to facilitate their involvement. Similarly, some federal agencies live within the spirit of cultural resource legislation, having progressive programs that seek to preserve, protect, and make resources accessible. Unfortunately, other federal agencies fail to acknowledge their legislative responsibility and do the minimum amount of compliance possible. And finally, we see that tribal rhetoric is refined, but the implementation of tribal ideas lags. It's time to bridge this impasse.

In part II we present ideas on ways to keep the tribal cultural resource movement growing. We begin with chapter 6, which focuses on starting a tribal program. Certainly, any band or tribe that has started a program could write its own book describing how it got the program started and how the program has influenced tribal members' personal lives and careers, their tribe, and the cultural resources of their area. In chapter 6 we present some of the issues that we have seen or heard about and offer suggestions regarding the key ingredients that are needed to be successful.

In chapter 7, we discuss the cornerstone of tribal cultural resource management: consultation. Our intent in this chapter is to persuade archaeologists, cultural resource professionals, and agency officials that consultation is nothing to fear. In actuality, it is something to treasure.

Through consultation, an environment conducive to creating synergy can result. That, of course, assumes that the consulting parties have laid the groundwork for productive consultation by developing relationships based on honesty, mutual trust, and respect. We also hope in this chapter to illustrate to tribal representatives the need to take consultation seriously and deliver the appropriate people to the table.

In chapter 8, we introduce the concept of the cultural landscape. This concept has been growing in popularity for several years and addresses many of the concerns expressed by American Indians in the past. Managing cultural resources by landscape and not property lines, however, is challenging and creates the need for creative solutions.

In chapter 9 we discuss the concept of cultural resource stewardship. We think Congress was quite clear that its intent in passing cultural resource legislation was to ensure that important cultural resources would be available for future generations. In implementing the legislation, we seem to have lost that intent, as archaeological interests took precedence over the people's interests, and bureaucratic pressures created a system that favored process over common sense.

Tribal cultural resource management is a natural outcome of many aspects of North American archaeology. In effect, it's archaeology that's come full circle by showing increased respect for today's native peoples and stewardship of their resources.

DEVELOPING A TRIBAL CULTURAL RESOURCE PROTECTION PROGRAM

Cultural resource programs operated by tribes come in many shapes and sizes and collectively make up what we refer to as tribal cultural resource management. Today, there are approximately one hundred tribal cultural resource programs. Some are successful, some are managing to stay afloat, and others continue to be challenged. Many other tribes would like to start a program, but have not yet done so. This chapter focuses on starting and developing a cultural resource program within a tribal structure.

Our concept of tribal cultural resource management is that tribal programs will generally need to interact with organizations outside the tribe. Even if a tribe is concerned only with protecting resources on its reservation, it will likely need to interact with agencies outside the reservation from time to time. For this reason, much of this book involves ways to work with others as effectively as possible.

To present our thoughts on developing a tribal cultural resource management program, we have organized the chapter as follows:

- Reasons for starting and supporting a cultural resource program
- Starting a cultural resource protection program
- Learning the cultural resource management system
- Becoming a THPO facing tribal programs
- Obstacles

Reasons for Starting and Supporting a Tribal Cultural Resources Program

There are many reasons why a tribe may choose to start a cultural resource protection program. One obvious reason is that the tribe thinks it can do a better job of protecting reservation resources than anybody else. If there are off-reservation resources of concern, which is often the case, the tribe may feel it needs to get involved in decisions being made about those resources, too. To ensure protection, some kind of program needs to be started, whether it is composed solely of a few people to oversee what others are doing, or whether it is a full-blown program that conducts all the various cultural resource protection activities.

Tribal programs tend to differ from nontribal programs in at least two important ways. Site protection and conservation of sites, especially sites that are directly involved in the ongoing culture, are usually emphasized more than research. The term *protection* is a key distinction between a tribal program and a nontribal program. Nontribal programs have traditionally placed greater emphasis on data recovery (i.e., inventory, testing, and excavation) and research for compliance and academic purposes. Tribal programs also undertake data recovery and research when necessary, but with a greater emphasis on the stewardship of the resources through careful, long-term avoidance, monitoring, restoration, and data control.

For many tribes, avoidance of the resource is frequently the preferred alternative. If a site does not have to be impacted, and subsequently mitigated (that is, excavated), then absolute avoidance of the resource is the best way to go. Avoidance of the resource saves time, money, and, most important, the resource itself. Protective measures include, but are not limited to: avoidance, site stabilization, public education, and law enforcement. Many times tribes advocate spending less effort to identify, evaluate, and mitigate resources, but spend greater effort and funding on monitoring, assessing site conditions, and devising and implementing protective measures to protect and preserve the resources.

A second reason tribes often want to start a cultural resource program is to provide economic opportunities for their tribal members. Many aspects of cultural resource protection are ideal for tribal members—jobs for tribal members and perhaps income from contracts that can be used, in part, to invest in tribal members to provide for their on-the-job education, training, and employment. In some tribes there may be certain activities for which use of tribal members is not appropriate, such as archaeological excavation or human remains recovery and handling. In these cases, nontribal members may need to be a part of the program. But other activities, such as archaeological surveying, construction monitoring, analyzing artifacts, consulting with agencies, maintaining the records and archives, curating collections, and conducting documentary research, provide tribal members with training and experience in pursuing careers. In a large program there are also a few administrative jobs, such as receptionist, secretary, and records clerk. And any program, regardless of size, will be able to develop many short-term paying opportunities for elders, who are needed to provide information, or advice, about a particular area, resource, or project.

Providing these opportunities for tribal members opens doors outside the reservations, too. A broad range of experience for tribal members, from the administrative office to the field and laboratory, is valuable in developing the skills wanted by off-reservation employers. Private contracting firms can provide subcontracting opportunities for the tribal program and education, training, and employment for individual tribal members. There are also advantages to getting tribal members employed with federal agencies like the U.S. Forest Service, Bureau of Land Management, U.S. Department of Defense, U.S. Department of Energy, and others. Not only do tribal members learn how to work in a variety of settings, they gain a wide range of cultural resource experience, and they can assist the tribe in developing relationships with these outside organizations.

Where does the money come from? Most reservations have ground-disturbing projects being undertaken every year, ranging from road construction, housing developments, water and sewer improvements, gravel mining, oil and gas exploration, coal mining, and timber sales. Whoever is paying for these projects, be it some U.S. government agency or the tribe itself, should include enough moneys to adequately review the project for impact on cultural resources and mitigate that impact as necessary. These projects could require a cultural resource inventory and possibly more, including ethnographic studies and oral history. For many tribes these services are still being provided by the Bureau of Indian Affairs or off-reservation contracting firms, or the work is not being done at all.

And don't forget the off-reservation projects. An agency undertaking any project on lands with resources important to the tribe should consult with the tribe about its plan. The Zuni Pueblo's tribal program figured that out early on (Anyon and Ferguson 1995, 919). Moneys should be provided for consultations, and if cultural resource work is needed, there is no reason that the tribe should not do it—no reason, that is, as long as the tribe has an adequately staffed cultural resource program with a good track record.

Federal land-managing agencies like the U.S. Forest Service and Bureau of Land Management have the potential to provide education, training, and employment through contracting for tribal members. Federal agencies like the U.S. Department of Defense have the potential to provide the same, along with grants for specialized services, including oral history, ethnographic studies, monitoring, and co-management of the resource base.

Other reasons for starting a cultural resource program include educational opportunities for tribal members, retrieval of cultural information that may have been or would likely be lost if someone did not start organizing it, interactions with elders, return of human remains and other items of cultural patrimony, and so on. For example, one effect of a tribal program is the way it helps tribal members reconnect with their heritage. Cultural resource projects create situations that require tribal staff members to learn about places that are important in their tribal history and culture. Perhaps the situation is a construction project in an area that was once used by a particular family, or perhaps it involves a threatened plant resource believed to have cultural importance. Whatever the situation, staff members must identify persons with knowledge about these things, interview them, and perhaps take them on a field trip. Such efforts are restoring a traditional role for elders as teachers.

Anyone who has ever participated in such an event knows that visits to cultural places often lead elders to remember things they may not have thought about for a long time. Discussions inevitably concern oral tradition, resources, aboriginal tools and techniques, and archaeological sites. The power of visiting places, observing resources not seen or thought about for years, and talking about such things is profound. Because of the numerous projects that are being undertaken, and because such projects generally focus on places and resources, these activities are affecting the way tribal knowledge is passed on to succeeding generations. Cultural knowledge used to rely almost solely on oral systems. Today, because of the system that is in place, this information must often be recorded on site forms or be taped for archives, recorded on maps, or videotaped. Cultural knowledge used to be restricted to certain people. While much of this knowledge continues to be restricted, there has been a relaxation of the rules about certain types of knowledge, to enable tribes to work within the governmental system and help save the resources.

These tribal staff members taking on cultural resource management roles are by necessity becoming cultural resource specialists in their own right. A new career path has emerged on and off the reservation. Specialists must learn why certain cultural sites are found across the landscape, learn how to identify information contained in the land and artifacts associated with a site, and try to understand the importance of these places in the culture today. Increasingly, we see tribal cultural resource specialists interviewing elders, taking elders to visit places, and taking the time to learn traditional technologies.

Other tribal members working in cultural resource management are becoming tribal liaisons, serving as intermediaries between the Indian and the non-Indian worlds. They routinely deal with non-Indians (such as federal agency managers, construction crews, city managers, looters, or lawyers) to explain why places and resources must be protected. They must also work with Indian elders and Indian youth to learn and teach about aboriginal ways, cultural sites, and working in the non-Indian world. They are learning how to forge agreements so that tribes can obtain funding to do more surveys, to monitor more construction projects, to train more tribal youth, and to do more oral histories. Learning to work in both worlds gives them a special set of skills that will be important to them and to their tribe in the future.

Each tribe has a different situation and codes for dealing with cultural-type places and information, so it is hard to be specific about what kind of program a tribe should have. But in most cases, tribes will benefit by developing some type of cultural resource protection program. Starting one and being successful, however, are not necessarily easy things to do.

Starting a Cultural Resource Program

Starting a tribal program begins by obtaining approval and resources from the tribe. Each tribe has its own organizational structure, so exactly who has the authority to grant this approval and dedicate funding and resources (e.g., offices) will need to be determined. The approval needs to be from "high up," because one of the first actions that might be necessary is to approve policies and procedures for conducting cultural resource work on and off the reservation.

For example, if the new cultural resource group intends to review future timber sales for the tribal forestry department, that requirement will need to be imposed on the forestry department from above. Likewise, staff from the new cultural resource group will be attending meetings about projects on and off the reservation to consult about needed cultural resource efforts. These individuals need to be empowered by the tribe to make decisions, or some process needs to be approved for bringing back information and communicating it to the individual or group (e.g., tribal council, cultural committee) that will make the decision.

The need for funding goes without saying. Even if the cultural resource group intends to pay its way through grants and contracts, there will likely be some lag time in which salaries will need to be covered until funds start flowing in. Even then, it is almost impossible to operate a program fully on contract dollars. Inevitably, once the program has started, the tribe will have occasion to need its services, requests from local schools will come in, or an agency will want to come by to discuss some of its future ideas. Adequate funding is needed to carry the program.

Staffing

Staffing is a major aspect of any cultural resource program, but especially on a reservation where a tribal employment office will be looking for tribal members to be given first choice at any available jobs. Tribal members should be involved in their program's cultural resource management tasks, planning their future, and educating the archaeological and Indian communities regarding their mutual concerns and differences. This is, in part, what a successful tribal program is. However, oftentimes no one on the reservation has experience in the cultural resource management profession as we know it today.

Cultural resource management is a highly technical field. Most state and federal agencies rely on the Secretary of the Interior's Standards and Guidelines for Archaeology and Historic Preservation, published in the *Federal Register* on September 29, 1983 (*Federal Register* 48[190]), to determine who qualifies to provide paleontological, archaeological, and historical services on their lands. If a tribal member does not have a university degree in anthropology or a related field, the tribe cannot obtain the archaeology permits needed by state and federal agencies to undertake a project. This is an ironic situation, in that American Indians believe they have been taking care of their cultural resources from time immemorial— long before the Secretary of the Interior Standards and Guidelines appeared. Cultural resource management is nothing new in Indian Country.

Nevertheless, the staff needs to be experienced in cultural resource management, whether its members have degrees or not. Training and experience are needed in areas such as archaeological surveying, identifying artifacts, completing site forms, conducting oral history, performing archaeological test excavations, describing artifacts, drawing artifacts, and so on. Various types of training are available, but person-to-person training works well, followed by on-the-job training.

Oftentimes, tribes build their initial staffs with university-trained archaeologists experienced in contract archaeology or the *business* of cultural resource management. Since the 1980s, many archaeologists have had the opportunity of working for Indian tribes, being asked either to develop the program for the tribe or to join an already existing program. These have generally been win-win arrangements. The archaeologist was afforded the opportunity of working with a native group, and the tribe needed university-trained archaeologists to round out its new programs, especially, when applying to the National Park Service for Tribal Historic Preservation Office certification.

Like the earlier cultural resource management days, this new job requires archaeologists to relocate or be on the reservation for extended periods of time. Many find working with Indian tribes immensely enjoyable. It's really just too much fun, but the cliché "no pain—no gain" comes with working in Indian Country. To be sure, working for Indian tribes is oftentimes demanding, complicated, and extremely difficult (Nicholas and Andrews 1997).

An archaeologist newly hired to begin the foundations of a tribal program may rely heavily on educating his tribal staff through "oral teachings." The method that the archaeologist was subjected to during his or her education—extensive reading requirements, papers, class debates—probably won't be appropriate for a room full of tribal youths who may or may not have a high school degree. On-the-job training may be more the norm. This initial assistance familiarizes tribal students and technicians with archaeology, anthropology, the cultural resource management process, and contracting with federal agencies for historic preservation services. Over time, tribal members will begin to understand the non-Indian ways of communicating (shake hands firmly; make eye contact; be cordial but confident; use lots of acronyms like BLM [Bureau of Land Management], NPS [National Park Service], NHPA [National Historic Preservation Act], and TCP [Traditional Cultural Property]; and carry a briefcase with all the necessary papers and files to surround yourself with).

All these activities help natives observe nonnatives in their professional environments and become better accustomed to speaking cultural resource management jargon. This is important because non-Indians may not know much about Indian languages, but they are proficient in cultural resource mumbo jumbo. They also know how to leave a paper trail recording their mumbo jumbo, and so should you when working with them. An Indian well-versed in mumbo jumbo can confuse his or her adversary, causing the person to withdraw, sullenly pondering, "How did this Indian become so skilled in mumbo jumbo?" Most likely, from a renegade Siyapo (nonnative) archaeologist, who's "gone Injun" and let the cat out of the bag, so to speak.

Other things to be learned include personal codes of behavior; being timely (i.e., Siyapo time vs. Indian time); regularly attending all meetings whenever possible; returning phone calls, e-mails, faxes, or letters; and generally mimicking how business is done in the bureaucratic scheme of things. Human relations become very important as a new tribal program identifies itself and works toward active and meaningful participation in the contract archaeology that is available to the tribe. Tribal staff members are encouraged to evaluate and sharpen their skills toward working more actively with the non-Indian community.

Many times tribal staff members may need to travel—say, to training sessions. This can be difficult, if they have not done this previously. There may be tribal members without a driver's license, identification, or a major credit card; the latter is required when renting a vehicle and oftentimes to check into a hotel. Generally, tribal members will have only cash from their per diem checks, issued by the tribal accounting department before their trip.

There are many great training and educational venues, which are excellent for tribal members just starting out in cultural resource management or already in a career. These classes and workshops are of short duration, between two and three days; are oftentimes held in different locations that are agreeable to travel; provide optional university graduate credit; and are presented in an oral manner that is amenable to tribal students, who are away from the reservation with little experience in such workshops. The more education and training opportunities are provided to tribal students, the quicker the results. But it is a full-time endeavor.

As pointed out by Jeff Van Pelt in his foreword to this book, tribal members are not the only ones who need training. An archaeologist brought in to help build the program needs training as well. How do you provide someone raised in middle-class white America with a tribal perspective? Again, on-the-job training seems the most effective. *Verbal whippings* is another term for it. After the tenth or twentieth time a tribal manager or elder "explains" to you how your logic is flawed, you start— and we mean, start—to get the picture.

Consequently, when a nonnative first begins working for an Indian tribe, there will generally be a period of adjustment and learning forthcoming. Edgerton (1965) discusses his fieldwork with the Menominee in 1959, and Nicholas and Andrews (1997) remind us that there is also a dark side of archaeological–aboriginal relations.

Any number of cultural differences, or inter- and intratribal politics, can become a contentious fact of life to deal with in building and maintaining a tribal program. Nothing new there, folks! More than one archaeologist newly working for an Indian tribe might think, "I seem to have slipped into applied archeology," or something. It's just the way it is in Indian Country, and sometimes the consequences of these cultural differences can be amusing. One of these amusing incidents originated from an encounter that an archaeologist had with an all-Indian crew (see sidebar).

Setting Up the Office

Several fundamental and practical requirements about starting a program need to be mentioned. An office needs to be established and staffed. There is nothing more frustrating

Indians One, Anthropologists Zero

Anthropology is the study of the many varied peoples and cultures around the world, right? And fieldwork among the natives is part of anthropology, right? Well, sometimes anthropology and undertaking archaeological fieldwork with the natives don't always mix—not in the Blue Mountains of northeastern Oregon, anyway.

Arrangements had been made with a gentleman working on his Ph.D. in anthropology to join our CTUIR field crew as the replacement principal investigator. The opportunity being offered this fellow seemed golden. Getting to work in the Blue Mountains of northeastern Oregon with an for someone trying to get hold of a cultural resource department than to have the phone ring and ring and ring. If there is insufficient funding for a person to be in the office who can answer the phone and take messages, make sure there is voice mail or an answering machine. And return those calls. You never know when it might be about an inadvertent discovery, a looting, or a potential contract. Regardless, all calls should be answered and returned.

A fax machine and a computer are also requisites for any professional program. E-mail is widespread, and you will miss out on a lot of communications if you don't have it. Items that can't be e-mailed can be faxed, making a fax machine indispensable.

These new technologies notwithstanding, many items still arrive via the U.S. mail: reports, scopes of

(*Continued*)

all-Indian archaeology field crew was an experience of a lifetime. This was field archaeology and anthropology. Apparently, it was an experience of this anthropologist's lifetime, as well.

He called from a pay phone booth somewhere in northeastern Oregon. After only several days on the job, our principal investigator had slipped out of the Indians' camp and was making his getaway, and fast. So fast, in fact, he took the project's field money needed for truck fuel, groceries, and the like. No pleading on my part could convince this guy it was okay to drop the moneys off at the CTUIR tribal offices where the crew could retrieve it. Nope, he was heading west out of Umatilla Country lickety-split, where an anthropologist could be an anthropologist without bothersome Indians—at least, without this bunch of Indians. He pledged to mail the funds to me once he safely arrived back on the Oregon Coast somewhere.

It's not that the crew was inhospitable or unaccepting of this academically advanced "student of mankind," but rather, the incident showed the anthropologist's unwillingness to adapt. And, in all fairness, it's not that he could not adapt; he just probably didn't give it a chance. Regardless, working with native peoples on reservations may not be everyone's cup of tea. In this case anyway, Indians 1, Anthropologist 0.

work, requests for proposal, letters inviting you to meetings, meeting minutes, requests for information, and announcements of training courses and conferences. Between e-mail, faxes, and the post office, the information flow is never-ending. What to do with it? It has to be filed so that it can be retrieved by whoever is handling that particular piece of business. Nothing is more embarrassing than to go to a meeting unprepared because you did not get the materials sent out before the meeting, or you could not find the necessary file.

Finally, we mentioned earlier that staff will need to make considerable effort to contact agencies and insist that they consult and make opportunities available to the tribal cultural resource program. It looks really bad when agencies or cultural resource firms contact a tribal cultural resource office to initiate discussions, propose work, and so on, and they never get any response, written or verbal. You have to actively interact if you want your program to be successful.

Documenting Known Resources

If a tribe is going to protect its cultural resources, its new cultural resource protection office will need to become expert about tribal history and resources on and off the reservation. This can be done by first collecting all known information, a process that seems never-ending. Then the program can embark on collecting new information—say, from interviewing elders or conducting archaeological and traditional cultural property surveys.

Much of this valuable information can also come from histories and records that are available on the reservation. There should be a tribal historian who can provide basic references and identify repositories of more information. Important information on the reservation can be difficult to find, however. Usually, there are several offices (e.g., administration, educational, land use, law enforcement, and others) that have information worth preserving. Oftentimes, an unpublished report or study will surface when a tribal member remembers to bring it in to share with others. Many tribal members own valuable one-of-a-kind historic photographs, too, but you seldom have the opportunity to see them.

In the late 1960s, John Adair, then professor of anthropology, San Francisco State College, was requested to assemble a bibliography of all anthropological research that had ever been done on the Navajo, including linguistic, archaeological, ethnological, and the like. The bibliography was being requested to allow the Navajo access to information not as yet assembled for use by future generations. Adair (1973, 108) supported the idea, saying, "I think it's enormously important and our responsibility as anthropologists—among our other tasks—is to help in just that kind of endeavor." Of course, there already are exhaustive bibliographies published for many tribes. *The Newberry Library Center for the History of the American Indian Bibliographical Series*, Indiana University Press, Bloomington, is excellent for American Indian bibliographical source material.

While collecting this archival information, bibliographies can be assembled in-house by tribal staff members who are becoming familiar with the literature. Computers now make this much easier than it once was. New entrees can be made with ease, and hard copy printed at any time. This allows the tribal staff to keep current on the literature, forms, records, and so on, that are applicable to them and their resources. Knowing your sources and keeping them well organized are fundamental to any tribal program and allow for more effective research.

Collecting all known archaeological information requires additional work. Tribal staff will be called upon to deal with hundreds of archaeological site forms, archaeological reports, U.S. Geological Survey quadrangle maps depicting site locations (i.e., the site atlas), and other published and unpublished information pertaining to a tribe's cultural resources. In 1998, for example, the Confederated Tribes of the Umatilla Indian Reservation (CTUIR) archives contained more than 4,000 site forms, hundreds of maps, dozens of oral history tapes, and numerous archaeological and anthropological reports, books, and photographs (Burney, Van Pelt, and Bailor 1998). This is in addition to the tribal archives maintained by the Tamástslikt Cultural Institute, also located on the reservation.

Although this kind of information can be gathered from many different sources, the most comprehensive repository of such information is usually the state historic preservation office. Each state has its respective State Historic Preservation Office, which performs lots of functions dealing with cultural resource issues. An important function is to serve as the statewide repository for all the cultural resources recorded within the state's boundaries, regardless of land ownership. So, all the lands within the state that were inventoried for cultural resources, and the recorded resources themselves, are on file in the State Historic Preservation Office library. The CTUIR staff leased its own photocopiers to minimize interference with the Oregon and Washington State Historic Preservation Office personnel who needed to make their own copies.

Federal agencies like the U.S. Forest Service, the Bureau of Land Management, the U.S. Department of Defense, and so on, also have valuable cultural resource information on their lands. Ideally, these federal agencies provide copies of all site forms and technical reports to their respective state historic preservation offices, but this frequently isn't the case.

Of course, all of this voluminous material has to be appropriately filed to be available to tribal staff for research and report preparation. These kinds of loose-leaf files are most appropriately stored in legal-size file cabinets using pendaflex vertical files. Tribal archives will also contain a number of books and other publications that are available through universities, historical societies, professional archaeological societies, and a host of other cultural resource management organizations; maps depicting the area under investigation (i.e., the reservation, ceded lands, ancestral lands, and aboriginal lands), oral history tapes, videos, and other materials relating to the tribe or tribe's culture history.

One type of resource that may be more difficult to identify relates to traditional cultural properties and sacred sites. Because these places tend to be culturally sensitive, not much of this information has been documented. There is often concern about sharing such information with nontribal members. Many times, such information is controlled by particular families and is not even shared with other tribal members. Protecting these places is the conundrum of tribal cultural resource management: Tribes want to protect these important places, but because they are culturally sensitive, few people know about them, making it hard to protect them. We'll talk more about this issue in chapter 9 on cultural landscapes.

Curating Collections

The tribe may have a museum already on the reservation that contains archaeological and ethnographic collections. If so, its members should be prepared to receive much more material if the tribe is interested in getting back collections made on its lands or related to its people. If no museum currently exists, some arrangements will need to be made to care for these collections. Collections require a lot of care, and if they are to be handled in a professional and culturally sensitive manner, considerable time and effort will be required.

Learning the Cultural Resource Management System

Knowing some of the technical attributes of archaeology and cultural resource management is important, but so, too, is learning about the cultural resource management system. Anyone working in cultural resource management needs to know the system—the laws that drive the system, the players, and how things work.

A tribal technician might wonder why the system is important to know. The answer reminds us of a story from the 1950s. Two good friends of Indian people—Rosalie Wax, an anthropologist, and her husband, Murray Wax, a sociologist—were conducting workshops for American Indians. One day, Murray began teaching the native students about the culture of the White Man: how white people worked, how they thought, and how they organized themselves. Some of the Indian students complained about the topic. Rosalie explained it quite simply. They would be able to exercise their options in life—assimilation, accommodation, encapsulation—if they studied the white man with the same care and patience that some of their ancestors had studied the buffalo (Parker 1992, 185).

The Laws

Laws are a dry subject, but really, anyone working in cultural resource man-

---

"This Is Where My Ancestors Are."

One area in particular where Wanapum are acquiring expertise is natural and cultural resource management. By gaining knowledge in ways to protect the environment, the burials, the archaeological sites, and the traditional plants and animals, the Wanapum are able to be more directly involved in decision making and doing the work. It is very important for American Indians to be part of the consultation process of such federal laws as the National Environmental Policy Act (1969), the American Indian Religious Freedom Act (1978), the Archaeological Resources Protection Act (1979), and the Native American Graves Protection and Repatriation Act (1990). The Wanapum work with the other tribes to gain experience in cultural resource management methods and to provide a united front on common issues.

The Wanapum excel in natural and cultural resource tasks because caring for the land, the spirits of the land, and the ancestors is something they have been taught to do all of their lives. It is a very satisfying job for them. As one of the staff, Jason Buck, explained when asked about his interest in cultural resource protection,

This is where my ancestors are. I just try to preserve it for future use and for the younger people, younger than I am. I'm still learning myself and that's why I wanted to do it, to learn more about myself and more about my people. (Reprinted from Longenecker, Stapp and Buck 2002)

agement needs to have a basic awareness of the main laws. Legislation that significantly contributes to cultural resource management's beginnings includes, but is not limited to, Sections 106 and 110 of the National Historic Preservation Act of 1966 (and the implementing regulations, 36 CFR [800] and P.L. 74–292); the National Environmental Policy Act of 1969; Executive Order 11593 of 1971; the Archaeological and Historical Conservation ("Moss-Bennett") Act of 1974, which amended the Reservoir Salvage Act of 1960; the American Indian Religious Freedom Act of 1978 (P.L. 95–341); the Archaeological Resources and Protection Act of 1979 (P.L. 96–95); and the Native American Graves Protection and Repatriation Act of 1990.

For just about everything you wanted to know about this legislation, and much more, particularly as it relates to Native Americans, you are referred to several informative new works. Thomas F. King's (1998) *Cultural Resource Laws & Practice: An Introductory Guide* does a tremendous job of assembling and explaining the complex array of cultural resource legislation. Dr. King has a companion volume titled *Federal Planning and Historic Places: The Section 106 Process* (King 2000), focusing on the management of impact on historic properties under Section 106 of the National Historic Preservation Act. Joe Watkins, a Choctaw Indian and federal archaeologist, published *Indigenous Archaeology*, providing a discussion of federal historic preservation legislation and how it relates to American Indians (Watkins 2000). For state statutes, see Carnett's (1995) publication *A Survey of State Statutes Protecting Archaeological Resources*. These are very useful when working in cultural resource management and tribal CRM.

Another useful guide that tribal staff can easily carry in that new briefcase is an alphabetized guide of the cultural resource legislation. Ladonna Brave Bull Allard, with the Standing Rock Sioux Tribe, Fort Yates, North Dakota, has put together a reference guide that is useful to tribal staff, titled *Cultural Resource Laws Relating to Indian Tribes and Indian Land Owners* (Allard 1996).

Developing Relationships

It is important to let other professionals know there is a new tribal program in town. It's important that other archaeologists, contractors, agency people, and tribes know that you exist. It's vital that tribal programs notify federal land-managing agencies in those states within aboriginal territories.

Developing working relationships with neighboring tribes is also necessary if resources are to be protected. The Northern Cheyenne Tribe, Lame Deer, Montana, for example, may claim all, or parts of, South Dakota, Montana, Colorado, Nebraska, Wyoming, Kansas, and other states as well, within their aboriginal domain. The Southern Ute Tribe, Ignacio, Colorado, may claim all, or parts of, Colorado, Kansas, New Mexico, South Dakota, Utah, and Wyoming. Of course, different tribes have utilized areas at different times, reflecting population movements, both native and nonnative, across the West. Consequently, if the Northern Cheyenne Tribe or Southern Ute Tribe would like to be consulted with regard to cultural resource issues by the Forest Service and Bureau of Land Management in their aboriginal lands, the tribes need to notify their respective states. The various State Historic Preservation Offices should also be kept apprised of these kinds of notifications to federal agencies.

Tribes can also help one another when expertise is not available on-staff. In 1997, a number of tribal members, primarily elders and assistants, who were enrolled with the Cocopah Indian Tribe of Somerton, Arizona, visited the Umatilla Indian Reservation. The Cocopah guests toured the reservation and were treated to a traditional dinner in the Longhouse. Gifts were exchanged and testimony given by the attendees. Although time was short, making it difficult to accomplish everything, it was a good intertribal experience. Sue Arbuthnot, of *Hare in the Gate Productions*, Portland, Oregon, filmed the event for both tribes' archives.

Training

Most tribal programs have a hiring preference for native staff members, to the greatest extent possible. Oftentimes, however, tribes may not have the required number of applicants needed to fill all the positions. It is not uncommon for tribal programs to be composed of tribal members, nontribal members, and tribal members enrolled on other reservations (Longenecker and Van Pelt 1999; Warburton 2000). For example, there may be tribal members enrolled with the Nez Perce or Yakama tribes working in the CTUIR's Cultural Resource Protection Program. One of the past supervisors of the CTUIR program was an enrolled Northern Cheyenne from Lame Deer, Montana. In 1995, the Zuni Cultural Resource Enterprise had 24 full-time staff members: 19 were Indian, all Zuni, except for one Navajo and one Mohawk (Anyon and Ferguson 1995, 918). Within the three offices of the Navajo Nation program, about half of the 90 part-time and permanent employees are Navajo (Warburton 2000, 96).

Extensive training for tribal staff is a high priority. Training pays off in many ways, one of which was when a CTUIR tribal monitor discovered a mammoth tooth during preparation of the CTUIR's new Wildhorse Golf Course. Calvin "Dino" Jones, a CTUIR tribal cultural resource technician, discovered a few animal bone fragments and a giant tooth about a meter below the original ground surface. The tooth was recognized as that of a mammoth. Dino realized the importance of the find and halted construction in the immediate area, allowing staff to further examine and evaluate the find.

The University of Nevada, Reno, has a Heritage Resources Management Program that provides really informative and useful cultural resource management classes that are well attended by native and nonnative students alike. There are a variety of courses, including, but not limited to, Introduction to Section 106 Review (one of the first courses that should be taken), Consulting with Native American Groups, Heritage Resources Management: Decision-Making in the Legal Environment, NAGPRA's Evolving Legacy, and others. The university hosted a workshop in 1996 to work on the training needs of Indian tribes in historic preservation. All thirteen tribes that attended have subsequently been certified as Tribal Historic Preservation Offices and have been supportive of Indian involvement in cultural resource management and the development of tribal programs.

To help with the business end of cultural resource management and tribal cultural resource management, the Society for American Archaeology, 65th and 66th Annual Meetings (2000 and 2001), Philadelphia, Pennsylvania, and New Orleans, Louisiana, respectively, cosponsored workshops with the American Cultural Resources Association (ACRA), titled "The Business of Cultural Resource Management." According to the workshop's description, "This workshop . . . offers a practical introduction to the business of archaeological and cultural resources consulting. Topics include how to read and respond to a scope of work, how to develop an appropriate cost proposal, and how to create overhead rates and other financial information." How to prepare a business plan and the important elements of project management, professional development, and strategic planning are also covered. In addition, of interest at the SAA is a sponsored forum titled "Native Americans Building Our Side of the Bridge: Efforts in Preservation of Cultural Resources." These would be worthwhile workshops for just about anybody working in cultural resource management, including tribal staff members working in their respective programs.

Office and fieldwork skills include a lot of writing (the oral tradition is a valuable one, but the written word is essential to a tribal program), attending meetings, giving presentations, organizing, and managing, to mention just a few. Consequently, it is oftentimes the responsibility of the consulting archaeologist to bring the staff up to a level of proficiency. Although the archaeologist can provide short training sessions for tribal staff at any time, it is the day-to-day interaction of staff members with the archaeologist that eventually develops the desired proficiency. This educational and train-

---

Sample Letter to Initiate Discussions with Neighboring Agencies

Date
Federal Agency
Address, Phone, Fax

RE: Request to "Federal Agency" or Government to Government Consultations with the "Tribe" Discussing Those Natural and Cultural Resources Administered by the Federal Agency.

Dear Sir or Madam:
I would like to respectfully request the "Federal Agency" begin conducting government to government consultations with the "Tribe" to discuss the natural and cultural resources administered under your office. The state of _____ , including those lands administered by the "Federal Agency," are within the aboriginal lands of the "Tribe." Consequently, the "Tribe" has considerable interest in any ground-disturbing activities on your property that have the potential to adversely affect resources significant to the "Tribe."

The "Tribe" has a compelling interest in the identification, evaluation, and stewardship of the natural and cultural resources, including traditional cultural properties (TCPs) and sacred sites located on "State's" public lands, including the "Federal Agency." My technical personnel, and elders of the "Tribe," would be pleased to cordially work alongside your staff toward the Tribe's interest in consulting, contracting, and participating in your overall long-term historic preservation needs, particularly those of Native American origin.

(Continued)

Please contact _____ at (—) _____; Fax (—)____ to arrange a meeting time and place to casually discuss how the "Tribe" can constructively assist the "Federal Agency" in conserving American Indian resources and supporting the right of American Indians to worship freely, access their traditional cultural properties and sacred sites, and provide the maximum protection for the preservation of these resources, places, and sites. Thank you.

Sincerely,

Mr. or Mrs. _____
President/Chairman
Tribe

cc: State Historic Preservation Office
 Advisory Council on Historic
  Preservation
 Individual Districts, Forests,
  and the Like

ing course of events is a long-term commitment, but one that works when developing a reservation cultural resource management program. It would not be unreasonable to estimate that many tribal programs could require between five and ten years before reaching their full potential and self-sufficiency (Warburton 2000, 97).

Additional training could be available through other tribes with programs, including the tribal historic preservation offices and the National Association of Tribal Historic Preservation Officers; by attending local university or college archaeology and anthropology classes and workshops or university archaeological field schools; by undergoing federal paraprofessional cultural resource management training sessions; by joining professional archaeological organizations (e.g., the Society for Applied Anthropology, the High Plains Society for Applied Anthropology, and the National Association for the Practice of Anthropology); by subscribing to professional archaeological journals; and by attending conferences to network with colleagues, listen, learn, and present papers.

Getting Contracts

Undertaking projects for tribal departments and private clients (e.g., coal, oil and gas, timber harvesting, developers, and sand and gravel companies) is also valuable to any tribal program. Again, it's imperative for a tribe to institute a policy on the reservation that requires a cultural resources process to be followed prior to any ground-disturbing activities. By the tribal program providing these services to private clients, the work gets done, thereby contributing to the reservation's cultural resource database (i.e., tribal archives), and another step toward the education, training, and employment of tribal members is achieved.

Obtaining archaeological contracts is always a necessity when forming a tribal program. Allowing tribes to share in the consulting dollars goes a long way toward achieving meaningful consultation. Excluding the cultural resource management being undertaken in conjunction with the Hanford Site, the fledgling CTUIR archaeological program first began contracting for archaeological services in 1989. Every contract negotiated by the CTUIR provided them with an opportunity to (1) preserve the spirit and intent of their legal treaty rights; (2) engage in government-to-government consultations; (3) provide the tribes with the ability to participate in meaningful consultations with state or federal agencies; and (4) provide education, training, and employment for tribal members.

Managing multiple project deadlines, including organizing fieldwork, analyzing field work results, and preparing reports, requires a certain level of organization to maximize labor, budgets, and office and laboratory space. In 2001, the CTUIR program had over fifty small and large projects ongoing. That's the up side. The down side, the work load continues to increase, but there never seems to be enough funding to provide the necessary office and laboratory space, overhead expenses, secretarial services, assistant services, or travel expenses that are required for many of the projects.

Attending Conferences and Publishing

Tribal program staff members should attend conferences, give papers, and publish their projects and other aspects of tribal cultural resource management. This is important to "to help provide better tools and knowledge to the next generation of anthropologists [and tribal staff] who will be working with Native Americans and other indigenous groups" (Stapp 2000, 76).

Some tribes prefer not to gain exposure for their activities. And that's okay, too. However, reports, journal articles, and books regarding the tribe's culture history or projects can make a contribution to the tribe and anthropology without necessarily being of a sensitive nature.

Becoming a Tribal Historic Preservation Office—To Be or Not to Be

The 1992 Amendments to Section 101 of the National Historic Preservation Act of 1966, as amended (P.L. 74–292), allow tribes to implement tribal historic preservation programs and assume all or any part of the management and compliance responsibilities exercised by state historic preservation officers on their reservations and other Indian-owned lands. These amendments represent a culmination of significant tribal historic preservation tion legislation over the past several decades, with an emphasis during the 1990s. Finally, Indian tribes are able to regulate the archaeological work undertaken on their reservations, as well as off reservation, including ceded lands, treaty lands, usual and accustomed lands, and aboriginal lands.

The advantages of becoming certified as a "THPO Tribe" are numerous, which may or may not be desirable to the tribe. Being certified indicates to everyone that the program has met the basic qualifications of the National Park Service. It also enables the tribes to conduct various activities, as noted in the sidebar.

Over thirty tribes have signed an agreement with the National Park Service to assume formal preservation

Indians Managing Indian Resources: Tribal Historic Preservation Offices

Not that long ago our country's native peoples had little influence, and even less participation, in how their ancestral cultural resources were identified, evaluated, managed, and, unfortunately, mismanaged. In 1992, legislative changes enabled greater involvement and participation of Indians in cultural resource management. Section 101(d)(2) of the National Historic Preservation Act provides that "A tribe may assume all or any part of the functions of a State Historic Preservation Officer . . . " This important legislation has authorized tribes to do the following once they have completed the process to become a Tribal Historic Preservation Office/Officer (THPO).

- The THPO coordinates its historic preservation activities with all applicable state (e.g., first and foremost, the SHPO) and federal agencies, local governments, private organizations, and individuals. This just makes good sense, in that it better positions the tribe to actively participate in local and regional historic preservation issues, many of which may be of direct concern to a tribe or tribes.
- One of these activities is undertaking an inventory of all prehistoric and historic resources on the reservation, and any other Indian lands, to determine

113

responsibilities under Section 101(d) (2) of the National Historic Preservation Act. In addition to the powers this provides the tribes, it also provides funding in the form of grants. Over $21.9 million in grant funds have been used to assist tribes in assuming state historic preservation office responsibilities, drafting preservation ordinances, implementing cultural resource management plans, identifying and protecting historic sites, and conducting preservation needs assessments. The average grant award is $35,000.

(Continued)
if significant resources exist that meet the National Register of Historic Places eligibility criteria—or the tribe's criteria, for that matter.
• In consultation with the SHPO, Advisory Council on Historic Preservation, Bureau of Indian Affairs, and other state and federal agencies, prepare a comprehensive reservation historic preservation plan. Preparing such a plan will significantly help the tribe in carrying out its historic preservation responsibilities. It will also help in developing and providing public information, education and training, and technical assistance in historic preservation.

The process for becoming a tribal historic preservation office is as follows:

1. The tribe's chief governing authority makes a request to assume the responsibilities.

2. The tribe designates a tribal preservation official to administer the tribal historic preservation program, through appointment by the tribe's chief governing authority or as a tribal ordinance may otherwise provide.

3. The tribal preservation official provides the secretary of the interior with a plan describing how the functions the tribal preservation official proposes to assume will be carried out (guidance for the plan can be obtained from the National Park Service).

4. After consulting with the tribe, the appropriate state historic preservation officer, the Advisory Council on Historic Preservation (if the tribe proposes to assume the functions of the state

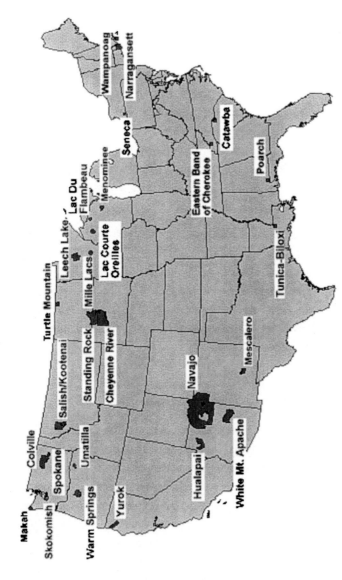

Figure 6.1. Map showing the locations of the tribal historic preservation offices (reproduced with permission of the National Park Service).

historic preservation officer with respect to review of undertakings under Section 106), and other tribes, if any, whose tribal or aboriginal lands may be affected by conduct of the tribal preservation program, the secretary determines:

- That the tribal preservation program is fully capable of carrying out the functions specified in the plan;
- That the plan defines the remaining responsibilities of the secretary and the state historic preservation officer;
- That the plan provides, with respect to properties neither owned by a member of the tribe nor held in trust by the secretary for the benefit of the tribe, at the request of the owner thereof, the state historic preservation officer, in addition to the tribal preservation official, may exercise the historic preservation responsibilities in accordance with subsections 101(b)(2) and (b)(3) of the Act.

5. The secretary approves the plan.

As mentioned previously, there may be reasons why tribes do not want to be certified as a tribal historic preservation office. There may be a perception that if they do, they need to abide by National Park Service rules. It simply may not be worth the bureaucratic hassle; the advantages may not be that great for a particular tribe.

Obstacles Facing Tribal Programs

One thing for sure, it's more difficult to start a cultural resource program without support from the tribal leadership. Tribal government support is an absolute must. No tribal cultural resource protection program can exist without it. Tribal politics can hinder and even prevent a successful program. While many of our preconceived ideas about tribal values lead one to think that such support would be easy to obtain, that is not always the case. For many reasons, tribal governments may not provide support for cultural resource programs in the beginning or while in operation. This has always been a mystery to us. Perhaps the reasons are similar to why nontribal cultural resource programs generally fail to receive widespread support from their governments.

Getting a tribal program off the ground can be tricky when trying to appease the concerns of all factions within the tribe or tribes. Unfortunately, the result of these politics can be harmful to beginning a tribal program for years to come. This is especially true for reservations that have significant ground-disturbing activities. These large projects have the greatest potential for adversely affecting Indian resources. Consequently, a range of cultural resource management studies is typically required, prior to commencing groundwork.

Sometimes tribes hesitate to support cultural resource programs because they perceive a conflict with economic-development goals: housing development, health clinics, gaming facilities with associated motels and golf course, and so on. The Seminole Tribe of Florida, for example, ran into a problem when ancestral human remains were inadvertently discovered during construction of a parking lot in Tampa (Cypress 1997, 159). The CTUIR ran into mammoth remains when building their new golf course. In both cases, solutions were found and the projects continued. Nevertheless, people who are responsible for economic development within a tribe often carry more power than those attempting to protect cultural resources.

Other causes hindering tribal cultural resource program development include the all-too-common interpersonal relations among competing tribal members for limited positions and funding; an unsupportive Bureau of Indian Affairs; lack of a tribal member, or tribal members, having the aptitude and interest in leading the development of the tribal program; and a shortage of physical plant facilities to house the tribal program.

Finally, poor management can stifle successful development of a tribal program. Because of the desire to hire tribal members, many times staff persons who are hired are unprepared for the challenge. Or those who are hired move onward and upward just as the program is growing. On this point we remain solutionless. Hiring experienced nontribal cultural resource employees until tribal employees can replace them is one common approach that has its advantages and disadvantages. We've also seen on-the-job education and employment of tribal members work. Whatever staffing strategy is employed, to build and sustain a tribal program for the long term, you must start by providing as much education, training, and employment to tribal members as reasonably possible. These students *are* the tribal program. If a tribal program is not investing in its tribal members, the program is not providing what it should.

Summary

Despite the rapid advances that tribes have made in cultural resource management, there is still much progress to be made. The vision is in place, the desire to apply tribal values to cultural resource management is entrenched, and tribal programs are functioning. As each day passes, more and more experience is being gained in incorporating tribal values into the existing cultural resource management framework. Some tribes have embraced tribal cultural resource management as a necessary part of their tribal administration of Indian lands and resources. Other tribes are less receptive to the idea.

Cultural resource management will most certainly continue to change as more tribes build their tribal programs and achieve tribal historic preservation office certification. America's cultural resources will be better served by providing a more favorable climate in the profession for meaningful participation by tribes. With the increased involvement of native peoples in cultural resource management, a synergy between indigenous peoples, university researchers, contract archaeologists, and state and federal regulatory agencies can begin to better protect and preserve important resources.

CONSULTATION: THE CORNERSTONE OF TRIBAL CULTURAL RESOURCE MANAGEMENT

> Consultation is an enhanced form of communication which emphasizes trust, respect and shared responsibility. It is an open and free exchange of information and opinion among parties which leads to a mutual understanding and comprehension. Consultation is integral to a deliberative process which results in effective collaboration and informed decision making. (Children's Health Initiative Program)

Consultation is the cornerstone of tribal cultural resource management. It is the interface where cultural resource staff, agency officials, tribal representatives, archaeologists, the public, and others can come together to participate in a decision-making process. During consultation, a tribe's interests, concerns, and expectations can be expressed, and a process leading to a decision can be agreed to among the parties. We have seen consultation work, and we have seen it fail. The key ingredient to success would seem to be sincerity. Does the agency or project proponent truly want to know what Indians think about a particular project or issue? Or are they simply checking the box "Have you consulted?"

Consultation is a many-sided process, with no cookbook approach. In this chapter we identify the ingredients for consultation and some of the recipes that have worked. In the end, the consulting parties will need to make up their own recipe, based on the meal that is most appropriate at the time. It might be a banquet, an informal dinner, a picnic, or a potluck. Regardless, consulting parties can be successful if they really want to be.

While the most important component of formal consultation is the decision-making process, in a stewardship setting, consultation should also be an ongoing process. You can't just consult when a project comes up or when a decision is needed. Consulting parties must maintain regular contact to share information, maintain follow-through on previous decisions and commitments, and cultivate relationships.

What Is Consultation?

Agencies and tribes have gained substantial experience in consulting over the last fifteen years. It 1987, we were introduced to the term *consultation* and how it was defined and applied when working with Pacific Northwest Indian tribes, specifically in regard to cultural resource issues. Terms that came to be used frequently by tribal staff when working with federal and state agencies include *treaties, sovereignty, government-to-government relations, meaningful consultation* (as opposed to pretty meaningless consultation), *funding, co-ownership, co-partners, co-management,* and *tribal contracts.*

A fundamental point is the role of consultation in decision making. In the past, consultation took the form of "decide and defend." In other words, an agency or government decided what it wanted to do and then "consulted" with a tribe by explaining the decision and answering questions. Most people today recognize that this approach is not consultation. Consultation is a process that enables one party to obtain input regarding interests, concerns, and expectations of another party and to integrate that input into the decision-making process. As stated in the Children's Health Initiative Program definition cited at the start of this chapter, consultation "is integral to a deliberative process, which results in effective collaboration and informed decision making."

There can be different levels of consultation, from government to government at the higher levels, to technical staff to technical staff at the lower levels. Generally, any communication among groups promotes the goals of consultation. However, there are often protocols, and it is imperative for all involved to know when Consultation with a capital "C" (i.e., formal Consultation) is required, and when consultation with a small "c" (i.e., informal consultation) is occurring.

For example, if technical staff and tribal representatives discuss a proposed project and indicate that the plan seems acceptable, the agency would not say Consultation has occurred and hence proceed with the project. Such a statement would not be made until appropriate communication with tribal officials had occurred, be it via letters or face-to-face meetings, according to the established protocol. Neither should a tribal official claim that consultation has not occurred on the project. It would be more appropriate to say that the project's consultation process has not been completed.

Consultation is many things to tribes, but, first and foremost, it may be "funding." Without financial assistance, most tribes simply do not have the financial wherewithal to genuinely participate in the requested consultation to the degree needed. Consequently, tribes may not be able to participate on an equal footing, addressing the many technical and complex issues facing them, in regard to the proposed project and eventual development. The development of tribal archaeological contracts can help provide some funding to further consultation efforts.

Through long-term extensive consultations, various tribes have continued their interest in managing their land-base and natural and cultural resources by exercising their ancestral and sovereign interests over their aboriginal lands, air, water, fish, minerals, timber, birds, and animals. Cultural resources have come to mean more than "stones and bones." Natural resources like huckleberry-gathering areas, or special places where limited amounts of "medicines" are gathered, could be as culturally significant as a prehistoric pithouse village site or cliff dwelling. The distinction between natural and cultural resources becomes obscured and less separable. Protecting these kinds of natural, yet cultural, resources on public lands requires extensive consultations with federal land-managing agencies like the U.S. Forest Service, Bureau of Land Management, U.S. Army Corps of Engineers, and other federal and state agencies.

Most tribal cultural resource offices are deluged with unsolicited mail—much of it, ideally, requiring a short response. Cultural resource management activities, such as reviewing draft environmental documents, can be time-consuming and costly. There are also potential contracts, scopes of work, scheduling, and budgets to prepare. Regardless, a tribal program should make every reasonable attempt to respond to everyday inquiries. The more proactive the office, the greater its influence will be. Here again, consistency is required in providing a professional response and efficient and timely dialogue; attending meetings, training sessions, and workshops; reviewing documents; and performing other essential duties. In short, play the game, to the extent possible. No doubt, it can be a daily juggling act.

Undertaking extensive consultations is hard work, requiring courtesy, patience, organization, consistency, and diplomacy. Even so, the process can be elusive and difficult to articulate. For meaningful consultations to occur, tribes should be approached as sovereign, independent nations on a government-to-government basis at the earliest possible time. The U.S. government has a unique and special trust responsibility to federally recognized Indian tribes as established by treaties, statues, court decisions, and the U.S. Constitution. For example, treaties are mentioned in Article VI, Section 2, of the Constitution as the "Supreme law of the land." Tribes should not be considered "interested parties" because of their sovereign status. Some tribes have treaties, which need to be acknowledged and understood. All parties must be present, active, and consistently participate in the deliberations and negotiations. Every consultation meeting is usually a learning experience in some aspect of human psychology, behavior, compromise, and intensive deliberations.

Francis B. Brown is an enrolled Northern Arapaho tribal member from Wyoming and chairman of the Medicine Wheel Coalition for Sacred Sites of North America. Francis has been a long-time negotiator advocating for the preservation and conservation management of the Medicine Wheel in Wyoming's Big Horn Mountains. He has commented, "When you do have consultations with federal agencies, you go in with honest and fair considerations, go in with an open mind and negotiate. Negotiate where you don't hurt any tribe, or yourself. Honest, fair negotiations really work" (Francis B. Brown, personal communication, Boulder, Colorado, November 5, 2000). The Medicine Wheel consultations undertaken between the Coalition, Big Horn County, and Big Horn National Forest, Wyoming, took about seven years.

Francis hits on an extremely important element in any consultation process, and that's honesty. Honesty is vital from the beginning to keep things on the right track and maintain credibility with tribes. Honest mistakes are always going to be part of consultations, but being forthright and open is always the best policy. If a site is damaged or adversely impacted in some way, it should be immediately acknowledged and dealt with to minimize complications later.

Meaningful consultation for the Confederated Tribes of the Umatilla Indian Reservation, as for many tribes, is where the tribes' point of view, recommendations, suggestions, and comments are carefully considered and incorporated. Conversely, when this is not the case, the consultations can be interpreted as pretty meaningless. There are cultural differences and similarities frequently seen when tribal and nontribal participants meet (see, especially, Wax and Thomas 1961). Some of the more common differences include the relative concept of time, the role of consensus decision making, trying to control and profit from the environment, and the connection of religion and other traditional aspects of culture to the environment (Russo 2000).

Why Consult?

There are many reasons to support the implementation of a meaningful consultation process with tribes. It's the legal thing to do, it's a good thing to do, and it's the right thing to do. Generally, tribes like consultations to begin just as soon as reasonably possible, from the very inception of a project. Tribal governments and state and federal agencies can be worlds apart in their understanding of what makes up the consultation process: Who should participate, when does it begin, how should it be conducted (what is the tribal government protocol?), what should it provide, and when does it end? Regardless, it's a process that can provide a meaningful experience for native and nonnative participants alike in their common interest of cultural preservation.

On January 24, 1983, the Reagan-Bush administration issued a statement on Indian policy recognizing and reaffirming a government-to-government relationship between Indian tribes and the federal government. This relationship was the cornerstone of the Bush-Quayle administration's policy of fostering tribal self-government and self-determination and was reaffirmed in September 1989. On June 14, 1991, President Bush issued his administration's official policy on American Indians, stating, in part, "This government-to-government relationship is the result of sovereign and independent tribal governments being incorporated into the fabric of our Nation, of Indian tribes becoming what our courts have come to refer to as quasi-sovereign domestic dependent nations." Domestic dependent nations, as declared by the U.S. Supreme Court in 1831 (*Cherokee Nation v. Georgia*). The president's policy builds upon the policy of self-determination first announced in 1970 and reaffirmed and expanded upon by the Reagan-Bush administration in 1983; and again, by the memorandum "Government-to-Government Relations with Native American Tribal Governments," signed by President William J. Clinton on April 29, 1994.

President William J. Clinton, on November 6, 2000, signed Executive Order 13175, which directs agencies to accommodate access to American Indian sacred sites by Indian religious practitioners, to provide additional protection for physical integrity, and, where appropriate, to maintain confidentiality of the locations of these sites. This Order also incorporates the Executive Memorandum of April 29, 1994, and emphasizes that "agencies" shall comply with that internal directive for the purpose of developing "Government-to-government relationships with Native American Tribal Governments." On May 14, 1998, President Clinton issued an Executive Order titled "Consultation and Coordination with Indian Tribal Governments," which, in part, was undertaken "in order to establish regular and meaningful consultation and collaboration with Indian tribal governments."

Five federal laws prompt consultations between federal agencies and federally recognized Indian tribes. They are: (1) the National Historic Preservation Act of 1966, including its 1992 Amendments and its interpretation in *National Register Bulletin 38* (Parker and King 1990); (2) the National Environmental Policy Act of 1969; (3) the American Indian Religious Freedom Act of 1978; (4) the Archaeological Resources Protection Act of 1979; and (5) the Native American Graves Protection and Repatriation Act of 1990. Each law can stand alone and trigger consultations under certain circumstances and for different purposes. In large projects all five laws can be invoked. When the latter occurs, the consultations and compliance process can become confusing for federal agencies and tribes alike.

As previously noted, federal historic preservation legislation passed between the 1960s and 1990s, some of it Indian-friendly, ushered in an increased need for state and federal agencies to more actively consult with Indian tribes on a number of cultural resource issues. Passage of the Native American Graves Protection and Repatriation Act (NAGPRA) of 1990, the publication in 1990 by the National Park Service on Traditional Cultural Properties known as *National Register Bulletin 38* (Parker and King 1990), the 1987 amendments to P.L. 93–638, the Indian Self-Determination and Education Assistance Act, and comprehensive amendments to the National Historic Preservation Act of 1966, as amended in 1992, including a number of provisions specifically relating to Indian tribes and tribal lands (Suagee and Funk 1990), were also helpful in advocating for a greater voice by Indian tribes in the management of cultural resources.

Consultation Examples

There are few model examples of what consultations are when carried out with tribes in a genuinely meaningful way. There are more examples across Indian Country of what consultation is not. The failure to implement intensive and meaningful consultation with federally recognized Indian tribes when working with their ancestral cultural resources and places is commonplace. Whatever the reasons, this lack of consultation has the potential of preventing tribes from receiving the education, training, and employment in historic preservation activities they might have otherwise. Consulting with Indian tribes could be as simple as just asking them to participate. But when no one asks, nothing happens to significantly involve the tribes.

Nevertheless, there are examples of cultural resource projects managed cooperatively by tribes and state and federal agencies.

The Hanford Site

The Middle-Columbia River of the Southern Plateau is home to the Hanford Site—a 560-square-mile federal piece of real estate straddling the Columbia River in southeastern Washington State (unlike our following Dowe Flats example, which consists exclusively of private lands). The environment there is very dry. The semi-arid climate supports various communities of shrub steppe and grassland. The Tri-Cities of Richland, Pasco, and Kennewick are at the very southern tip of the Hanford Site, and the Washington and Oregon border lies a short distance farther south. Priest Rapids, home of the Wanapum people, is just to the west.

The Columbia River is always a captivating sight, effortlessly dominating your attention whenever you are within its view. Large numbers of native peoples from different families, bands, and tribes have relied on the Columbia River for life itself, celebrating its salmon, eels, and other life-giving resources through reverence and ceremony. Archaeology and Indian oral history have recorded native peoples' relationship with the river as ongoing for many centuries.

The Hanford Site is squarely in Indian Country, surrounded by a number of federally recognized Indian reservations: the Yakama, Colville, Spokane, Coeur d'Alene, Nez Perce, and CTUIR. The Wanapum, residing at Priest Rapids, Washington, have never signed a treaty with the

United States government and are not federally recognized. Since encountering the Lewis and Clark expedition in 1805 (Corps of Discovery), the tribes here have a history that is inextricably connected with European newcomers. Nearly 150 years later, these Middle-Columbia native cultures have suffered unimaginable losses.

The Yakama Nation and the Confederated Tribes of the Umatilla Indian Reservation are treaty tribes that have ceded lands within the Hanford Site. Relinquishing vast areas of their ancestral aboriginal homelands during various treaty councils in the mid-1800s, in exchange for certain promises, was one approach to early consultation. From the tribes' viewpoint, these early consultation efforts were way too one-sided, and the tribes were on the wrong side. Not what you would call meaningful consultation by today's standards.

The Hanford Site, a U.S. government nuclear facility, came to Indian Country in 1943. In response to the war effort, the United States needed to develop a nuclear capability, and Hanford was chosen as one place to do it. The approximately 358,400 acres of sand and sagebrush seemed ideal for a project of such immense proportions that demanded extremely tight security. To many of the native peoples in this general area, the land fenced by the federal government was more than just sand and sagebrush. In current language, it is better known as a cultural landscape (see chapter 8 for a more detailed discussion).

A cultured landscape supports the cultural (e.g., fishing, gathering, habitation, ceremonial, and other sites) and physical remains (burials and associated goods) of past and present Indian communities. The development of the Hanford Site not only disrupted past and present native life and routines, but also caused the displacement of nonnative communities, such as Hanford and White Bluffs, by requiring the local citizenry to relocate elsewhere.

Beginning almost from the time of European contact, the Columbia River and its environs have given up immense amounts of native cultural items and burial remains to vandals, collectors, development, dams and reservoirs, natural erosion, and, to some extent, archaeological projects, including those undertaken at the Hanford Site. This history between a U.S. government-owned and -managed operation and native peoples provides one of our two examples chosen to exemplify what makes for meaningful consultations.

Consultation between Hanford's federal personnel and neighboring Indians, including the Wanapum, began in 1943 when the U.S. Army Corps of Engineers met with Wanapum Band leaders regarding the federal government's need for the land to develop the top secret Manhattan Project. Some seven years later, in 1951, Puck Hyah Toot (also known as Johnny Buck), a late leader of the Wanapum of Priest Rapids, made known his concerns about graves being looted in Priest Rapids Canyon and Wanawisha Cemetery in Richland. Puck Hyah Toot suggested fencing the areas and marking them with signs warning that "digging was prohibited." Despite Puck Hyah Toot's pleas, neither the Atomic Energy Commission (a predecessor agency to the U.S. Department of Energy) nor the Bureau of Indian Affairs took any action.

In 1953, Puck Hyah Toot's concerns were revisited when he and Tamalawash, another native gentleman having ancestral family ties in the Richland vicinity, requested to tour the Hanford Site to inspect additional Wanapum cemeteries (figure 7.1a). As a result, Puck Hyah Toot, Tamalawash, a Hanford representative, and Click Relander, a journalist from Yakima, Washington, toured Hanford. Through this joint effort, five cemeteries were visited, mapped, and noted to be in good condition. Mr. Relander later published much of this event in his book *Drummers and Dreamers* (Relander 1956). Almost twenty years later the government finally marked the corners of these five cemeteries to better establish their locations at Hanford, without drawing attention to them (Nickens 1998, 1–3).

In the late 1970s, David G. Rice (University of Idaho), an archaeologist who had been working in the area, prepared an archaeological overview of the Hanford Site along with a cultural resources assessment of the Hanford Reach (Rice 1980a and b). In 1986, Rice advocated for the need to study the history and character of American Indian usage of the area. Rice noted that in contrast to the number of recorded archaeological and historical resources, little ethnohistoric or oral history data had been collected that documented uses of specific places across the landscape. More was required to identify traditional cultural places and other sensitive areas, too, like the cemeteries, and very sacred and revered places like Gable Mountain, Gable Butte, and Rattlesnake Mountain. Unfortunately, for reasons that remain unclear, little apparently came of Rice's worthwhile proposal.

Despite the Hanford Site suddenly appearing in Indian Country, and the subsequent *loss of access to traditional native places and resources*, matters

Figure 7.1a. Puck Hyah Toot and Tamalwash at the Hanford security gate, ca. 1955 (courtesy of The Relander Collection at Yakima Valley Regional Library).

slowly moved in the right direction during the next two decades. Around 1980, the U.S. government selected the Hanford Site as one of three potential sites for a deep-storage repository of high-level radioactive waste. The Nuclear Waste Policy Act of 1982 included a provision for those federally recognized Indian tribes at possible risk from the undertaking to receive "affected tribe status," making them eligible for funding. The Yakama Nation, the Nez Perce Tribe of Idaho, and the Confederated Tribes of the Umatilla Indian Reservation (CTUIR) applied for and received "affected tribe" status. Almost overnight, this newly designated status provided these three tribes with a level of consultation and funding not previously enjoyed. For the CTUIR, anyway, this funding started their tribal cultural resource protection program. Although Hanford funding was temporarily halted it would later return and continue to be an important source of revenue for tribal cultural resource management.

With funding, things began to happen. Different administrative and technical staff were brought together; numerous meetings were attended; letters, memos, and reports were written, and phone calls made. In short, money allowed the tribes better representation and input when addressing issues that resulted from activities undertaken at the Hanford Site. The tribes tried to increase the federal agency's cultural awareness of the aboriginal cultural landscape making up the modern-era Hanford Site. Through these more responsive and focused consultations, the tribes pressed the U.S. Department of Energy to incorporate their native values into Hanford's decision-making process (figure 7.1b).

At one point, the affected tribes were asked to distinguish which parts of their ancestral landscape were sacred and which were not. For Gable Mountain, at least, no parts were viewed as more sacred than others or devoid of sacred value. These different worldviews represent one example of the fundamental differences of opinion that are most challenging to many consultation efforts, including those undertaken at the Hanford Site.

Figure 7.1b. Tribal cultural resource technicians working at Hanford, 2000.

Sacred Gable Mountain became host to a large mine shaft, a water line, a gravel quarry, and installation of communication towers, without consultation. Consultations, during a following project, resulted in a major effort to repair and restore the mountain. Since then, it should be noted that Gable Mountain has been off limits for most governmental activities, out of respect for tribal wishes.

By the late 1980s the aforementioned consulting tribes had developed some form of tribal archaeological operation that responded to Hanford's cleanup efforts and protection of cultural resources. In 1987, the U.S. Department of Energy, at Hanford Site, moved toward establishing a more formal cultural resources program, the Hanford Cultural Resources Laboratory. Two years later, and after extensive input from tribal staff, the *Hanford Cultural Resources Management Plan* was issued (Chatters 1989). The creation of the plan was a major achievement for the Hanford Site, though it was not without controversy. Were the Indians' review comments really incorporated into the plan? Many legitimate concerns had been expressed, only some of which were incorporated. These concerns would form the basis for future consultation, though with the management plan issued, the urgency to resolve such concerns dissipated.

Your Driver's License, Please

Being an American citizen without your driver's license, or other photo identification, can pose problems, especially when entering a secure federal nuclear facility, as a group of Indian elders once found out and as Michael Burney recalls here.

During one of our very first trips in the latter 1980s to visit the Hanford Site with a group of elders from the Umatilla Indian Reservation, I was amused when trying to get through Hanford's initial security checkpoint. All visitors must produce some form of picture identification—generally, your driver's license—and answer some questions so that a record about you can be established and an ID badge issued, to be worn while visiting the facility. At first, this request didn't appear problematic, except that none of the native elders could produce a driver's license or any other form of picture identification. Like all of us, they were also questioned as to whether they were American citizens or not. Hearing this question while in the presence of this group of elderly Indian gentlemen, sporting long braids, struck me in a way I hadn't felt before. These First Peoples may be on the outside, but they would forever be a part of the land.

By 1989, Hanford was no longer a candidate for a high-level waste repository. Now there was a new mission—clean-up of the chemical and nuclear wastes generated during the previous forty-five years of plutonium production. This new emphasis that was placed on the Hanford Site further stimulated the need for intensive consultations and participation by the affected tribes.

During the late 1980s and early 1990s, the consultation process between the Hanford Site and affected tribes assumed a rather routine nature: the Department of Energy sent out reports to the tribes for review and comment, the tribes responded, Hanford Site staff considered the review comments, and so on. Meetings were attended and occasionally a field visit was arranged. Regardless, substantive results were slow in coming. Nevertheless, the Hanford Site, by providing participation to the tribes in establishing and maintaining long-term and meaningful relationships, remained committed to making consultation work.

The fundamental nature of Hanford Site consultations changed somewhat in 1994, when the Department of Energy decided to update the 1989 *Hanford Cultural Resource Management Plan*. A series of meetings was held with the individual consulting tribes to solicit their comments on the plan and the overall program. Overall, it would be fair to say the tribes did not feel that the resources were being managed adequately. It wasn't that the plan needed to be rewritten, but rather, it just needed to be followed as written. The tribes requested specific items: earlier notification of Section 106 projects; a broader definition of cultural resources that was more inclusive of cultural and natural places and resources; and greater participation in the actual fieldwork. Clearly, this opportunity to consult with the Hanford Site on such an important guiding document provided a positive avenue to influence the way native resources were being perceived and managed.

Consultations on these issues continued in a collective manner at the technical level. Staff from the Hanford Site and individual tribes met on a regular basis. Ironically, during the first "Tribal Issues Meeting," an event occurred that would consume the tribal representatives for the next year. Before an hour had passed, a messenger reported that human remains had just been unearthed at the construction site of the new multimillion-dollar Environmental and Molecular Sciences Laboratory. The meeting's attendees converged on the construction site to begin implementing the inadvertent discovery process required under the Native American Graves Protection and Repatriation Act of 1990.

Through extensive consultations, it was mutually agreed to collect the burial remains, stabilize the site, construct the laboratory in a new location, and restore the disturbed area using native plants. The reburial was completed with minimal difficulties, and the laboratory relocated, although not without scheduling delays and significant additional costs. The native plants concept proved more elusive, however. Employing native plants as part of environmental restoration had been frequently discussed, but practical experience in such an endeavor was in short supply. Regardless, forging ahead, the U.S. Department of Energy provided funding to support an intertribal team to restore native plants. The cooperating tribes worked together toward their common goal, and by 1996, the revegetation was completed.

The Hanford "Tribal Issues Meetings" were also back in swing, with between six and ten meetings taking place annually. The group worked on Section 106 concerns; the new draft of the *Hanford Cultural Resources Management Plan*; strategies for recording traditional cultural places, determining inventory areas and methodology to be used; developing a geophysical test bed; and putting together a course for law enforcement about looting Indian sites. The Hanford Site now provides immediate notification of all 106 undertakings, has broadened the definition of cultural resources to better reflect the native point of view, supports regular visits by tribal elders, and stresses a stewardship model emphasizing the protection of Hanford's 560-square-mile cultural landscape rather than individual sites. By applying sound principles of stewardship across the overall landscape, the Indian places and resources enjoy long-term conservation and preservation not otherwise possible.

Since the pioneering efforts of Puck Hyah Toot and Tomalwash half a century ago to protect cemeteries from harm, Hanford Site personnel may have participated in more consultation efforts than just about any other federal facility anywhere. This is especially true during the last fourteen years. Several major revisions to the *Hanford Cultural Resources Management Plan* have been produced, hopefully making it more responsive to the consulting tribes. The "Tribal Issues Meetings" continue, primarily as information-sharing get-togethers. Despite this extensive history of consultation, much of it taking place over the years with the same individuals, there will always be differences on the table. That's what makes consultation necessary. Mutual respect, trust, honesty, and a willingness to learn are some of the "right stuff" that supports mutually beneficial and meaningful consultations.

The Dilemma over Sharing Cultural Information

It is no secret that American Indians regard much cultural information as sensitive and are often reluctant to share such information with others unless absolutely necessary. In the following passage from a newspaper article concerning archaeology in Washington State, the reporter captures the essence of how one tribe, the Wanapum, grapples with sharing cultural information with archaeologists.

The archaeologists who study the artifacts are not always sure what they are or how they were used. Sometimes the Wanapum will tell them, sometimes not. They are careful. Objects may have been used for good and bad, [Rex Buck] said.

"You may not want to disturb something you cannot control," he said. "Maybe you get sick or a child gets sick. Maybe something happens. We are concerned about this for someone who takes it . . . Something was put here for a reason."

But the Wanapum have other reasons for holding their history close. They don't lightly share the stories that form their cultural heritage. "You don't say a lot. Then you say a little more. Pretty soon someone wants to write a book," Buck said.

That's not how the Wanapum want the children to learn about their heritage. "It takes away something sacred to us," he said. "When you learn the oral way, it's living. Read it in a book, that's not there. (If) our children come to depend on archives and resources, they do not have that meaning."

The Dowe Flats Project

The Dowe Flats Project in northern Boulder County, Colorado, involved a private company undertaking extensive, and expensive, cultural resource consultations with thirteen federally recognized Indian tribes. These tribes were the Southern Ute and Ute Mountain Ute of Colorado; the Northern Ute of Utah; the Jicarilla Apache of New Mexico; the Rosebud and Oglala Sioux of South Dakota; the Northern Cheyenne of Montana; the Eastern Shoshone and Northern Arapaho of Wyoming; and the Southern Cheyenne, Southern Arapaho, Comanche, Kiowa, Kiowa Apache, and Pawnee of Oklahoma. Local Indian residents in Lyons, Longmont, Denver, Boulder, and other communities also participated.

The company, Cemex, Inc., (formerly, Southdown), had been producing cement since 1969. To ensure adequate materials for the future, the company needed additional reserves of limestone for its production process. The Dowe Flats limestone was desirable because it was close to the existing plant; the closer the deposit to the cement plant, the lower the transportation costs. Dowe Flats held an estimated twenty-eight years' worth of the required limestone and was close enough to the production facility to allow an enclosed conveyor system to transport it from the mine to the plant.

(Continued)
Instead, Buck wants to give Hanford historians and archaeologists just enough information to help them think about what they are working with—"to step back and look around, see how everything ties together." It's a balance that Stapp and Buck work together to find.

Sometimes Hanford workers will not be told by the Wanapum that an area has cultural significance until work there starts, and even then they may not be told much. To protect sites during future generations, cultural resource workers may need more information, Stapp said. In that case, "We take a little bit of that living [story] and put it in him," Buck said. "We're doing the same thing to him as we might do to our children." (Cary 2001)

As part of developing this open-pit limestone mine, various permits, of which cultural resources were a component, were required from Boulder County and the State of Colorado. Boulder County, as a Certified Local Government under the National Historic Preservation Act, was the lead governmental agency with respect to the management of Dowe Valley cultural resources. No federal permits were required. Consequently, Cemex, Inc., undertook several archaeological and historical inventories of the proposed mining site (locally known as Dowe Valley or Dowe Flats) to identify the archaeological and historical resources on its property (Burney 1989). A number of American Indian localities were recorded, which contained ancient fire pits, chipped stone tools and debris, and manos and metates, or ground-stone tools.

Perhaps the most spectacular prehistoric area was discovered because broken pieces of ground-stone were strewn on the surface of the plow zone along a fence line. Limited subsurface testing of this site, consisting of a single 1m x 1m excavation unit that exceeded almost four meters, or about twelve feet, revealed a continuous archaeological record of several thousands of years. The test excavation unit was back-filled and a recommendation made that the site not be subjected to further disturbance. For now, the site remains undisclosed and undisturbed.

Although Cemex, Inc., needed to develop the nearby open-pit limestone mine, the company was simultaneously interested in identifying the cultural resources (and paleontological resources, requiring the appropriate specialist) within its mine permit boundary and preserving them as well. The company rightly assumed that Dowe Valley was important to those tribes claiming historical indigenous rights to the land and their cultural resources. It was this perception of respect and sensitivity toward the archaeological past and contemporary present (i.e., the consulting tribes) that guided Cemex, Inc.'s consultation efforts. To say the least, it was astonishingly new territory for the company. Yet Cemex, Inc., proceeded, primarily through the efforts of the plant manager, John W. Lohr, who eagerly moved forward not knowing what might be accomplished or the ultimate outcome.

Fortunately, the cultural resource inventories, including information gleaned from early newspapers, other written sources, and consultations with knowledgeable locals (a separate historical study was completed, too), suggested that the potential was low for undisturbed cultural deposits in the valley proper. Years of artifact hunting, moss-rock mining, ranching, and farming had effectively obliterated an area rich in American Indian history. From early personal accounts, we knew Dowe Valley was once home to dozens, perhaps hundreds, of stone tipi rings—the remains of intense prehistoric occupation not that long ago. Today, only a few tipi rings remain and their numbers have decreased during the past fifteen years. Most of them were quickly destroyed through early farming efforts when fields were cleared for cultivation and fencing. All of the valley had been under cultivation and grazing since the mid-1860s.

Regardless of this past historic land use, Cemex, Inc., as a further precaution to avoid disturbing buried archaeological materials, undertook an extensive geomorphological inventory of the mine permit area. This study was to further assess the potential for there being buried as yet undetected cultural deposits, including human remains. To the greatest extent possible, the geomorphological inventory likewise suggested a low probability for undetected and undisturbed cultural deposits on the valley floor.

As a result of the archaeological, historical, paleontological, and geomorphological studies Cemex, Inc., had gathered a substantial amount of information. Subsequent meetings with the Colorado State Historic Preservation Office led Cemex, Inc., to begin consultations with Colorado's only two land-based Indian tribes, the Southern Ute (Ignacio, Colorado) and Ute Mountain Ute (Towaoc, Colorado), regarding the cultural resource findings. As a result of further recommendations advanced by the Colorado Commission of Indian Affairs, the Wyoming Indian Affairs Council, and individual tribal members themselves, the list of federally recognized Indian tribes that Cemex, Inc., would ultimately consult with *increased to thirteen Indian nations from seven states*. All of these tribes considered themselves indigenous to the state of Colorado, including Boulder County. This is not to say that these thirteen tribes are the only tribes native to Colorado (e.g., there is the Navajo Nation), but, rather, they were the ones participating on this particular project.

Cemex, Inc., kicked off its consultation efforts by requesting from each of the tribes an introductory meeting *on their respective reservations* to share information on the proposed undertaking (i.e., the open-pit mining), the cultural resources that could be potentially adversely impacted, and measures to mitigate that impact. Avoidance of the cultural resources was the company's preferred and optimal form of mitigation to best ensure long-term preservation. Specifically, Cemex, Inc., requested that these initial meetings meet the following ten goals:

1. Personally meet with tribal government representatives (i.e., tribal councils) during one of their regularly scheduled monthly meetings and with appropriate technical staff, including NAGPRA representatives, Cultural Committee members, elder groups, and others;

2. Introduce the company's perception of how the consultation process should be conducted;

3. Solicit tribal recommendations on how *tribes believed* the consultation process should be conducted. This was essential, in that Cemex, Inc., recognized early on the *sovereign nation status* of each of the thirteen tribes. In short, the consultation approach, or protocol, for each of the tribes may have shared similarities, but nevertheless remained quite distinct and separate from one another;

4. Provide an overview of the company's proposed undertaking to develop open-pit mining to extract limestone for cement production;

5. Disclose all the cultural resources identified and recorded for Dowe Valley, generally, and the mine permit boundary, specifically. Most of the adverse impact would occur within the mine permit boundary;

6. Provide suggestions for short- and long-term preservation and conservation of these resources;

7. Discuss when and what nonburial items might be collected during inventory or excavation, for eventual curation in an accredited museum facility; or *if collection of any artifacts was even supported at all;*

8. Discuss where the nonburial artifacts might be curated. The University of Colorado Museum, Boulder, was finally chosen for artifacts already collected during previous studies;

9. Identify goals best representing the tribe's interests in preserving *its* historic and sacred sites, traditional cultural places (i.e., all of Dowe Valley), and other places of tribal concern; and,

10. Incorporate the tribe's feedback to formulate a better plan to ensure long-term protection and conservation for the native resources, using conservation easements with Boulder County, monitoring of mining activities, and facilitating present-day use of portions of Dowe Valley for the tribe's educational, cultural, and spiritual needs. For example, very private locations are provided for sweat lodges utilized by native participants from on and off the reservations.

Following these introductory reservation meetings, Cemex, Inc. requested that each of the tribes attend an intertribe conference in Longmont, Colorado, to further examine the company's project and cultural resources. Although each of the thirteen tribes was clearly acknowledged for its sovereignty and subsequent independent status, the company felt that bringing all the tribes together would be a mutually beneficial event, providing a win-win situation for all—a recommendation first advanced by Wallace Coffey, then chairman of the Comanche Nation of Oklahoma. Not only would the proposed mine and cultural resources be examined and discussed, but the numerous tribes would have an opportunity to visit one another, renewing old ties, and establishing new ones.

This first intertribal gathering hosted by Cemex, Inc., (all expenses, including mileage, air fare, ground transportation, meals, lodging, and consulting fees, were provided for) took place in Longmont, Colorado, on October 1st and 2nd, 1993. Longmont is a small community located within a short driving distance from the company's plant, Dowe Valley, and Boulder, making it ideal for the meetings. Because of the company's intense efforts and willingness to fully fund the conference, there were 45 tribal attendees, representing 9 of the 13 identified federally recognized tribes. In addition, Southdown similarly funded the participation of the president of the Governor's Interstate Indian Council; 6 Commission of Indian Affairs executive directors from Colorado, Montana, Oklahoma, South Dakota, Utah, and Wyoming; and the president of the Medicine Wheel Coalition for Sacred Sites of North America. What a gathering it was!

During these two days in October, Cemex, Inc., continued to solicit tribal representatives for their help in determining management options for the preservation of the cultural resources and the contemporary use of Dowe Valley for educational, cultural, and ceremonial purposes. Furthermore, Cemex, Inc., asked tribal representatives to evaluate the company's performance after the conference by distributing a three-page questionnaire with inquiries, including, but not limited to, "Has the company's tribal consultation process been meaningful for you?"; "How could the consultations be improved for your involvement?"; "Would your tribe be interested in further consultations . . . beyond this October Inter-Tribe Gathering?"; "Is the company's policy of avoidance of the known Indian sites adequate?"; "Should these protected Indian sites remain closed to the general public?"; "Is the proposal for the monitoring of ground-disturbing activities in the 315-acre mine quarry adequate?"; and so on. The results of these questionnaires were an integral part of the company's future consultation efforts.

Tribal representatives and other attendees were provided with additional voluminous information about the project and cultural resources, in-

Well-Done, Please!

Despite the best of intentions to really put out the red carpet and support meaningful consultations, there is always the possibility that something will go wrong. Cemex, Inc. (formerly, Southdown, Inc.), discovered this when hosting a large evening meal with, primarily, northern and southern Plains Indian tribes, as Michael Burney relates.

Cemex, Inc., once hosted several days of consultation meetings with thirteen federally recognized Indian tribes that were assisting with numerous historic preservation issues, from curation, monitoring, and preservation, to long-term stewardship. One evening, the company threw a fantastic dinner for the fifty or so Indian guests from seven western states. The evening meal was buffet style so everyone lined up to walk down the length of tables to choose what they wanted. At the end of the line were assistants ready to slice off a big ol' piece of juicy-red roast beef from a gigantic hindquarter of beef. Yumm, yumm! Wait a minute! "Juicy-red" roast beef?!

As I sat down to join my Northern Cheyenne and Rosebud Sioux companions, I soon noticed my friends had pushed their juicy-red roast beef aside and were intent on not eating it! I was quietly informed that their preference was for a big ol' piece of "well-done" roast beef. Perhaps not a super-major point, but, then again, why throw a feast when folks won't eat what's being served?

It was about this time that I also found out these Plains Indians weren't keen on salad bars. Kind of like having to attend morning meetings without coffee and donuts. By the way, the next all-tribes dinner hosted by Cemex, Inc., was held outdoors, and the buffalo was cooked to everyone's liking: well-done!

cluding copies of the archaeological inventories (e.g., Burney 1989) and limited site testing (e.g., Grant 1990), a three-ring binder of all site and isolated find forms, professional papers regarding the project and cultural resources, the consultation process, an ethnobotanical literature review (Lederer and Figgs 1994), a pollen and macrobotanical analysis (Cummings 1991), the paleontological survey (Carpenter 1994), the geomorphological study (Rushmore 1994), and an ethnographic/ethnohistoric file and literature search (Burney and Lovejoy 1994).

Not content with just passing paper around, Cemex, Inc., also professionally documented the conference by producing a 27-minute video titled *Dowe Flats Native American Tribal Consultations: The October 1st and 2nd, 1993, Inter-Tribal On-Site* (produced by Thomas Howard Imaging, Boulder, Colorado, from eight hours of filming). Over seventy copies of this video were distributed. As the title notes, an all-day on-site visit was

Figure 7.2. Participants in the Dowe Flats consultations (courtesy of Cemex, Inc.).

provided to the attendees for their personal inspection of the proposed mine site and cultural resources. To enhance the day's activities, Cemex, Inc., generously provided a lavish catered lunch and entertainment by the Catchin Eagles Singers from the Ute Mountain Ute Tribe of southwest Colorado. An eight- by ten-inch color photo of the group was also provided to all attending members to commemorate such a grand event. Upon request by tribal members, Cemex, Inc., assisted several tribes by making contributions toward a Sun Dance held during the summer of 1994 and toward the Medicine Lodge Peace Treaty Council, Medicine Lodge, Kansas (September 23–25, 1994). From never having worked with tribes before, the company had quickly adapted itself to a policy of being Indian-friendly.

The nine tribes quickly responded to Cemex's needs, identifying several responsibilities to include, but not be limited to: (1) Guiding and continuing the consultation process initiated by the company; (2) reviewing any proposals regarding anticipated future archaeological undertakings; (3) advising on the selection of archaeological monitors; (4) managing any archaeology conservation easements; (5) directing the reinterment or curation of artifacts; (6)

providing input on the Colorado Historical, Prehistorical, and Archaeological Resources Act regarding the reinterment of human remains; and (7) managing educational, cultural, and ceremonial activities proposed for Dowe Valley. Furthermore, as a result of this momentous on-site gathering the consulting tribes advanced six recommendations as follows:

1. Continue the consultation process by supporting the tribes as active participants in a meaningful and cooperative co-partnership and genuinely addressing the native cultural resources;

2. Consult with local native peoples for their input into the consultation process. (The communities along the Colorado Front Range have a large number of native residents.);

3. Preserve the known native resources as they now exist. Do not subject them to disturbances from development or additional archaeological excavations. That is, encourage an environment for cultural preservation, not cultural disintegration;

4. Prior to initiating mining activities, develop a geomorphological program to inspect areas within the mine permit boundary that are most likely to yield buried undisturbed resources;

5. Develop a monitoring program to address unknown buried resources that are exposed during ground-disturbing activities; and

6. Attempt to identify an Indian-run, nonprofit organization to manage the native resources within Dowe Valley, including contemporary use of a portion of the valley by native peoples for educational, cultural, and ceremonial purposes.

Subsequent consultation conferences of a similar nature were hosted by Cemex, Inc., in October and February 1994 and November 1995. Between these conferences, all the tribes' representatives were kept informed by phone, fax, mail, and additional personal visits to various reservations. It was during the October 7th and 8th, 1994, meeting that the thirteen consulting tribes convened as the Dowe Flats American Indian Advisory Council. Twenty-four individuals representing eleven tribes attended. A smaller meeting was held on February 10th, 1994, but only a few tribal representatives were present, including the Northern Cheyenne, Rosebud Sioux, and Medicine Wheel Coalition for Sacred Sites of North America. Finally, eleven tribes were represented during the November 4th and 5th, 1995, meeting.

As a result of these consultation efforts, a number of issues of concern had been brought to Cemex, Inc.'s attention by consulting tribal members, which proved beneficial to Dowe Valley and the native cultural resources. Not the least important was the protection and preservation of the known Indian sites. The Dowe Flats American Indian Advisory Council was unanimous in its request that the sites not be disturbed, *even for further academic research*. Cemex, Inc., responded by preparing a protection plan for all the significant sites within its project area, including conservation easements conveyed to Boulder County on the native sites on Indian Mountain; providing an annual inspection of the native sites in the project area by cultural resource personnel; fencing and posting for "no trespassing" on the company's property; and conveying to Boulder County, in fee title, the Indian Mountain properties. These properties contain most of the significant prehistoric sites in the project area, and public access would be limited or prohibited altogether.

Additional mitigating measures implemented by Cemex, Inc., were the completion of two geomorphological studies to further examine the potential for buried sites within the mine area and monitoring topsoil removal by the project archaeologist or qualified American Indians (determined exclusively by the Dowe Flats American Indian Advisory Council) during the life of the mining operation. The project archaeologist would also instruct the quarry crew in applicable cultural resource laws and artifact recognition; would adhere to Colorado law regarding the accidental discovery of any human remains and associated burial goods and, to the greatest extent possible, to the wishes of the Dowe Flats American Indian Advisory Council; would support and provide the opportunity for tribally approved and sponsored educational and traditional ceremonial activities to take place on Indian Mountain; would undertake the reburial of previously collected artifacts curated at the University of Colorado Museum, Boulder; and would prepare an *Employees and Contractors Cultural Resource Management Manual for the Dowe Flats Project*.

These consultation efforts put forth by Cemex, Inc., for a small, but very culturally significant, valley in northern Boulder County fostered tremendous goodwill, not only among a private company and thirteen American Indian tribes, but among the tribes themselves. The company's efforts provided a rare opportunity for so many different tribes to simultaneously gather together on a cultural landscape that was considered a "crossroads" for all the tribes present, and some that were not.

The archaeological evidence was abundant throughout Dowe Valley, despite much of it being obliterated or carried away over the past 150 years. Regardless, because of Cemex, Inc., and the tribes' willingness to learn from one another through mutual care, respect, and cooperation, the valley and American Indian places it holds prevail. This was one time the White Man had ears and listened to what the Indians had to say, a big heart to understand their concerns, and a big wallet to transport, house, and feed the People.

It should be noted that the Dowe Flats American Indian Advisory Council went from assisting Cemex, Inc., to engaging the U.S. government in extensive consultations regarding a possible medicine wheel located at 325 Broadway in Boulder, Colorado. Subsequently, the Council shed its earlier title, replacing it with the United Tribes of Colorado, or UTC, to better reflect the organization's stewardship interest in its ancestral places throughout the State of Colorado, in addition to Dowe Valley. Consulting with private, municipal, state, and federal interests in all aspects of cultural resource stewardship in Colorado and other states within its aboriginal sphere of influence is the primary focus of the UTC. As described in its bylaws:

> The purpose of this organization [United Tribes of Colorado] shall be as an intertribal charitable, educational, and advocacy organization of Native American Indian Tribes, established in order to form a central voice for (1) the protection of Native American Indian traditional, historic and aboriginal homelands in Colorado; (2) the protection of the associated cultural resources of these places; (3) and protection of sacred lands, and ensuring appropriate trusts; and (4) ensuring the participation of Native American Indian Tribes in the repatriation of ancestral remains, burial items, and sacred objects.

The UTC is presently working with the Boulder County Parks and Open Space Department on issues of cultural resource protection, including the cultural resources of Dowe Valley. It had its most recent meeting in

143

Boulder, Colorado, on October 27, 2001. Additional tribes having ancestral ties to Colorado are encouraged to become members of the organization.

Suggestions to Consider in Formulating Consultation Approaches

In most cases, the agency, corporation, or government proposing an action is responsible for initiating consultation with a tribe. In this section, we direct our comments to those who will be contacting tribes and attempting to establish a consultation relationship. Remember, however, that while one party may ultimately be responsible for "consulting" as part of a regulatory requirement, if consultation is to achieve its goals, both parties must be responsible for making consultation work.

Just as each tribe should be considered a unique nation, in itself the consultation protocol may also be unique. Clearly, the tribe or tribes to be consulted are the ones to provide their processes. All federally recognized Indian tribes have a tribal government administered by a tribal council or board of trustees. As noted elsewhere, many tribes now have a Tribal Historic Preservation Office, cultural resource protection office, historic preservation office, culture commission, elders' advisory group, treaty commission, NAGPRA committee, traditional military societies, or other group that may require notification. Any one, or all, of these tribal components can, and usually do, play a major role in the consultation process. There is no easy formula to provide for the perfect consultation protocol. However, the following suggestions may help the responsible party initiate and establish a consultation relationship:

- Obtain recommendations from the relevant State Historic Preservation Office(s), Commission of Indian Affairs (every state has one), and applicable federal agencies regarding which tribe or tribes should be contacted for the consultation process. Oftentimes, the initially identified tribal representatives will also have a recommendation regarding other tribes not identified by the previously noted groups;

- A vital ingredient necessary to consultation success, however, is supporting (i.e., funding for travel, per diem, consultant's fee, and the like) the tribe's participation in the consultation process and incorporating its concerns, recommendations, and solutions to meet tribal and nontribal needs. Just as Sol Tax had to make financial arrangements for Indians to cover their week in Chicago while they attended the American Indian Chicago Conference in 1961 (Ablon 1962, 19), proponents of consultation projects will want to consider paying attending tribal members for mileage, plane tickets, ground transportation, lodging, time, and meals.

- Tribes want to be part of a project in its initial planning stages, not solely as reviewers of already prepared draft material of which they had no meaningful input. The more typical scenario provides the "consulting" tribe or tribes with a copy of the already completed draft environmental assessment or environmental impact statement for their review. Tribes will be in a better position to evaluate and possibly support a particular project if they are well informed and an active part of the decision-making process and assembly of deliverables.

- The initiation of consultations with tribes should begin as early as possible. That is, in the earliest design conception phase. For example, when it's determined that an environmental assessment or environmental impact statement is going to be required, the consulting tribes should be notified. Many consulting tribes can be viable subcontractors in producing parts of these documents and should be; examples of such input can be cultural overviews, archaeological overviews, ethnographic descriptions, and current social conditions. The cultural preservation category is especially amenable to tribal input and participation.

- Each federally recognized tribe is a sovereign nation; many have viable treaties and treaty rights. Consultations should be conducted on a government-to-government basis (see previous), following the tribal government's preferred formal protocol for such an activity;

- Tribes prefer to conduct business on a face-to-face basis to better understand the project being discussed. Letters, faxes, phone calls, and e-mails, by themselves, do not generally constitute meaningful consultation. And, oftentimes, you may not be provided with a reply anyway. During the start-up of the consultation process, it may require extra effort and diligence to properly connect with tribal contacts and government. Once contact has been established and some familiarity found, it generally becomes easier to regularly talk with tribal representatives. Nevertheless, an adequate amount of time needs to be allocated for this oftentimes labor-intensive process;

- Call tribal offices and inquire with whom you should be talking, at least initially. Let them know who you are, what your project is, and your interest in consulting with the tribe. Obtain their input as to whether they are the appropriate tribal contact persons for your particular needs. They may have additional suggestions as to other contacts within the tribe who should at least be provided with copies of all project correspondence. The tribal chairperson is always provided with a copy of everything, unless he or she requests not to be;

- Prior to any on-reservation meetings, copies of all information regarding the proposed project and any previously gathered archaeological information should be made available to the consulting tribe or tribes. Lots of copies may be required to provide the consulting tribe with all the necessary background information. This advance information can assist the consulting tribe in better preparing for the introductory meeting, providing its members have the staff, funding, and time. Full disclosure of all cultural resource project information to the tribes should be a standard practice.

- Try to maintain a flexible schedule. As a general rule, do not expect to be called upon at the time your meeting was scheduled; you may not be called upon at all. Once, one of the authors was scheduled to meet with the Rosebud Sioux Tribal Council. After flying from Denver to Rapid City, South Dakota, renting a vehicle and driving to the Rosebud Sioux Reservation, and spending two days waiting, the archaeologist returned to Denver, unsuccessful. Another attempt to meet with the Tribal Council would have to be made. Although disappointing, this time does not have to be wasted. This can be an excellent opportunity to visit with tribal members, read bulletin boards, or just tour the tribal complex and offices. Information can still be obtained that will be useful to better understand the tribe, historically and today.

- Frequently, it's much less costly in time and money for tribal representatives to meet on their reservation than to engage in extensive travel. Tribes generally have adequate meeting space and are eager to host meetings. Meeting on the reservation also means that elderly representatives can attend, whereas if they had to travel, especially by plane, they might not be able to. In addition, when elderly tribal members travel, they frequently require one or two additional individuals to assist them during their trip.

- Offer to provide an introductory meeting at tribal offices with any tribal member wishing to attend. This meeting will generally be with your tribal contact, culture committee, tribal historic preservation office, cultural resource protection office, treaty commission, and others. It is not uncommon for any number of tribal members to show up for your presentation. Take the time to introduce yourself, say where you're from, and explain why you are there. Meet everyone and gently shake their hands to get things started. This first meeting allows tribal members to see and meet you and get some idea of what you and your project are all about. You can solicit tribal input at this time for what activity should come next. At some point a presentation to the full assembly of the governing body, tribal council, or board of trustees will be likely.

- Make your presentation before the tribal council in its chamber. Tribal councils are typically very busy, so keep the presentation brief and to the point—that is, about ten to thirty minutes in length. Visual aids can be helpful, such as large aerial photographs, maps, and other means to explain the project.

Talk plainly and to the point. Never make a promise or commitment you cannot honor. At the close of your presentation, take the time to shake everyone's hand and thank them for their time.

- Afterward, visit the tribe's museum or cultural center, including its gift shop. Sometimes it's a good place to obtain some obscure literature about the tribe and reservation. It's always useful to try and get a tour of the reservation, too—things like the administration buildings, schools, and gaming and other recreational facilities.

- When you visit the reservation, tribal staff members often are available to provide a tour of their tribal facilities, including their gaming facility and reservation. Try to take advantage of these offers to better familiarize yourself with where they live and what they have to work with. This personal perspective can greatly assist you in your understanding of the folks you want to develop strong relationships with, in order to optimize your consultation efforts. Consultation is a lot about developing professional and personal relationships, so have fun with it! If invited, participate in one of the reservation's events. Maybe there's a powwow or somebody is hosting a sweat that night. Dr. Omer Stewart, founder of the University of Colorado Anthropology Department, Boulder, and champion of Indians' right to use peyote (Stewart 1973), participated in a Sun Dance and many Native American Church gatherings for years. Dr. Stewart was a member of the Native American Church. Participating in a sweat is a good way to put your mind in a good place.

- Tribal representatives can also meet off their reservation, but funding to undertake the trip (mileage or airfare, meals, lodging, ground transportation) is almost always required. The folks requesting consultations with these tribes can deny their request for travel funding, but as a result, there may be few, if any, Indians attending. And if you don't have good, consistent cooperation and participation with the consulting tribe or tribes, the consultations are less than meaningful. In fact, the "consultations" are of little value.

- State or federal agency staff that host tribal representatives at their offices will always want to have ample amounts of coffee and tea available for the meeting, especially if it is a morning meeting. Don't forget the donuts, bagels, fruit, or other continental breakfast items as well. Tribal representatives might travel a number of hours to reach the meeting, so having hot coffee and something to eat is very welcome. Soft drinks, juices, and bottled water are commonly provided during afternoon meetings. Tribal elders oftentimes attend consultation meetings, so it's good to have light refreshments to help them get through the sometimes lengthy meetings. Taking breaks every so often during long meetings is always good for everyone, too. It's very important to create a warm and comfortable environment where everyone is well taken care of and refreshed. If treated properly and hospitably, tribal representatives will be more likely to attend future consultation meetings as well.

- When providing travel funding, arrange to pre-pay for tribal members' electronic plane tickets, or if they are driving, pay their round-trip vehicle mileage in cash soon after they arrive at the meeting. Tribal members traveling by air will typically not be renting a vehicle, so their ground transportation needs must be prearranged and prepaid. It's preferable to have someone meet tribal representatives as they arrive at the airport. This individual can provide the necessary transportation to the meeting location or direct them to the shuttle service. Lodging needs to be prearranged so that tribal representatives can simply check in. Again, some tribal members may be elderly, requiring additional privacy and rest during their stay. Always take great care to assure that their comfort is provided for. It's also helpful to have meeting representatives greet tribal personnel upon their arrival to the hotel, in order to deal with unforeseen problems or answer any questions. All meals need to be provided for, if advance moneys are not made available. When meals are being provided, especially the evening meal, be sensitive to what's being served. Menus can vary, depending on the geographic area and tribes attending. For example, many of the Rocky Mountain and Plains tribes enjoy meals with medium- to well-cooked beef or buffalo. Pacific Northwest tribes oftentimes serve fish with their meals. Alcohol is neither encouraged nor provided.

- Follow up after the initial rounds of meetings on and off the reservation. The tribal contacts should be kept current on every aspect of the project by phone, fax, U.S. mail, or e-mail. Copies of all correspondence should be maintained in the project file to accurately document the consultation efforts. Additional on-site visits by tribal representatives may be necessary, depending on the events during the life of the project. For example, human remains may be accidentally discovered anytime during the project. It's important that consulting tribes are afforded the opportunity of actively participating in the cultural resource management being undertaken, including, but not limited to, the Class I file and literature search, overviews, oral histories, ethnographic studies, inventories, testing, and mitigation.

How long can consultations take? There is no hard and fast answer here. One thing is for sure, the consultations will most likely require more time than was allowed for. Many projects can require a year or two to reasonably consult with tribes. Not providing for sufficient time can be particularly harmful to the tribes and the consultation process. Tribal officials may be forced to point out to agency representatives, "Your schedule and deadlines are not the tribe's." There is a compelling reason for engaging tribes early in the conception phase of a project. Tribes can then better cooperate in establishing the project's issues, schedule, deliverables, and deadlines. A tribe, or tribes, may also be available to contract some of the work required of the project.

Summary

Consultation must be an open-ended process. You don't make a decision, consult with people, obtain their input, and then stick with your decision.

You must be open to change. Through consultation, you may learn of a group's concerns about a project or event that you were not aware of. These may be easy to address, or they may not be. You might learn about other ideas that you had not considered, which may allow you to meet your goals and reduce costs or types of impact. Many times over, we have found this to be true.

Meaningful consultation should be approached in this spirit. As partners, we must realize that we are in this together. True, the agency may be legally responsible for making a decision that won't please everyone. However, if the partnership is based upon trust, honesty, and mutual respect, the relationship will endure. In the end, if you consult with sincerity, you will succeed.

CULTURAL LANDSCAPES AND THE CHALLENGE OF PROTECTION

One of the newer approaches to managing cultural resources is the cultural landscape concept. Different terms and definitions are used, including, but not limited to, ethnographic landscapes, storyscapes, rural historic landscapes, and ecological landscapes. Regardless of how historic preservationists choose to identify a particular piece of Mother Earth, we are simply referring to geographical areas that possess special meaning to those who have ancestral ties to the area in question. We could just as easily supplant cultural landscape with more Indian-friendly terms, perhaps, like landscapes of the heart, ancestral landscape, aboriginal landscape, sacred geography, usual and accustomed areas, and so forth.

Generally, a cultural landscape would be all-encompassing, composed of smaller interconnected places that relate to the people's economic, social, and spiritual lives. A good example of such a place would be the Black Hills of South Dakota and Wyoming: *Paha Sapa* to the great Sioux Nation and *Moxtavhohona* to the *Tsistsistas* branch of Northern Cheyenne (Lazarus 1991, 3; Schlesier 1987, 211). All of the Black Hills are considered sacred to these tribes.

Cultural Landscapes in Cultural Resource Management

The movement toward cultural landscapes in the context of tribal cultural resource management accelerated when the notion of traditional cultural properties took hold (Parker and King 1990). That concept dramatically changed cultural resource management by expanding the *types of places* to be managed. Special *places* devoid of artifacts and features could now be acknowledged and eligible for the National Register if they had been important in the past and were important to the people's future. For example, traditional resource-gathering areas where plants, medicines, and minerals are collected for secular and sacred purposes are special places that are traditional cultural properties. To learn about such places, cultural resource professionals would now have to actually interact with American Indians.

The concept of cultural landscapes is again altering cultural resource management by affecting *the way* these places are identified and managed. The landscape concept shifts the unit of management from individual sites to larger areas that can include many types of interconnected sites. We refer the reader to a recent article by Evans, Roberts, and Nelson (2001), regarding these concepts as adopted by the National Park Service.

The idea of geographical areas having cultural significance is hardly new. American Indians have been trying to educate non-Indians about this ever since European contact. Indians have always attached significant sacredness and cultural significance to specific features on the landscape and the overall landscape itself, embodied in the concept of Mother Earth.

Unequivocally, America's First Americans believe Mother Earth, in Her entirety, to be sacred, although certain mountains, mountain passes, rivers, cascades, waterfalls, lakes, springs, and other special places might harbor special power. Scott (1907, 559), when communicating in sign language with the Arapaho chief Left Hand, in 1897, was told, "We used to have a great many medicine places; any place where there is a high hill or water by itself is a place where one can be helped by the medicine. We worshipped the earth also, but nothing beneath it." Upon inquiring of Anthony Sitting Eagle, Northern Arapaho elder, Wyoming, whether he was aware of any special or sacred mountain peaks west of Boulder, Colorado, he commented, "The whole Colorado Front Range is sacred" (Burney 1994, 249).

For the rest of us, however, the landscape concept first appeared in the Department of Interior's National Park Service 1980 guidelines, which at that time related specifically to farming and rural areas. The idea emerged as preservationists realized that their goals were only partially met when they narrowed their focus to whether or not a building was eligible for the National Register of Historic Places. Rather, they preferred to include buildings in their natural setting to better represent and preserve the overall character of the place. Thus arose the cultural landscape alternative.

The landscape concept was easily adapted to American Indian cul-

tural issues. Indians, archaeologists, and anthropolo-
gists had similar concerns
about the adequacy of cultural resource protective
measures. Recommending a
specific site as eligible for
the National Register or
grouping a number of sites
together as a National Register District were both useful tactics, but they still had
limitations when it came to
protection.

Previously, impact to
archaeological sites more or
less occurred only when
there was direct impact,
such as a road or pipeline.
Direct impact is usually immediate and the results are
clearly seen within several
minutes. Any kind of heavy
equipment can irreparably
damage, or outright destroy,
the integrity of a cultural
resource. Just about any
ground-disturbing activity
you can think of easily qualifies as a direct impact,

The Micaceous Clay of Picuris Pueblo and a Traditional Way of Life

Archaeology has now come to mean so much more than just "stones and bones," if you will. Greater sensitivity and respect are now provided cultural resources, which may include geological materials, plants, fish, birds, animals, and the like. One such cultural resource, but so much more, is the mica-ceous clay deposit vital to the Picuris Pueblo.

Picuris Pueblo in Northern New Mexico has a traditional cultural place where tribal members collect a specific kind of mica-laden (micaceous) clay. This resource is ex-tensively used by Picuris potters and mica-clay sculptors. The significance of this place is not due to it being a point-specific collec-tion of artifacts and features, but rather be-cause of the actual mica-clay resource and its importance to the artisans of Picuris Pueblo.

Despite the aid of three environmental law firms and the area's extreme value to a Pueblo around for over 1,000 years, the New Mexico Supreme Court refused in Oc-tober 2001 to hear Picuris Pueblo's lawsuit against the mica mine operation irreparably damaging this important resource (Matlock 1999, A9; Maxwell 2001). Not an unusual ending to these kinds of situations. As a side note, the micaceous clay deposit is an excel-lent example of a natural resource that can also be viewed as a cultural resource under the broader definition of cultural resources.

including archaeological excavation, whether undertaken professionally or not.

With traditional cultural properties, various types of indirect impact that include, but are not limited to, audible and visual effects could be con-sidered adverse. There are many examples of indirect impact that affect traditional cultural places within a cultural landscape; only several will be noted here, however, for illustrative purposes. Bear Butte ("where people are taught," or *Nowah'wus*, a term of the *Tsistsistas* branch of the Northern Cheyenne; Schlesier 1987, 211), north of Sturgis, South Dakota, is a small hill revered by many northern and central plains tribes. This is especially true for the Northern Cheyenne tribe in Montana and the Southern Cheyenne tribe in Oklahoma. Despite years of the tribes trying to sensitize the State of South Dakota to this fact, the State nevertheless developed Bear Butte State Park as a tourist attraction for the small nearby community of Sturgis. Consequently, Bear Butte, a sacred place on Montana's aboriginal cultural landscape, was directly impacted through the development of access roads, parking areas, hiking trails, and observation facilities. Indirect impact was realized through vehicular traffic, tourism, and the ability of nonnative visitors to observe and interfere with native peoples participating in their various ceremonial activities, including the sweat lodge.

As another example, several years ago the U.S. Air Force proposed northern New Mexico as a training area for low-flying aircraft. The town of Taos, Taos Pueblo, and the Taos Mountains would be regularly impacted by these low-flying training exercises. Needless to say, the native inhabitants of Taos Pueblo were less than enthusiastic about the proposal. Although there was uncertainty about whether the flights had the potential to actually cause long-term damage to the pueblo's adobe architecture, the bigger issue centered on the visual and audible impact on this part of northern New Mexico and its inhabitants.

In this regard, there was considerable outpouring of concern not only by native peoples but by the Hispanic and Anglo citizenry as well. On this issue, the majority of Taos Valley folks did not support the U.S. Air Force proposal because of the indirect impact the flights would have on the area's character. Similarly, some southwestern tribes of the Four Corners area have expressed concern over the increasingly dirty air generated from coal-fired power plants that is appearing over their aboriginal homelands and ancestral communities.

The point is, as noted by the native worldview, *all of Mother Earth is sacred*, not just archaeological and historical sites or traditional cultural places. One tribal cultural specialist once told us, "How can I say over here is important and over here is important, but in between is not. It is all important. That is like asking me which part of my body is less important so you can cut it off. My fingers? My toes? My breast? My head?"

Defining Cultural Landscapes

As previously noted, Native American cultural landscapes contain a variety of natural and cultural resources that tribes consider part of their heritage: This is where their ancestors lived and died and important events took place, including the actual place where the People originated from. Frequently, in less disturbed regions the remains of this indigenous past can be seen, and where access is possible, the landscape continues to be used by Indian people today. The land, its resources, and special places are vital in maintaining Indian values and lifeways. The Columbia River (*Nch'I-Wana;* Hunn 1990), or *Chiawana,* the Wanapum name for "The Big River" (Relander 1956, 21), is such a place.

Cultural landscapes can be viewed as analogous with ecosystems: an inseparable single unit of an ecological community with its physical environment. Clearly, a cultural landscape includes the entire territory that is utilized by a specific group, and as partially illustrated earlier, there are individual places within the overall landscape that are identified by name, oftentimes through oral tradition. Several examples of these kinds of sacred places are provided as follows:

- The point where an indigenous group originated;

- The underground, the surface, and the air;

- Villages;

- Burial places and cemeteries;

- Sites of ceremonial structures (e.g., medicine wheels and Sun Dance arbors);

- Petroglyph and pictograph locations;

- Large anthropomorphic and zoomorphic rock features;

- Vision-questing places;

- Sweat bath sites;

- Culturally important plants, animals, birds, and fish and their habitats;

- Camping areas, including those associated with the culturally important resources;

- Monumental geological features, including mountains, hills, unusual geological formations, volcanoes, and the like;

- Rivers and their confluences, lakes, springs;

- Caves;

- Places where important events took place (e.g., treaty councils and battlefields); and

- Trails and roads.

These few examples of sacred and culturally significant native places are inextricably entwined with the other interconnected places across the aboriginal cultural landscape. To native peoples, it is utterly illogical to isolate them from one another. Mother Earth doesn't work that way. At least, that's what thousands and thousands of years of observation have led them to believe.

It has only been since about 1970, when America's fledgling environmental movement began gaining momentum, that non-Indians attempted to embrace this viewpoint with the recognition that all aspects of our planet may be systemically related. The analogy of a spider's web is useful. It's difficult not to focus on the individual components or patterns making the web, but once the web is completed in its entirety, these individual parts become obscured, less noticeable than the finished creation.

Identifying Landscapes

While it is useful to identify the overarching cultural landscape that has traditionally encompassed a group's territory, in a more contemporary setting it is often necessary to define a set of landscapes that has meaning today. Except in the most remote areas, traditional cultural places have undergone extensive change. Entire portions of traditional landscapes have been heavily developed by modern-day society and may have reduced significance to present-day native peoples.

Regardless, for most North American native groups their reservation and, in some cases, adjacent lands ceded to the U.S. government, via treaty, are all that remains of their original cultural landscape. For those tribes exiled great distances from their aboriginal homelands (e.g., for those tribes forcibly relocated West since European contact on the Eastern seaboard and the many tribes that were forced to relocate to the present-day state of Oklahoma), the situation is even more difficult. Even the tribes themselves struggle over preserving environmentally what little is left versus attaining greater prosperity through economic development of their land and resources.

It should go without saying that Indian tribes must be included when one is identifying cultural landscapes that are important to them. Therein lies a dilemma. Native peoples rarely need to explicitly identify these kinds of places, much less publicize their whereabouts. To the contrary, it's non-Indians who want to identify, catalog, record, photograph, and, whenever possible, publish their findings. These situations cause confusion and distress to Indian people.

For the most part, sensitive information such as that usually surrounding traditional cultural areas may not be freely shared, even among tribes themselves. Some tribes deal with this delicate situation in a variety of ways. They may work closely with state and federal agencies to ensure the greatest degree of confidentiality that is reasonably possible, while others develop their own tribal historic preservation programs. In the latter case, tribes can more effectively control what information is collected, how it's used, where it's stored, and so on. This is especially true on their own reservations or on other lands under their control.

In particular, tribal members don't discuss human remains and burial locations. Likewise, they are cautious about divulging locations where food and medicines are procured. This information can also be sensitive and confidential. The Creator could take these necessities away if they are shared with others. Maybe not, but better safe than sorry.

Sometimes the reasons are more practical. Revealing the locations of huckleberry patches, piñyon pine nuts, or medicinal plants that are sought after by pharmaceutical companies will, more often than not, lead to their demise. Several examples that immediately come to mind are the huckleberries noted previously, edible fungi, and the sacred Grandfather Peyote so revered by the Native American Church. We all know what happened to the beaver, salmon, and buffalo when they became economically desirable. Anything with a price on its head is likely to become very scarce in a hurry.

Actually identifying cultural landscapes and the associated archaeological remains and traditional cultural places does not necessarily require disclosing why the area is important. Anthropologists who work closely with tribal communities have developed approaches that are helpful to state and federal agencies and the tribes. Examples include cognitive mapping (Austin 1998), resource importance (Stoffle and Evans 1990), resource inventory and assessment (Stoffle, Halmo, Evans, and Austin 1996), and many others. And, of course, anthropologists don't always have to be involved. Many federal land-managing agencies are content with simply noting the general location of the "place" for avoidance purposes and letting it go at that.

When attempting to identify cultural landscapes, traditional cultural places, or other sensitive locations, non-Indian cultural resource personnel may find it useful to consider the following suggestions:

- Work with those knowledgeable about the area, its resources, and places and activities associated with past and current use. Kooistra-Manning, Deaver, and Quirt (1993, 85–86) designate those places and activities currently being used by native peoples as "contemporary use areas." Due to the sensitive nature of sharing much of this information with non-Indians or even among other Indians, the data may be confidential and under tribal control. Note that different people may have used the same area for more than one activity, resulting in a variety of experiences, stories, and attachments.

- Coordinate frequent visits for tribal members to the area when soliciting information. Again, if tribal members, including elders, are not involved in such an endeavor, it is, for all practical purposes, a futile exercise. If, that is, your goal is to gather information about indigenous cultural landscapes and traditional cultural properties. The more tribal members visit the area in question, the more recalling of past stories and experiences will be afforded. Providing bus tours for tribal elders, children, and others is usually an excellent means of getting things started and an appropriate first step. Such efforts may foster a rekindling of the past and may support future use of the area. As noted in the Hanford, Washington, and Dowe Flats, Colorado, examples in chapter 7, not only were Indian sites and places identified and recorded, but Indians were provided access and allowed use of their aboriginal cultural landscape. Despite the stringent security needs required of the Hanford Site, tribal members are encouraged to partake in on-site visits, tours, and the like. More specific activities are also accommodated. As for Dowe Valley, Boulder County (thanks to Cemex, Inc.) has provided tribal members with the use of Indian Mountain for ceremonial activities. In the latter case, this is particularly helpful, in that the large American Indian population residing along Colorado's Front Range appreciates a *place* to go to conduct these activities.

• Undertake archaeological and historical inventories to identify isolated finds, features, sites, and other cultural phenomena, working with tribal representatives. This fieldwork will provide the data needed to generate maps illustrating site-distribution patterns. Geographical information systems (GIS) are useful for managing large databases and are gaining in popularity. Many tribes, however, have concerns regarding the security of their information relative to electronic storage.

Protecting Cultural Landscapes

The preferred alternative when managing any cultural resource, including a traditional cultural place or cultural landscape, is protecting and preserving its integrity and overall character. This is an easier task when managing smaller areas such as a farm or a ranch, but is most difficult when measuring hundreds of miles in size. Having multiple ownership by private landowners and municipal, state, and federal agencies only compounds the situation.

Cultural landscapes everywhere are evolving. Across the United States, there is increasing competition for the land and resources. Can cultural landscapes anticipate any kind of long-term preservation under such

Evolving Traditions

A common criticism from cultural anthropologists concerning the traditional cultural property concept is its relatively static view of tradition. A place is a traditional cultural property if it was used in the past and is needed for the future. But places change and so do traditions, as one cultural anthropologist, Robert Winthrop, explains here.

All traditions reflect adaptation to changing circumstances, whether the change is incremental or catastrophic. Few would suggest that the Catholic monastic life is [inauthentic] or nontraditional because the form it takes in the late twentieth century is distinctive, diverging in many respects from the particular observances of several centuries ago, or because at various periods in its history it suffered radical dislocations in its observance. The same logic would seem to apply to American Indian societies.

This is not to suggest that anthropologists should abandon critical thinking or scholarly standards when involved in cultural resource management studies. Nonetheless, where American Indian communities (or any other communities) are concerned, the objective of cultural resource management policy should not be to ensure the strict perpetuation of earlier practices, or to demand an unbroken continuity of ritual observance. Rather, to the extent feasible federal policy should be directed toward protecting and extending access to those resources and landscapes through which traditions can be adapted and renewed. In this context the words of the philosopher Miguel de Unamuno seem very apt: "We live in memory and by memory, and our spiritual life is simply the effort of our memory to persist, to transform itself into hope, the effort of our past to transform itself into our future." (1972, 11–12) (Winthrop 1998, 27)

pressures for economic development? Development is difficult to contain within these large landscapes unless an area is designated a National Monument or National Park—and even that does not always assure protection. In fact, artifact collecting, tourist development, and the visitors themselves represent significant adverse impact on these federal recreational facilities.

Preserving a cultural landscape involves more than simply protecting specific places within it. As noted previously, all of the individual places are interconnected. Adverse impact to any one of the parts affects all of the landscape. Eventually, the overall effect of this cumulative impact degrades the landscape, diminishing its integrity to the point that it loses its natural setting and character. Minimizing visual and noise impact is equally important when attempting to preserve cultural landscapes.

The National Park Service wants snowmobiles out

of certain parks (e.g., Yellowstone National Park): The noise, pollution, and visual impact are deleterious to the park's natural setting and character. The National Park Service also purchases private lands within its parks and removes buildings, when attempting to restore the park to its "precontact" setting. A recent example is the Antietam National Battlefield near Sharpsburg, Maryland. Officials "are restoring vast swaths of the park to look as it did in April 1862, when one of the bloodiest battles in American history was fought there. The plan includes buying more land within the park's boundaries to restore woods" (Associated Press 2001, 8A).

Preserving cultural landscapes, or restoring them to their pristine settings, is a great idea but seldom a reality. In that native peoples now retain only about *3 percent* of their aboriginal territory (Utter 1993, 169)—it only stands to reason that most of their aboriginal lands, traditional cultural places, and cultural landscapes are under non-Indian control. Ownership may be private, municipal, county, state, federal, or all of them combined. The Columbia River Gorge in Oregon and Washington and the Middle Missouri River in South Dakota are examples of such multiple land ownership.

Conflicting interests may also arise regarding cultural resources. Nonnatives may propose monuments to commemorate their history or may restore buildings or whole neighborhoods (e.g., revitalize downtown), or researchers may undertake various archaeological studies, including excavation, on native sites. For this reason, it behooves tribes to establish strong working relationships with these entities so that their interests and concerns can be better understood and taken into account.

When landowners' competing interests collide, maintaining any real integrity of a cultural landscape becomes challenging and elusive. Cultural landscapes on federal lands, or those eligible for federal funding, may fare better than nonfederal projects. Federal facilities and projects must adhere to federal legislation that addresses cultural resource issues and concerns, including cultural landscapes. Expending the effort necessary to getting a landscape listed on the National Register of Historic Places (and, simultaneously, on state and tribal registers) further establishes some level of protection. As noted elsewhere, however, this course of action may require obtaining culturally sensitive information. Virtually any undertaking within an American Indian landscape can potentially affect the area's character and setting. Consequently, it is essential that Indians be actively involved in reviewing any proposed undertakings (preferably in their conceptual planning stage) and their possible adverse impact.

Interestingly, many federal facilities established in years past have inadvertently preserved large portions of their land base, due to security requirements that limit access to the general public. The Rocky Flats nuclear facility between Boulder and Golden, Colorado, is such an example. Without this federal oversight, less effort and funding that addresses cultural landscapes would be the norm. Although the Dowe Flats case discussed in chapter 7 was not a federal undertaking, the project followed federal cultural resource guidelines and legislation.

And, as noted previously, even cultural landscapes under Indian ownership and control are subject to modification over time. To say the least, Indian communities on reservations desperately need economic development. The United States is currently experiencing a recession, in which the nation's unemployment of around 6 percent is of some concern. Well, try 70 percent and then some, a level of unemployment not uncommon on many of America's Indian reservations.

Few reservations, if any, are not supportive of more economic development. This goal of greater self-sufficiency and prosperity may be achieved by allowing the extraction of natural resources from Indian lands (e.g., coal and timber) or developing ski resorts, cultural centers, museums, and other recreational facilities on the reservation. Indian gaming facilities, including conference centers, hotels, and golf courses, are certainly popular. Most states are now endorsing the gaming industry, provided that states get their share of the take. Considering what American Indians have lost since they encountered non-Indians, a reasonable argument could be made that the state should not receive any portion of the gaming moneys.

All of these developments, however, modify the landscape. Again, encouraging economic growth while maintaining the native land base can be tricky at best. Although this dichotomy is often viewed as the "progressives" versus the "traditionalists," it is not that simple. Regardless, lands controlled by tribal governments will more likely ensure that tribal values are taken into account during development of their reservation, ensuring that their cultural landscape's integrity is maintained to the greatest extent possible. Native and nonnative cultural resource managers may consider the following types of activities to better protect and preserve those cultural landscapes within their purview:

- Ensure that all proposed projects conduct cultural resource reviews to consider their impact on the cultural landscape. Federal undertakings must comply with the National Environmental Policy Act, the National Historic Preservation Act, and other applicable federal legislation before they are given approval. Agency officials must consult in a meaningful way with tribal leaders concerning any project that potentially affects Native American resources (cultural or natural). Tribes may request to be kept informed throughout the project and may ask for greater involvement, as necessary.

- Monitor sites at regular intervals to provide early warnings of potential impact. These various types of impact can result from flooding, fires, earthquakes, or other natural events or from human intervention, such as dams and reservoirs, recreational activities, artifact collecting, or digging.

- Work with local law enforcement to enlist its support in monitoring sites susceptible to illegal activities. This cooperation may involve the training of law enforcement personnel under the Archaeological Resource Protection Act. As noted in chapter 5, the Confederated Tribes of the Umatilla Indian Reservation, Cultural Resource Protection Program, actively provides Archaeological Resource Protection Act training to various local, state, and federal law enforcement agencies.

- Likewise, work with local, state, and federal organizations to promote public education in Native American relations, archaeology, and historic preservation in general. Many states now have programs celebrating "Archaeology Month" that are designed to support long-term public education, with an emphasis on schools and civic organizations.

- Implement a stabilization effort to identify, assess, and restore sites that are adversely impacted. Impact that is injurious to the resources should be noted and corrected whenever feasible.

A major benefit of the cultural landscape approach is that it enables tribes, cultural resource personnel, and other stakeholders to collectively consider the effects of just about any project within, or adjacent to, the property in question. The bottom line is, tribes can be more involved in the overall management and protection of the landscape. That's a good thing.

Summary

In this chapter we have advocated for the management of cultural resources through large geographic areas, be they called cultural landscapes, ethnographic landscapes, storyscapes, rural historic landscapes, ecological landscapes, landscapes of the heart, or whatever. Although relatively new to historic preservation, the concept appears to be gaining support as the profession, state, and federal regulatory agencies, Indian tribes, and others incorporate it into their historic preservation strategies. Advocacy for the cultural landscape concept and its success will require a preservation consortium composed of all those interested in pursuit of cultural and natural preservation.

CHAPTER NINE
PROMOTING A CULTURAL RESOURCE STEWARDSHIP AGENDA TO ADDRESS TRIBAL INTERESTS AND EXPECTATIONS

Steward: A person who manages another's property, finances or other affairs. (*The American Heritage Dictionary*)

Cultural resource stewardship at the federal level is not a new concept. Effectively, it began with the passage of the 1906 Antiquities Act. In passing this Act, the U.S. Congress confirmed that American society had an obligation to protect and conserve the nation's cultural resources for current and future generations. As archaeologists took on the stewardship challenge, the goal of stewardship evolved into saving archaeological resources for information purposes. Then, with greater influence from American Indians, the goal started to evolve toward saving cultural resources for people first and information second.

In this chapter we present an approach to stewardship that addresses the fundamental needs of American Indians to preserve, protect, and have access to culturally important resources. Our approach, however, is not restricted to places with American Indian resources. The stewardship approach presented here is targeted to places with lands that are overseen by some responsible organization. It may be a reservation, a federal land unit, or a landscape managed by a consortium of agencies, tribes, local governments, and so on. The point is, someone is responsible for protecting resources contained in a particular area.

The stewardship approach we advocate is an integrated approach that improves protection of cultural resources. The approach results from interactions among American Indians, federal agencies, cultural resource professionals, and others. It is one of the many benefits of different groups working together for a common goal, what we refer to in this book as synergy.

We begin this chapter by defining cultural resource stewardship and then focus on the ingredients of a good stewardship program. We discuss some of the requirements that a stewardship program must meet if it is to be successful and follow this with the functions a stewardship program needs to fulfill. We close by illustrating how these functions are combined to perform common cultural resource tasks.

Defining Cultural Resource Stewardship

The concept of cultural resource stewardship arises because cultural resources are a threatened resource. They are extremely fragile; they are non-renewable. They are finite. Loss of the resources is inevitable. We can't stop meandering rivers, forest fires, floods, and other natural forces. We can't stop development. And we probably can't stop looting and vandalism. But we can try, nevertheless.

One of the first cultural resource definitions for stewardship came out of the U.S. Department of Defense Cold War Legacy Project. That project was conceived to care for the many sites and collections that represent and symbolize the nation's fight against the Soviet Union and its communist agenda between 1945 and 1990. The Department of Defense defined stewardship as:

> *the faithful management of resources as assets that must be turned over to the next generation.* (DOD 1994)

Three aspects of this definition inform us about the notion of stewardship. The words *faithful management* remind us that one must have a vision that goes beyond simply following established procedures by rote. It is a spirit that one must possess in doing one's job, similar to that of a medical doctor whose primary goal is to save the patient. The term *asset* gives a different twist to cultural resources. Assets are generally inventoried and actively managed to ensure that they stay in good condition; asset preservation is usually a primary goal.[1] The phrase *must be turned over to the next generation* reminds us that we are the caretakers, not the owners, of those cultural resources we are helping to manage.

A definition that focused on archaeological resources appeared from the Society for American Archaeology, which identified stewardship as the centerpiece of all its principles. The Society defined stewardship as follows:

> Stewardship: The archaeological record, that is, in situ archaeological material and sites, archaeological collections, records and reports, is a public trust. The use of the archaeological record should be for the benefit of all people. As part of the important record of the human cultural past, archaeological materials are not commodities to be exploited for personal enjoyment or profit. It is the responsibility of all archaeologists to work for the long-term preservation and protection of the archaeological record. Although archaeologists rarely have legal ownership of archaeological resources, they should practice and promote stewardship of the archaeological record. Stewards are both caretakers and advocates for the archaeological record. As they investigate and interpret the record, archaeologists should also promote its long-term conservation. Archaeologists should use their specialized knowledge to promote public understanding and support for the long-term preservation of the archaeological record. (Lynott and Wylie 1995, 23)

For many archaeologists:

> the archaeological record (specifically the primary record—archaeological deposits) is a fragile and irreplaceable resource for the understanding of human populations, cultures, communities, and sometimes agents, whose lives are very largely unknown or inaccessible by any other means. From the perspective of archaeological science, the value of archaeological research is measured by the information it yields about the past. (Lynott and Wylie 1995, 29)

From the tribal perspective, however, the value of archaeological resources is not measured by the information it yields about the past. American Indians have uses for archaeological sites related to their ancestors, and we would cite their interests above those of archaeologists. For American Indians, the uses may be to protect spiritual integrity for the ancestors and those unborn; it may be to visit former living areas with elders or children to teach and learn.

We are encouraged by one recent trend in the archaeological profession. Fagan (1993) has argued that in accepting the conservation ethic, there must be a fundamental reorientation of archaeological practice:

He is particularly concerned that the issues and basic values of conservation become a standard part of archaeological curricula, and that priority should be given to "fundamental research" addressing questions about the conditions responsible for the destruction of archaeological resources, about looting practices, and about the effectiveness of various educational and legal strategies for protecting these resources. (Lynott and Alison Wylie 1995, 32)

If this were to happen, it would help preserve the archaeological record, which is certainly in line with cultural resource stewardship goals. Fagan's motivation may differ from that of American Indians, but it is a start in the right direction.

Based upon our experiences and understanding of the needs of American Indians and other descendent populations, we propose to define cultural resource stewardship as follows:

Cultural resource stewardship means preserving, protecting, and ensuring that cultural resources are accessible, as appropriate, for present and future generations, especially descendent communities.

Preserving is important to secure the integrity of the resource as we find it. *Protecting* is important to keep the integrity from being impaired or destroyed. *Ensuring that cultural resources are accessible* implies their availability for use, whether for on-site ceremonial visits, family educational or recreational purposes; information about the resource on a website; or even archaeological excavations to recover data to answer meaningful questions about the past. *As appropriate* indicates that proper behaviors and conduct must be exercised; there may be places that are not appropriate for on-site visits or sharing with the public. And finally, *for present and future generations* reminds us that people, especially descendents, wish to have access to sites today, as well as in the future.

Stewardship Principles

Every cultural resource program will likely develop its own set of principles, based upon the types of cultural resources, the needs of tribes, the needs of interested parties, the level of public access, and the various other program-specific circumstances. The following list is our general set of principles that we strive to follow to make a stewardship program successful:

- Listen to those who have attachment to the cultural landscapes and balance their interests with the interests of people who desire lands for uses that may impact the landscape;

- Accommodate the rights, religions, traditions, and interests of those living cultures that have connections to the resources, whenever possible;

- Avoid disturbing objects, locations, and sites of cultural significance, unless these face unavoidable destruction or harm;

- Mitigate all avoidable damage and threats to important cultural and historic resources;

- Adhere to all applicable cultural and historic resource laws and regulations—both in the absence and in the presence of external enforcement.

Principles, while important, are just words. They are easy to say and write, harder to live by. In reality, the principles listed previously are not all that different from ones identified by the Society for American Archaeology in recent years. Few would argue, however, that the archaeological community has been effective in adhering to its principles as stated. You have to believe the words if you are going to live by them. As we look back on our careers and transformations, it was probably the first word of the first principle, *Listen*, that was the most important. Listening to those whose *lives* depend on the resources, and not just to those whose *livelihood* depends on them, will have the biggest effect on making a stewardship program successful.

Defining Stewardship Requirements for a Cultural Resource Program

In this section, we identify a set of requirements that a facility must meet to be a good steward for cultural resources. We have developed these from the set of cultural resource laws with which a federal agency must comply.

Personal Reflections on CRM: Part III

In this third installment from Evan DeBloois, he calls for all facets of cultural resource management to be brought to bear in better ensuring the future preservation and conservation of our nation's prehistoric and historic sites.

Land management agencies have a direct public responsibility to manage cultural resources in the nation's interest, assuring that sites are protected and preserved, and access and information are made available to the public now and in the future. Although the term "stewardship" is considered by some as overly broad and over used, I think this is the one of the prime objectives of the National Historic Preservation Act as defined in the preamble. I define stewardship to encompass those activities that led to the protection and preservation of cultural resources for present and future generations. The land management agency also has a responsibility to the public to provide access to and interpretation of cultural resources. The Forest Service's Heritage Resource Management Strategy tries to address the entire range of a land management agency's responsibilities, and attempts to distinguish stewardship responsibilities from public service.

I began my career as a prehistoric archaeologist and ended up as a heritage (cultural) resource manager. I started out looking for prehistoric sites and ended up developing national policy and procedures for a comprehensive heritage management program. There are many roles to be played in a cultural resource management program, and all of them can be seen as segments of CRM, but to do CRM you have to put all of them together. As I see it, CRM is something land management agencies do, and they use a variety of people/resources in getting it done—contract archaeology, regulation, Section 106 compliance, historic architecture, cultural anthropology, interpretation, research, planning, and budgeting.

We propose these as a generic set of requirements to consider; each setting will likely vary according to state laws, agency policies, and other situation-specific criteria.

Requirements are extremely important to define. Facility managers, and particularly budget managers, seem to always be looking for the absolute minimum the facility must do to comply with the law. Cultural resource staff will typically roll out the list of laws, implementing regulations, executive orders, and agency policies to justify the cultural resource program activities. Some are very specific, while others are general and tend to overlap. By distilling the regulations, we can identify a series of high-level requirements that can be used to develop a comprehensive program. The requirements can also be used to evaluate the completeness of an agency cultural resource program.

We propose the following requirements as examples, along with ques-

tions that can be asked of a program to see if the requirements are being met:

- *Develop and maintain a cultural resource program*—Is there a
  reasonable-sized program? Is annual funding in place, with
  committed staff and procedures for ensuring that resources are
  preserved, protected, and made accessible?

- *Involve tribes and interested parties in the preservation planning
  and implementation*—Did tribes and interested parties participate in the planning of the program? Are they consulted regularly on program matters, both short term and long term?

- *Identify cultural resources and gain an appreciation for their significance*—Has the program conducted enough inventory and
  analysis to gain a good understanding of the location of archaeological sites, traditional cultural properties, and cultural
  landscapes? Is there an understanding of which sites are most
  important to tribes and interested parties, including scientists?

- *Consider the effects of agency undertakings*—Is a 106 process in
  place that addresses agency projects early on so that cultural resource input can be considered? Are tribes and interested parties being consulted as required by law?

- *Protect resources and mitigate unavoidable threats and impact*—Is
  a site and cultural landscape inspection program in place to determine whether the cultural resources are being adversely impacted by natural forces, such as erosion, or cultural forces, such
  as recreational activities or looting? Are mitigation efforts in
  place, especially creative ones (derived in consultation with
  tribes) beyond artifact recovery, such as public education, law
  enforcement training, and site stabilization?

- *Make resources available to Americans Indians and others*—Have
  tribes and interested parties been consulted to inquire about on-
  site visits and use? Have these requests been accommodated?

- *Return human remains and associated materials and objects of cultural patrimony*—Are there still American Indian human re-

mains in facility collections? Are inadvertent discovery procedures in place in case remains are encountered? Has tribal cultural affiliation been determined for the facility?

- *Maintain collections and records in good condition*—Are artifacts
and ethnographic collections being stored appropriately? Are
site records stored according to regulations?

If a cultural resource program review can answer these questions reasonably, then chances are the program is well on its way to meeting the
spirit of stewardship. In reality, many programs have some pieces of the
stewardship puzzle in place, while other pieces are missing. The remain-
der of this chapter provides input on how to ensure that a program com-
pletes the entire picture.

Functions to Be Performed in a Stewardship Program

Functions are things that need to be performed to successfully carry out a
specified mission and achieve the program goals. The functions provided
here come from a broader environmental stewardship vision and have
been adapted for cultural resource management (Jarvis and Bilyard 1998).

The thirteen stewardship functions described are, for the most part,
not new. In cultural resource management, however, they are not always
identified as such. More typically, cultural resource work is described and
organized by the types of activities performed, such as site inventories, 106
reviews, and collections management. Identifying the functions is useful
because it allows one, whether on the inside or the outside, to assess a particular function to ensure that it is adequately staffed and funded and that
proper procedures are in place. Furthermore, it enables one to track costs
according to function, which is useful for planning and budgeting purposes. To facilitate discussion, the functions are divided into three cate-
gories: (1) direction functions; (2) technical operations functions; and (3)
administrative functions, as shown in table 9.1.

Finally, in stewardship some required functions are not typically identified in archaeology-based cultural resource management. Examples include long-term monitoring, designing engineered solutions, or science
and technology. Reviewing the thirteen functions defined in the following

Table 9.1   Functional Elements of Cultural Resource Stewardship

sections enables program managers to assess exactly what they are accomplishing in the cultural resource program they are managing.

Direction Functions

Provide Guidance and Oversight [Guidance & Oversight]: This is perhaps the most important function of all, because it sets the direction and the agenda for the cultural resource activities on the site and holds program participants accountable for progress. Where does such direction come from and who makes the decisions? A common problem for cultural resource stewardship in the past has been the burying of the program in the organization. Key to raising the importance of the cultural resource program within the organization is garnering support from the outside and making sure these persons' interests are clearly conveyed to upper management. It's also important to find advocates within upper levels of management.

An effective strategy is to establish a leadership council of sorts, a kind of board of directors. This would be a group composed of upper-level managers and representatives from the key stakeholders that, ideally,

would meet six to ten times annually. The group can look at the broad regulatory requirements, capture the interests of the outside groups, consider
the needs of the agency, and provide direction. The more authority the
group is given, the greater its ability to provide financial resources and
strengthen the program.

Perform Management Duties [Management]: This function recognizes
both the need to manage the people who work in the cultural and historic
resource protection process and the tangible assets required for success.
This function houses the necessary tasks of an operation (i.e., duty as-
signments, tasking, payroll, vacation scheduling, retirement administration, office space, and equipment purchase).

*Assure Compliance with Regulations and Agreements [Requirements and
Drivers]:* Being able to demonstrate that the program is in compliance is
an important element of a successful stewardship approach. This function
provides for the effective interface with the regulatory community. It includes the reviews of undertakings to comply with Section 106, provides
an interpretation of NAGPRA and other regulations when events tran-
spire, and evaluates changes that are needed when new regulations are issued or old ones revised.

Infusion and Transfer of Science and Technology [Science and Technology]:
Stewardship processes and decisions can greatly benefit if science (including ethnoscience) and technology are incorporated. Investments in basic
science and applied science are a fundamental part of an effective stewardship policy. To the degree that we better understand the nature of the
cultural resources, as well as the forces that impact them, the better we can
protect the resources. It is important that state-of-the-art science and
technology be communicated to the appropriate staff members so they
can work more effectively. It's also important that needs are communicated from the program to scientific and technological institutions, the
public, and stakeholders so that they understand what's necessary. Finally,
as knowledge about human behavior, archaeological manifestations, and
methods is gained, it is important to share this with others through publications and attendance at professional meetings.

Technical Operations

Conduct Inventory and Status Investigations [Inventory and Status]: Land managers need to accurately inventory their lands and identify the cultural resources that exist. The agency also needs to know the status or condition of the resources to be managed. Identifying archaeological sites, traditional use areas, and buildings is a critical first step. Many times, if sites were recorded over twenty years ago, the information is minimal and not up to current standards. It's often necessary to re-record these sites so that a more contemporary baseline can be established, using the newest recording standards.

Conduct Surveillance and Monitoring [Surveillance and Monitoring]: This function addresses the need to periodically ascertain the status of any damage or threat to known cultural sites and structures. If a baseline exists, site re-visits can be scheduled on a regular basis, depending on how often the impact is predicted to occur. The purpose is twofold. One is to provide feedback as to the current status of the archaeological and historical resources, and the other is to compare the current status to the previously predicted status. This function also coordinates inspections in which mitigation has occurred, to ensure that the chosen solution is effective.

Perform Data Interpretation and Prediction [Interpretation and Prediction]: There is a need for interpretation of the data and information that is collected about archaeological sites, traditional cultural places, national register districts, cultural landscapes, and historic buildings. Some data interpretation and prediction could involve understanding the settlement pattern so that additional inventories can be targeted in high-probability areas (e.g., predictive models). Other types of interpretation and prediction relate to understanding data that is collected during long-term monitoring visits. The analysis of types of impact leads to formulating conceptual models regarding actual or expected damage and/or threats (i.e., the adverse forces working at the site, such as erosion, looting, or inadvertent recreation impact). These conceptual models predict expected damage over time so that there is a context for understanding the findings that result from monitoring. In addition, this function predicts the expected outcomes of planned mitigation measures.

Address Impact and Recommend Solutions [Decision and Procedure]: This function addresses types of impact that are determined unacceptable. The main activity is developing and evaluating alternative approaches to mitigating impact. For example, if human remains are eroding out of a river bank, these may need to be removed and the bank stabilized. If looting is occurring in an area, patrols may need to be increased. If recreation activities are impacting sites, recreation sites may need to be moved. In these cases there are likely several alternatives for accomplishing the objective. Developing solutions and evaluating the costs and benefits are the thrust of this function.

Execute Designed Solutions [Construction and Maintenance]: This function recognizes the need to actually implement one of the mitigation solutions. Typically, the solution will be an engineered approach to control erosion or control site access, archaeological excavation to remove materials before they are lost, additional law enforcement patrols, or public education to raise awareness and minimize inadvertent destruction.

*Protect the Public, the Personnel, and the Site [Site and Personnel Protection]:*Many archaeological and historical resources require continuous and active guarding to prevent trespass and vandalism. In addition, there may be a continuing need for monitoring access across large areas. This function houses the routine or repetitive in-the-field activities of the project and provides traditional safeguards and security-type operations.

Administrative Functions
Sustain Archives and Distribute Records [Archives and Records]: This is another critical function for stewardship. Keeping well-maintained and complete archives and records is vital because historic preservation protection entails working with irreplaceable information and objects over very long time periods. This function is the starting point for most actions and an important input to decision making. As such, archives and records serve as the central repository for all information about the landscape. Security is paramount.

Track Accountability and Report Status [Accountability and Reporting]: The historic preservation protection program is accountable to the tribes and others. This function recognizes this responsibility for accountability and makes reporting on status a formal part of the stewardship program.

Ensure Fiscal Resources [Fiscal]: Historic preservation protection requires consistent and adequate funding. This function gives formal recognition to the need to secure funding for current and future operations, as well as unplanned protection efforts.

Cross-Cutting Operations

Most work involving cultural resources cross-cuts two or more of three functions. The purpose of this section is to identify example activities conducted during the management of a facility's cultural resource program. Emphasis is given to new ways of doing things within the stewardship perspective. Flow charts are included to illustrate where particular functions connect.

Conducting Historic Preservation Planning

The process laid out in the secretary of the interior's guidelines for historic preservation planning is a good start. From a stewardship perspective, the weakness is that, oftentimes, input from tribes and stakeholders did not occur, the input is not part of an ongoing process, or the involvement was insufficient. Many times, people who care about the resources have not participated in planning their future. This could be for many reasons: They did not know about the planning, they did not fully understand how valuable their input was, or they just could not afford the time or did not have the money. Furthermore, too many agencies did some level of planning, only to stop, but planning is an ongoing process. Remember, planning is an ongoing process requiring a long-term commitment.

Historic preservation planning is the most important part of an overall stewardship program because it defines what minimal compliance is. In most organizations, those on the budget side of the fence want the minimum. "We are not in the cultural resource business. . . . What is the minimum we must do? What do the regulations say we are required to accomplish?" Except for Section 106 of the NHPA, the regulations don't have an answer to these questions. However, the regulations are clear in one regard. You need to establish a viable cultural resource management

Table 9.2   Conducting Program Planning

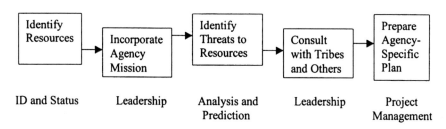

Identify Resources	Incorporate Agency Mission	Identify Threats to Resources	Consult with Tribes and Others	Prepare Agency-Specific Plan
ID and Status	Leadership	Analysis and Prediction	Leadership	Project Management

program to preserve, protect, and make accessible the cultural resources. How is a program defined? Get a handle on the resources to be managed, identify the threats and damage, work with agency officials to understand the agency mission and future plans, consult tribes and interested parties about their needs, and develop a program that best protects the resources. That's minimum compliance, in our book.

Identifying Resources

Early cultural resource management focused heavily on identifying sites and conducting archaeological and historic building inventories, for obvious reasons. You need to know what cultural resources you have as a first step in their management. Many agencies are still undertaking inventories because few facilities have completed the process for all their lands. Most agencies have not inventoried anywhere near all their property. Acres already inventoried, however, have high site densities. More recently, the legal recognition of traditional cultural properties requires these types of resources to be identified and recorded along with their counterparts. As noted in chapter 2, ethnographic surveys became more commonplace during the early 1980s.

A common deficiency in federal historic preservation is failure to evaluate the cultural resources. From a stewardship perspective, evaluations are less critical. All sites are important, being related across the landscape. If a federal (or other) undertaking develops, the impact on the landscape and resources must be considered. In other words, although sites may not be eligible for the National Register of Historic Places, this does not necessarily mean that an undertaking can proceed without review. The National Environmental Policy Act does not, for example, restrict itself only to eligible sites. It therefore becomes questionable whether or not time and

Table 9.3 Identifying Resources

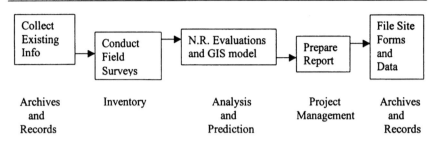

Collect Existing Info	Conduct Field Surveys	N.R. Evaluations and GIS model	Prepare Report	File Site Forms and Data
Archives and Records	Inventory	Analysis and Prediction	Project Management	Archives and Records

money should be spent evaluating sites until these become at risk. Don't forget, significance can vary culturally. A site may not have archaeological value, but it might have cultural value to a tribe. Significance can also shift over time (i.e., what did not seem significant years ago might be today, and vice versa.)

The rapid advances in geographic information systems are making it easier to understand where cultural resources are located across the landscape. This can help prioritize survey areas and sites to be protected and identify correlations with environmental conditions. There are, however, many concerns about converting information into electronic forms, and for this reason, many tribes hesitate to endorse geographical information systems for sensitive cultural data.

Conducting Section 106 Reviews

Conducting Section 106 reviews is the hallmark of modern cultural resource management. This legislation is the strongest and drives most of the work. Agencies are required to consider the impact of all undertakings, resulting in more sites being protected than by any other measure. There has been a tendency to procedurally encumber the process, though programmatic agreements can streamline the process.

From a stewardship perspective, the Section 106 process has been enormously effective. Two areas for improvement are noted. First, we need to better consider the effects of undertakings on cultural landscapes. Second, we need to continue the trend toward creative mitigation. Some people are critical because they feel that all the mitigation work done through archaeological excavation over the years has been of limited value.

Table 9.4   Conducting Section 106 Review Requests

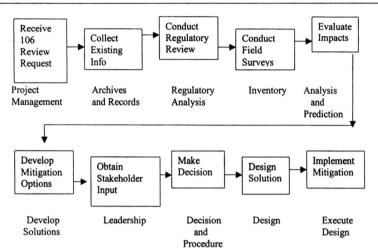

Long-Term Monitoring of Sites and Landscapes

To ensure that sites and landscapes are not being impacted by erosion, looting, vandalism, or recreation, they need to be regularly inspected. Depending on the frequency and nature of the disturbance, such inspections could be required every few months or every few years. Monitoring of site or landscape conditions needs a baseline for comparative purposes. It also requires a conceptual model of various types of impact so that findings can be compared against what was expected. For example, if minor recreational impact is predicted, and accepted, along a stretch of river, the leadership council won't require mitigation. Conversely, if the impact is significantly greater than predicted, action may be needed. Without conceptual models in place, project staff is at a disadvantage to determine when, and what, actions are needed. Developing a long-term monitoring program requires considerable effort. Which sites should be monitored, how frequently, what data should be collected, how the data should be analyzed, and how the results should be presented all depend on the situation at hand.

Summary

A successful cultural resource stewardship program requires a mind-set, a perspective, a paradigm that recognizes and advocates preservation, pro-

Table 9.5   Conducting Long-Term Monitoring

Develop Monitoring Plan	Collect Existing Info	Conduct Field Surveys	Assess Damage	
Project Management	Archives and Records	Inventory	Analysis and Prediction	Choose Impacts to Address
Develop Mitigation Options	Obtain Stakeholder Input	Design Solution	Implement Mitigation	
Develop Solutions	Leadership	Design	Execute Design	

tection, and access for American Indians, descendent groups, and others. Most cultural resource programs already include many of the components of a stewardship program. Generally missing is the mind-set, which requires greater involvement from tribes, interested parties, and the public in the program before it can be ingrained in the resource managers. Also commonly missing are those aspects of stewardship that concern long-term monitoring and condition assessments, as well as repair and stabilization when conditions warrant. One factor preventing these types of activities is cost, which again requires involvement of American Indians, other descendent communities, the public, and professionals, to develop and implement cost-effective strategies.

Note

1. We recognize that the term *asset* has connotations that imply property, which sometimes is contrary to Native American concepts. In this case, the word helps to draw a distinction to the notion of "resource base," used in natural and cultural resource management, which does not give the same sense of a need to actively manage. Regarding Native American concerns over the notion of property, readers will note that we often use the term *traditional cultural places* in place of *traditional cultural property* whenever possible.

Part III
THE FUTURE OF CULTURAL RESOURCE MANAGEMENT

Cultural resource management is a much different field today than when we started over twenty-five years ago. Having reviewed its development in parts I and II, we are encouraged about the future direction of cultural resource management. The field is much more inclusive than it used to be; tribes and other descendent groups are actively involved in making decisions about their resources, and even the public is frequently involved. There is more focus on protection of important places than there used to be; many land-managing agencies are expanding their cultural resource programs beyond Section 106 compliance by monitoring the long-term condition of sites and taking protective action when necessary. In fact, more agencies are complying with cultural resource regulations, and state and local governments are increasingly developing measures to protect their cultural environment. And the methods we are using are more sophisticated, enabling us to identify, manage, and preserve resources in ways never before possible.

Cultural resource management is stronger today than it ever has been and is well on its way to achieving greater stewardship for America's cultural resources. We still have a ways to go, however, if cultural resources important to American Indians and other groups are to be preserved in the face of development and other destructive forces. The public, for example, may question why cultural resources are important and does not value them as it might. Not all federal agencies fully comply with federal historic preservation legislation, and regrettably, some still don't really even try. Even those agencies with strong programs might begin to falter as budgets are reduced or new managers are hired. And there are still too many situations where tribes do not actively participate in managing and protecting resources that are important to them.

PART THREE

To conclude our book, we highlight some of the changes that working together has produced. We then present the challenges that remain and offer recommendations for future consideration. In the final analysis, working together to preserve, protect, and make accessible cultural resources has been a good strategy. There is no reason to stop now.

THE FRUITS OF SYNERGY

We attribute the successes of tribal cultural resource management to a powerful process called synergy: people gathering, sharing ideas, looking for solutions, and coming up with better answers collectively than any of them could have developed individually. It doesn't always happen; in fact, it's rather rare. But when it does, you know you have achieved something special.

Tribal cultural resource management has all the ingredients for creating synergy. It begins with the tribal representatives, the archaeologists and anthropologists, agencies, and others all interacting to protect important resources. To foster an environment for synergy, there must be three key ingredients from all sides: honesty, understanding, and mutual respect. You don't usually find that at the first meeting. Not even at the second.

Changes in Cultural Resource Management

In this section we identify various changes that have occurred in the way we manage cultural resources. We focus on those changes that relate to tribal cultural resource management, but in many cases, the changes benefit other cultural groups as well. One of the most important changes is in how we define cultural resources. Most of us today understand that cultural resources are not just stones and bones; they are the cultural landscapes of the earth—home to traditional use areas and the plant and animal resources themselves, as well as places where we used to live and dispose of our material goods.

Another important change is in the way professionals perceive the value of cultural resources. Many of us non-Indians have changed our understanding of the fundamental role these cultural resources play in culture. And we recognize that American Indian resources, for example, are not simply interesting historical places, but rather are integral parts of the living society. The Indian people today have a responsibility to care for the remains of those from the past; they need these resources to maintain and continue their cultural traditions today; and they have a responsibility to ensure that future generations will have access to the resources.

We have come to better appreciate the instructive role that cultural resources play in our own culture. Historic sites are great places to take our children, parents, and grandparents to learn about our own history and culture. We need the resources that relate to our cultural heritage if we are to continue our own traditions and values.

Those funding and conducting cultural resource activities have gained a better sense of the sensitivity of cultural resources and appropriate ways they should be handled. Non-Indians have increased their sensitivity to American Indian human remains and sacred sites and even passed laws to address these concerns. Much of this is due to the American Indians' special relationship with the American people. Books, videos, movies, and television documentaries are more frequent, and understanding is becoming more sophisticated.

Tribes and others have helped strengthen cultural resource management by applying political influence. These efforts have led to new local, state, and federal legislation and guidelines that encourage and support the preservation, protection, and access to all cultural resources of interest to Indians and non-Indians. These ideas have trickled down to land managers, who are now aware that cultural resources exist, have significance to living peoples, and need to be protected to ensure their availability to future generations.

Many land-managing agencies now have increased funding dedicated to on-the-ground protection. In the past, many agencies had a tendency to expend their time and money preparing plans, attending meetings, and doing anything but watching out for the cultural resources. Now, we are spending more time in the field, particularly on monitoring the condition of sites and taking protective action when necessary. Another example is the effort to combat looting of archaeological sites and burials. Agencies are issuing more citations for Archaeological Resource Protection Act violations and getting more convictions. Tribes have devoted extensive efforts to educate agency and law enforcement officials that looting is *not a victimless crime*; Indian people are seriously hurt by such violations.

Most land managers and cultural resource professionals now understand the need and value of undertaking meaningful consultations from the very beginnings of a project and of maintaining these relationships. These consultations help to eliminate the distrust and false assumptions that arise when people do not know what is being done. These consultations also help ensure that the right activities are done. Another benefit of consultations with tribes has been the systematization of cultural resource management practices across the region. Agencies generally manage by property lines, even though cultural landscapes transcend these boundaries. Tribes are pushing for consistent approaches among landowners and agencies.

We could go on, but the point has been made. Cultural resource management is a dynamic field and is getting better and stronger. American Indians have made significant contributions to the field, and as they increase both the extent and vigor of their presence at the cultural resource table, more contributions will come.

Tribal Developments Related to Involvement in Cultural Resource Management

Prior to 1906, there really was no substantive legislation that afforded protection to American Indian–related cultural resources. Since that time, however, the preservation, protection, and access of resources to Americans Indians have steadily improved. As a result, many federal agencies and, increasingly, tribes and state and local agencies have institutionalized cultural resource protection, including consultation with native people. Many sites have been saved, though the rate of loss across the continent stays high.

The consultation process itself has affected tribes. Requirements to consult that are found in most all of the legislation have encouraged tribes to identify points of contact, obtain expertise, and develop policies and procedures for handling the various cultural resource issues that repeatedly arise. This has led tribes to consider many issues: who can speak on the matter of human remains, how much cultural knowledge can be shared, what can be documented, and so on. Elders, possessing the kind of knowledge needed to resolve cultural resource issues, have regained some of their prominence of former years. Other tribal members have found new positions as keepers or gatherers of knowledge and as liaisons (Stapp and Longenecker 1998).

Many tribes have used these opportunities to develop full-fledged cultural resource programs, affording economic, educational, and training opportunities for tribal members on the reservation. Some of the positions are useful simply because they teach tribal members how to work and provide opportunities to apply their newfound skills. Often, tribal members who fill these positions are ignited by the exposure to cultural knowledge and use the opportunity to connect with their cultural roots, specializing in aspects of their culture. Cultural resource programs have become initiators, or at least partners, in teaching aspects of tribal history and aboriginal lifeways to tribal youth. In many ways, the emergence of tribes into cultural resource management has helped feed the tribal revival of recent decades.

Goals for Achieving the Stewardship Vision

The twenty-first century may or may not be good for cultural resources. We've had four decades of positive growth in the development of cultural resource management as a formally recognized field. Will this growth and development continue? Will the trend toward increasing historic preservation legislation end? Will all the gains we've made in the past forty years be lost? Not knowing the answer, we optimistically keep moving forward, advocating for better stewardship of the resources through the cumulative efforts of the American Indian and non-Indian communities.

Regardless, identifying and protecting cultural resources will be a very steep uphill battle as the U.S. population continues to grow and suburban sprawl consumes thousands of square miles of rural countryside. One incredible suburban sprawl is the 600-mile string city stretching between Raleigh, North Carolina, and Birmingham, Alabama. Another is the Colorado Front Range between Fort Collins to the north and Colorado Springs to the south. Immense areas are being developed along Interstate-25, parallel to the Rocky Mountains, including the New Denver International Airport, a 56-square-mile facility east of Denver. Is it worth even talking about stewardship issues in areas of such neverending development? Yet how can we not, if we care about the quality of life for these future communities?

Budgetary issues will likely continue to put pressure on cultural resource budgets at all levels. We will need to find ways to get more for our dollars—working together instead of against one another is a good start. We need to fight for our share, however. When people ask, "How can we afford to protect these places?" We'll need to respond, "How can we afford not to?" Do we really want sterile communities that have lost their historical and cultural roots? It is up to those who understand the implications of such decisions to fight for what is right.

In this concluding chapter of *Tribal Cultural Resources Management: The Full Circle to Stewardship*, we present four key goals we need to achieve, to meet the needs of American Indians relative to cultural resource preservation, protection, and access.

- Ensure that federal agencies comply with cultural resource regulations;

- Increase public awareness of and appreciation for cultural resources;

- Foster the relationship among American Indians, archaeologists, anthropologists, and others; and

- Keep the tribal cultural resource management movement going.

These goals are relevant, regardless of what the next few decades bring to cultural resource management: continued growth, stability, or retrenchment.

Getting Federal Agencies to Comply with Federal Legislation

A recent meeting between agency archaeologists and a tribal cultural resource protection manager exemplifies the different approaches the two take to protecting cultural resources. The tribal representative asked the agency archaeologist how much funding he had to identify cultural resources on the lands he managed, as called for under Section 110 of NHPA. The reply was, "$30,000 annually." "For how many acres?" "About 4 million throughout the West." "Do you think that is complying with federal law?" "That's all we have." "Well, maybe we will need to see what a judge has to say about that."

This is an excellent example because those of us working for an agency are often powerless when it comes to budgeting. We do the best we can, but if it is inadequate, if resources are compromised, lost to erosion, or destroyed by looters, or a burial is unearthed by a construction project, it is not the end of the world for us. We—at least, those of use who are not indigenous to the area—may be upset, but we are not affected as much as people who grew up in the area, live there now, and will be buried there. In the previous example, the agency archaeologist is resigned to the fact that he has an inadequate budget; to the tribal representative, it is simply unacceptable. There needs to be more pressure on agencies to comply with federal regulations. In the end, it comes down to people demanding that their resources be protected.

Increasing the Public's Awareness of the Value of Cultural Resources

The public is an important component to the future of cultural resource management. First, the public—and by extension, the many cultural and special interest groups that comprise the "public"—provides important input to agencies. Public groups can influence the cultural resource programs and actions of the agency by being explicit about their interests, concerns, and expectations. If, however, the public has no interest in the resources or their ultimate fate, people will not participate with the agency. The result will be that the agency will do as it chooses. Therefore, it's important to continue educating the public about what cultural resources are and why these are important to society and to future generations.

Second, the public can assist in preserving and protecting cultural resources. Public agencies (federal, state, county, and municipality) will never be able to fully fund adequate stewardship programs. Public support (beyond tax dollars) is needed, either in the form of financial support or, more likely, from in-kind support, primarily volunteer labor. Many examples exist of public groups serving as stewards. They are needed to look out for problems, help solve those problems, and continue the education programs to both school-age children and adults. Such efforts must be done in concert with descendent communities.

The third reason people need to be involved is simple—diversity of ideas. Agencies and professionals often fall into the rut of repeatedly doing things the same way. With new people come different perspectives and ideas on what can be done and what should be done. Such participation can help ensure that not only are things done right, but the right things are done. These goals need to be met if the nation truly wants to meet the challenges we face in protecting our cultural environment.

There has been significant progress in educating the public about the importance of cultural resources in recent decades. The public seems to appreciate cultural resources and what these mean to American Indians. There needs to be more public education about why cultural and historical places are important to everyone, regardless of ethnic background. We need people to understand how places that represent their own heritage function within their culture. Do these places represent key events in their history, reveal traditional cultural ways, or provide resources for them to continue their cultural beliefs? It's fine for non-Indians to appreciate Indian resources and visit and learn about them, Mesa Verde National Park being a prime example. But those are Indian resources. The notion that "these are America's resources" is only partially correct. Non-Indians should learn about their own cultural resources and how important these are to their own cultural system and heritage.

We agree with Fred Blackburn and Ray Williamson in their recent book *Cowboys and Cave Dwellers: Basketmaker Archaeology in Utah's Grand Gulch*. As they say, we must:

> increase people's appreciation of history in much the same way the environmental movement has heightened the public's understanding of how to use our lands, lakes, and rivers. By making ordinary citizens aware of environmental damage and how it affects their lives, natural history writers, educators, biologists, and geographers have sensitized us to the steady loss of our quality of life. Americans began to have better environmental preservation when thousands of people in communities everywhere started to take responsibility for their own local environment. In a similar way, the preservation of the historical record is up to us all. Those who care about preserving America's historic and prehistoric legacy must begin to share their views with others. (Blackburn and Ray 1997, 164)

This is a monumental challenge, but one that will reap enormous rewards if it can be met. The bottom line is that all of us, as individuals, are stewards of the land and its abundant resources. Only when we agree to that personal level of responsibility can we hope to achieve the comprehensive stewardship that our present and past deserve.

Fostering the Relationship among American Indians, Archaeologists, and Anthropologists

Archaeologists, anthropologists and American Indians have had conflicts in the past (Downey 2000; Thomas 2000; Watkins 2000). Archaeologists, for example, felt that they had a right to excavate sites, when and where they wanted to, in their quest for knowledge. American Indians felt that their responsibility was to protect sites, and usually that meant the sites were best left undisturbed. Many still feel the same way. Some archaeologists respect tribal concerns, but some don't.

Anthropologists also felt that they had the right to conduct studies of American Indians to learn about culture. American Indians resented the intrusion into their privacy and eventually refused to cooperate with many anthropologists. Some professionals, such as the action anthropologists and the applied/practicing anthropologists of today are adopting a different perspective: They use their skills and knowledge to improve conditions for tribal members. These days, proposals will be approved or disapproved by tribal governments. If an anthropologist and a tribe have a good working relationship, built on trust, honesty, and mu-

---

The Anthropology of Sol Tax

This brief bit of guidance, based on the principles of the late Sol Tax, provides a glimpse into one man's anthropology, or at least a way for the anthropologist to approach his relationship with his fellow man. He calls for courage, intelligence, patience, respect, and humility. We find these principles invaluable for guiding us through the challenges we face regularly as professionals in tribal cultural resource management.

To serve one's fellows,

- Contribute as you can knowledge of the choices available to them; to learn about one's fellows, observe the choices they make.
- Have the respect not to decide for others what is in their best interests; assume you will never understand them that well.
- But do have the courage to protect wherever possible the freedom of others to make those decisions for themselves, and even to make mistakes.
- For oneself, avoid premature choices and action; assume there always is more knowledge to be brought to bear on any matter than is currently available. (Adapted from Hinshaw 1979)

tual respect, synergy will be achieved, making for better results. Ideally, both parties will be rewarded, and the tribe will be provided with a copy of the report.

Archaeologists might follow the success of applied anthropologists in working collaboratively with American Indians (Harrison 2001). Archaeology since the 1960s (when the culture history approach was abandoned and replaced with the New Archaeology) has not been particularly effective. We would argue that archaeologists have produced voluminous information from their investigations, but have they contributed new knowledge? Maybe, but only at a certain level. Certainly, no wisdom has emanated from the halls of archaeology that Indians or any other group will necessarily benefit from. Perhaps archaeologists could try something new. They could engage Americans Indians to pursue research collaboratively. Both groups stand to benefit from such interactions and constructive synergy.

In one sense, the power of archaeologists has diminished as cultural resource management has flourished. Cultural resource managers now make the decisions, and archaeologists are but one of many voices that need to be considered. But in reality, archaeologists are an important voice. It is still the situation, although this is changing, that cultural resource managers are trained by archaeologists and indoctrinated into the "archaeology is data" mentality. Furthermore, when archaeologists do something that angers and offends American Indians, it hurts the ability of all non-Indians to pursue relationships. But more important, it hurts Indians, or whatever group is at odds with the archaeologists.

Some of the efforts of archaeologists have been beneficial to American Indians. Consider the efforts archaeologists have taken to combat looting (SAA 1995). Their goals are compatible with those of American Indians, even if their reasons for saving sites differ. How curious, though, that the archaeological community does not engage the Indian community in its struggle. American Indians can be powerful allies. Consider the effectiveness of the Confederated Tribes of the Umatilla Indian Reservation, who have taken up the challenge to educate law enforcement officials about the Archaeological Protection Act of 1979 (Longenecker and Van Pelt 1999). The training is effective in convincing officers and judges that looting is not a "victimless crime." Real people do get hurt—Indian people. We venture to speculate that an archaeologist could talk until he or she is blue in the face and not make anywhere near the impact on officers and judges that American Indians can when they explain the harm that looting causes Indian people.

Other archaeological efforts that are useful to Indian people pertain to the public being educated about cultural diversity and specific tribal histories. Much of this history comes from the archaeological record, as museums around the country and globe testify. Tribal museums now often communicate their past by using the information and knowledge contributed by archaeologists. But archaeologists don't always use common courtesy when writing someone else's history or investigating someone else's site. Don't the descendents have a right to say whether they want their ancestors' village or fishing camp to be excavated? Shouldn't they have a say in the excavation protocols to be followed, what research questions could be considered, how the information should be portrayed, and how the artifacts will be displayed and stored? If archaeologists don't have a legal responsibility to engage descendent populations, don't they at least have an ethical or moral responsibility? How about the common courtesy Dr. Sprague alluded to, by simply providing the tribe with a report copy (Sprague 1974)?

Former president of the Society for Applied Anthropology Anthony Paredes said it well: "Archaeologists should behave as if their own Grandmother had an interest in the site" (Stapp and Longenecker 1999). What if your Grandmother didn't want you poking around the town's seventeenth-century mayor's house, or she wanted her peers to have the oppor-

To Tell or Not to Tell

For decades there have been non-Indian archaeologists and anthropologists working for tribal governments. These professionals are using their education, knowledge, and skills to help tribes protect resources, as well as their right to be involved in decision making on projects that might impact their resources. These professionals have learned a lot about anthropology, people, culture, and working with other cultures. They have experienced things that most university anthropologists never have an opportunity to experience, and they understand aspects of culture in ways other professionals do not.

One of the tenants of action anthropology is that the action anthropologist will bring his or her experiences and ideas back to the university to aid in the development of anthropological method and theory. We wholeheartedly concur with this goal, but there is a problem.

Action anthropologists have not as a rule shared much of their knowledge and wisdom

(Continued)
with the profession. It does not appear to be in their nature to do so. There are many reasons: the close relationships developed among action anthropologists and the people they work with inhibit sharing too much information, there simply is no time to write for others when every minute is spent solving day-to-day problems, the closeness to the situation obscures the relevance to anthropological theory, and the distance from academia takes away motivation.

We view this potential loss of knowledge gained by these action anthropologists as a crisis for anthropology in the twenty-first century. For example, one of our colleagues has worked for a tribe for two decades. He has seen it all. The intertribal politics, the struggle to identify sensitive resources, the outside anthropologist who found an informant and wrote a tell-all book about tribal culture, the never-ending battles with government agencies to take tribal comments and wishes seriously, and the challenges of developing expertise within the tribe.

What will happen to all this information, knowledge, and wisdom that lies buried in our friend's head? Will he take it to his grave? That would indeed be unfortunate because what he has learned could benefit other tribes and future anthropologists. But is it his responsibility or the profession's responsibility to capture his thoughts? That's a good question. We lean toward the latter. He's paid his dues.

tunity to excavate, or she wanted a pretty book written about it, or she didn't want the artifacts stored at the university, or she wanted proper and immediate burial of any human remains? Wouldn't you try to respect her wishes and accommodate them? Of course, you would. Would you avoid her so that such matters would not come up? No. Would you agree to her wishes and then violate them because she was not checking up on you? Of course not. Any descendent population should be handled similarly.

The question, of course, is ownership—who has the right to enforce these types of decisions. Although ownership of archaeological sites—and we are obviously not talking about strictly legal ownership—can be complex, it's safe to say that archaeologists are not the highest on the list, despite what they think.

Keeping the Tribal Cultural Resource Management Movement Going

American Indians and the cultural resource management profession are inextricably linked. True, many resources in North America have no relationship to American Indians, but there are so many that do, it's hard to imagine in the future not actively including their participation. That's good, because Indians provide a rich, diverse perspective, making the field stronger and certainly more interesting.

American Indians have done more than play the role of stakeholder or interested party, as many groups do. Tribes in numerous cases have established their own programs and do their own work. Sometime this is done under the guidelines of the National Park Service through the Tribal Historic Preservation Office Program, but sometimes tribal programs have no one to answer to but themselves. In either case, we feel that getting tribal cultural resource programs up and running, staffed by tribal members, and keeping them economically viable will benefit everyone.

Why? First, it's the right thing to do. Resources are always better managed by those who are closest to them. They know the resources better, and they know how best to use them. Early on, tribes had no choice but to rely on non-Indians to provide cultural resource expertise.

Today, tribes vary in their approaches: Some tribes hire non-Indians, some train tribal members to be cultural resource technicians, and some push tribal members to achieve college and graduate degrees. It's the tribe's choice to determine what is best for it, especially on Indian lands. It's incumbent upon state and federal agencies, the academic community, and the cultural resource management profession to assist in any way they can.

Without question, tribes need to be involved in the work if possible and if this is something the tribe wants to do. There are ample opportunities for agen-

CRM as a Life Affirming Goal

The following is excerpted from a commentary by Phil Cash Cash [then Minthorn] on a special collection of papers on tribal issues in cultural resource management published in Practicing Anthropology *(Minthorn 1998). As a person of Cayuse and Nez Perce tribal descent who has committed himself to strengthening Native involvement in cultural resource management, cultural preservation, and repatriation-related issues, Phil provides a much needed perspective during a time of rapid growth of tribal historic preservation programs:*

The critical importance of cultural resource initiatives to the Native community rests on the fact that [these support] the recognition of Native peoples as living, viable cultures possessing human rights and dignity that deserve equal protection in the implementation of cultural resource laws and policy. . . . In the spirit of envisioning a broader, more inclusive cultural resource management in the Native community, I would like to offer the following suggestions for enhancing the ongoing interactions between the CRM professionals and Native communities:

(Continued)

- Build working relationships that are based on ability of the Native American community to participate fully as active partners in cultural resource management programs and goals.
- Establish a process to empower Native communities and cultural resource programs through active consultation, mutual decision-making, and the adoption of cooperative agreements for the promotion of long-term resource protection strategies.
- Create greater opportunities for the professional exchange, adaptation, and innovation of cultural resource management principles that utilize the experience, knowledge, and history of participating Native communities.

Native American cultural resource management is now poised for unlimited growth and development that will broaden and diversify the CRM discipline. More importantly, the lessons learned from our interaction will bring meaning to the words of the elders who often say, "It is good that you are listening" (Minthorn 1998, 32).

cies to contract with tribes. Generally, more work can be done for less money. Whether it's using tribal technicians to monitor construction or inspect the condition of sites, hiring tribal elders to help identify traditional use areas, or utilizing tribal senior staff to produce technical documents, contracting with tribal programs should be active.

Although situations vary, there is a great range in the degree to which tribes have moved into tribal cultural resource management. Some, like the Navaho Nation and the Confederated Tribes of the Umatilla Indian Reservation, have established programs and are working day in and day out to protect resources. They continue to provide opportunities for tribal members to gain the experience and qualifications they need to foster growth of functional tribal programs.

Other tribal programs are in their infancy. Typically small in size, these programs might focus more on participating in consultation than actually doing the work. The key point is that they are beginning to interact with state and federal agencies, or whoever, to develop a strategy for their tribal cultural resource protection program.

Then there are other tribes that are yet to start their programs. Agencies may not consult with them, or perhaps agencies have attempted to initiate consultation and the tribes failed to respond. Many tribes simply do not have the funding or personnel to get started.

How do we keep the movement going? It goes without saying that money is certainly needed by the tribes to provide for their full participation. But before money becomes an issue, opportunities must arise for agencies and tribes to work together. It begins with consultation and continues when agencies provide tribes with opportunities to do the work. Creating partnerships between the tribes and agencies facilitates the successfulness of this endeavor.

The key to a partnership is a good relationship. Relationships can form between organizations, but they strengthen when individuals form relationships as well. First and foremost, we return to consultation. Consultation needs to be ongoing, it needs to be sincere, and it needs to involve people at the appropriate level for the issues being discussed. At times, the heads of the organizations are the ones consulting, but in cultural resource matters, more commonly it is the cultural resource managers and their staffs.

For tribes with no cultural resource programs or just getting started, there needs to be more assistance. We recently heard from one young tribal woman, "My tribe lives next to a National Park where we have ceded lands. They never contact us about the things they are doing. Part of that is our fault. We just don't know how to get started." She was pursuing a Master's degree in resource management, so that particular problem may be well on the way to being fixed. But the problem for others will still remain. The National Park Service's Tribal Historic Preservation Program is not currently structured to meet this need. It could be, or some other solution could be found.

As tribes often point out, it is the responsibility of the agency to initiate consultation. That's true, but from a practical standpoint agencies typically do not pave new ground unless forced to. Tribes need to proactively lobby and educate agencies to be accountable for their actions, meet their commitments, and comply with federal historic preservation legislation. Information is the key. Tribes need to ensure that agencies share as much information about their activities as possible.

Cultural resource protection is just one of many issues confronting tribes. One underrealized benefit of cultural resource legislation is that it opens the door to consultation. Once a relationship starts with an agency, it becomes easier to talk about other issues concerning the tribe, including, but not limited to, environmental degradation, portrayal of tribal history and culture, economic opportunities, and so on. In other words, by capitalizing on the narrow definition of cultural resources and using the legislation to convince agencies to consult, a tribe can call upon the relationship to address other needs.

Summary

In conclusion, cultural resource management should be done in collaboration with native peoples, whenever possible. American Indian tribes have rapidly become more active and visible as participants, reviewers, contractors, and regulators in the cultural resource management process. Many of their projects, whether by design or accident, provide education, training, and employment for archaeologists and tribal members alike. More Indians are obtaining formal education and training in archaeology than ever before, but the collaboration is more than that. Tribes, as equal historic preservation partners, can bring their perspectives to the effort to protect cultural resources. By working together in a spirit of cooperation, we can accomplish more for future generations.

The tendency by many will be to question how all this can work. Many cultural resource people, especially non-Indians, want specifics, formulas, and guarantees. What we are advocating is more of a philosophy. Let go of the need to be in control. Forget formulas; there are too many variables and unpredictable situations. What we advocate is more of a process. Consult with an open mind, sincerely and honestly. Create an environment that promotes synergy. Keep in mind the primary goal: cultural resource preservation, protection, and access for future generations.

AFTERWORD

I am honored to author this afterword on tribal cultural resource management because I believe that this topic and this book represent a profound challenge to the way archaeology and cultural resource management are currently done.

Tribal cultural resource management represents the greatest change in the discipline of archaeology since the development and expansion of cultural resource management as a career field of study, research, employment, and the de facto basis and funding source of contemporary archaeological fieldwork, analysis, and reporting.

The concepts that are addressed in this book span the spectrum from consultation, co-management, tribal cultural resource management programs, tribal curation of collections, treatment of human remains, and approaches to excavation, to examining the fundamental goals of archaeology as a scientific discipline in generating knowledge about the past.

As a professional archaeologist and one who has been involved in cultural resource management and in many of the cases described in this book, I have seen firsthand the difficulties, profound emotions, and cultural clashes these topics expose. It is a very hard road to pioneer and to follow. There are no easy or simple solutions. To succeed, it will take sustained commitment, hard work, learning from failures, and faith that a shared effort will benefit all.

I believe that cultural resource management offers great opportunities not just for archaeologists and tribal members, but for all Americans. The daily dialogues that occur in cultural resource management today confront the main cultural assumptions we have as a society. Perhaps the most profound is the challenge to our concept of place. We are a mobile society.

Any number of studies, current newspaper articles, and media shows reveal the ubiquitous nature of suburban America. The nature of sprawl as a faceless, placeless repetition of fast food outlets, shopping malls, faux New England/Bavarian/Old West facades buries local histories and distinct cultural landscapes under the latest contemporary market-tested theme.

Tribal cultural resource efforts confront that directly by giving voice to local history and a sense of place. The concern with evaluating archaeological sites on criteria other than "D," as a data source, reflects the profound need to develop a method for looking at archaeological sites and the place of local histories in our collective experience from a human and a community standpoint.

Clearly, from the nature of historic preservation and cultural resource management controversies in today's papers, this topic requires the attention of the field. Archaeological sites as historic places provide the symbolic link to a common human past. The story revealed by archaeology and by tribal history provides the means to dramatically demonstrate American history at the local level. How that is to be accomplished and integrated into larger society is unanswered.

Archaeologists first approached site protection as a means of assuring places to excavate in the future. Tribal perspectives recognize them as places of the ancestors that deserve respect and protection in their own right. While such places have prominent status in tribal communities, archaeologists have their work cut out for them in helping to create a similar ethic in the larger society. Too often, archaeological sites reflect the tragedy of the commons—a vandalized, littered, and trampled open space. State Archaeology Month and Archaeology Week are two successful efforts to build an ethic of site respect and honor on a local level.

As Darby and Michael emphasize, both archaeologists and tribal cultural staff share that common goal in protecting archaeological sites. Such joint efforts are bound to reinforce the sense of stewardship for these sites and increase a sense of place at the local level. The joint efforts have already borne fruit in the battle against archaeological vandalism. It is recognized widely for what it is: a criminal activity.

Perhaps the greatest divide is how archaeologists and tribal members approach the topic of knowledge and information. Knowledge is such a culturally and professionally loaded topic, which is reflected in numerous disputes and high-profile cases such as the Kennewick Man.

In American society and among archaeologists, the goal is to discover and create new knowledge and information. One is rewarded for discovering new knowledge by gaining peer recognition, grants, tenure, publications, and ultimately celebrity status. The operating assumption is that not all is known and there are ideas and information about the past to be discovered, learned, and shared. Old knowledge can be discarded.

In traditional societies, knowledge and information are kept and handed down by the elders. Knowledge and information are not discovered as much as transferred. That information is not necessarily public.

Thus a fundamental cultural conflict is at the foundation of archaeological and tribal interaction. I don't know how such irreconcilable differences will play out. But given the scope and influence of American culture on a global scale, and how other European, Asian, and African countries struggle with American economic and cultural domination, tribal societies will have a much more difficult time.

I think it is incumbent upon those archaeologists who are committed to working with tribal programs to at least recognize the cultural assumptions they bring to the table. And to be honest about the overarching structure of the entire cultural resource management process: It is designed to get the projects to proceed.

Even when the process is working at its best, projects are most often redesigned or derailed by factors other than cultural resources. Increasingly, tribal cultural resource staff members will be the mediators between the larger society and tribal society. It will not be an easy road for them. We must recognize and support their successes when these occur.

The demands for information and the widespread globalization of that information, both cultural and archaeological, will dramatically increase in the future. The burden of tribal cultural resource staff members will also increase exponentially.

Finally, the context of the title of this book—*The Full Circle to Stewardship*—implies a diversity of approaches. Archaeology and cultural resource management are global disciplines. All over the world, agencies and individuals are working in the field and in offices, experimenting with and designing ways to protect archaeological, historic, and traditional cultural places. The diversity of approaches and the global recognition of protect-

ing such special places are important factors in promoting tribal participation. This book documents the pioneering efforts to make that a reality.

Robert Whitlam, Ph.D.
State Archaeologist
Washington State Office of Archaeology & Historic Preservation
Olympia, Washington

TRIBAL HISTORIC PRESERVATION OFFICES

Catawba Indian Nation
611 East Main Street
Rock Hill, SC 29730
(808) 328-2427

Cheyenne River Sioux Tribe
P.O. Box 590
Eagle Butte, SD 57625
(605) 964-7554

**Confederated Salish and
Kootenai Tribes of the Flathead
Indian Nation**
P.O. Box 278
Pablo, MT 59855
(406) 675-2700

**Confederated Tribes of the
Colville Reservation**
P.O. Box 150
Nespelem, WA 99155
(509) 634-2692

**Confederated Tribes of the
Umatilla Indian Reservation**
P.O. Box 638
Pendleton, OR 97801
(541) 553-3266

**Confederated Tribes of the Warm
Springs Indian Reservation**
P.O. Box C
Warm Springs, OR 97761
(541) 553-3266

**Eastern Band of Cherokee
Indians**
Qualla Boundary
P.O. Box 455
Cherokee, NC 28719
(828) 488-5537

Hualapai Tribe
P.O. Box 310
Peach Springs, AZ 86434
(520) 769-2223

**Lac Courte Oreilles Band of
Lake Superior Chippewa Indians**
13394 W. Trepania Road
Hayward, WI 54843
(715) 634-8934

**Lac du Flambeau Band of Lake
Superior Chippewa Indians**
P.O. Box 67
Lac du Flambeau, WI 54538
(715) 588-2139

Leech Lake Band of Chippewa Indians
6530 Hwy 2 NW
Cass Lake, MN 56633
(218) 335-2940

Makah Tribe
P.O. Box 160
Neah Bay, WA 98357
(360) 645-2711

Menominee Indian Tribe of Wisconsin
P.O. Box 910
Keshena, WI 64135-0910
(715) 799-5258

Mescalero Apache Tribe
P.O. Box 227
Mescalero, NM 88340
(505) 464-9279

Mille Lacs Band of Ojibwe Indians
HCR 67, Box 194
Onamia, MN 56359
(320) 532-4181

Naragansett Indian Tribe
P.O. Box 700
Wyoming, RI 02898
(401) 364-9873

National Association of Tribal Historic Preservation Officers
P.O. Box 19189
Washington, DC 20036
(202) 628-8476

Navaho Nation
P.O. Box 4950
Window Rock, AZ 86515
(520) 871-6437

Poarch Band of Creek Indians
128 Olive Street
Pineville, LA 71360
(318) 641-5773

Red Cliff Band of Lake Superior Chippewas
883835 Pike Road, Highway 13
Bayfield, WI 54814
(715) 779-3648

Seneca Nation of Indians
794-814 Broad Street
Salamanca, NY 14779
(716) 945-1738

Skokomish Indian Tribe
N. 541 Tribal Center Road
Shelton, WA 98584
(360) 426-4232

Spokane Tribe of Indians
P.O. Box 100
Wellpinit, WA 99040
(509) 258-4060

Squaxin Island Tribe
SE 70 Squaxin Lane
Shelton, WA 98584
(360) 426-9781

Standing Rock Sioux Tribe
P.O. Box D
Fort Yates, ND 58538
(701) 854-2120

Timbisha Shoshone Tribe
P.O. Box 206
Death Valley, CA 92328
(760) 786-2374

Tunica-Biloxi Indians of
Louisiana
P.O. Box 331
Marksville, LA 71351
(318) 253-8174

Turtle Mountain Band of
Chippewa
P.O. Box 900
Belcourt, ND 58316
(701) 477-6003

Wampanoag Tribe of Gay Head
20 Black Brook Road
Aquinnah, MA 02535
(508) 645-9265

White Mountain Apache Tribe
P.O. Box 507
Fort Apache, AZ 85926
(520) 338-3033

Yurok Tribe
1034 Sixth Street
Eureka, CA 95591
(707) 482-1822

REFERENCES CITED

Ablon, Joan. 1962. "The American Indian Chicago Conference." *Journal of American Indian Education* 1(2):17–23.

Adair, John. 1973. "Commentator." In *Anthropology and the American Indian*. Edited by James E. Officer, 107–98. San Francisco: The Indian Historian Press.

Adams, E. Charles. 1984. "Archaeology and the Native American: A Case at Hopi." In *Ethics and Values in Archaeology*. Edited by Ernestine L. Green, 236–42. New York: The Free Press.

Aikens, C. Melvin. 1986. *Current Status of CRM Archaeology in the Great Basin*. Bureau of Land Management, Nevada. Cultural Resource Series, no. 9. Reno: USDI-BLM, Nevada State Office.

AILTP (American Indian Lawyer Training Program). 1988. *Indian Tribes as Sovereign Governments: A Sourcebook on Federal-Tribal History, Law and Policy*. Oakland, Calif.: American Indian Resources Institute Press.

Allard, Ladonna Brave Bull. 1996. *Cultural Resource Laws Relating to Indian Tribes and Indian Land Owners*. Ms. on file. Standing Rock Sioux Tribe, Fort Yates, North Dakota.

Anyon, Roger, and T. J. Ferguson. 1995. "Cultural Resources Management at the Pueblo of Zuni, New Mexico, USA." *Antiquity* 69(266):913–30.

Associated Press. 2001. "Across the USA, News from Every State: Maryland." *USA Today*, Monday, November 26, 2001, 8A.

Austin, Diane E. 1998. "Cultural Knowledge and the Cognitive Map." *Practicing Anthropology* 20(3):21–24.

Barkley, Lloyd. 1998. "Confederated Tribes of the Umatilla Indian Reservation Contributions." In *Tribal Cultural Resource Studies at the Hanford Site, South-Central Washington*. Edited by Paul Nickens, 62–64. PNNL-12032. Richland, Wash.: Pacific Northwest National Laboratory.

Barney, Ralph A. 1974. "The Indian Claims Commission." In *American Indian Ethnohistory: Indians of the Northwest*. Edited by David Agee Horr, 13–16. New York: Garland.

REFERENCES CITED

Becker, Alice M. 1986. "Nevada." In *Current Status of CRM Archaeology in the Great Basin*. Edited by C. Melvin Aikens, 7–39. Cultural Resource Series, no. 9. Reno: USDI-BLM, Nevada State Office.

Binford, Lewis R. 1983. *In Pursuit of the Past: Decoding the Archaeological Record.* New York: Thames and Hudson.

Binford, Sally R., and Lewis R. Binford. 1968. *New Perspectives in Archaeology.* Chicago: Aldine.

Biolsi, Thomas, and Larry J. Zimmerman, editors. 1997. *Indians & Anthropologists: Vine Deloria, Jr., and the Critique of Anthropology.* Tucson: University of Arizona Press.

Blackburn, Fred M., and Ray A. Williamson. 1997. *Cowboys & Cave Dwellers: Basketmaker Archaeology in Utah's Grand Gulch.* Santa Fe, N.M.: School of American Research Press.

Brooks, Robert L. 1997. "Compliance, Preservation, and Native American Rights: Resource Management as a Cooperative Venture." In *Native Americans and Archaeologists: Stepping Stones to Common Ground.* Edited by Nina Swidler, Kurt E. Dongoske, Roger Anyon, and Alan S. Downer, 207–16. Walnut Creek, Calif.: AltaMira.

Brown, Dee. 1971. *Bury My Heart at Wounded Knee: An Indian History of the West.* New York: Holt Rinehart & Winston.

Burney, Michael S. 1989. *A History of Archaeological Investigations and Inventory of American Indian Resources of Dowe Flats, including Indian Mountain to the West and Rabbit Mountain to the East, Northern Boulder County, Colorado.* Report on file, Colorado State Historic Preservation Office, Denver, Colorado.

Burney, Michael S. 1991. "The BIA Agency Campus of the Umatilla, Cayuse, Walla Walla People: A Plea for the Preservation of Historic Buildings Administered by the Bureau of Indian Affairs." A paper prepared for the 44th Annual Northwest Anthropological Conference, Missoula, Montana, March 28–30, 1991.

Burney, Michael S. 1994. *An Ethnographic and Ethnohistoric Literature and Records Search, including Consultations with 14 American Indian Tribes, Regarding the Alleged "Rock Feature" at 325 Broadway, Boulder, Colorado* (draft report, December 1, 1994). Report on file, Colorado State Historic Preservation Office, Denver, Colorado.

Burney, Michael S. 2000. "Ohio Burial Grounds to Tribal Historic Preservation Programs: Action Anthropology and American Indian Tribes in the Year 2000." *High Plains Applied Anthropologist* 20(1):78–89.

Burney, Michael S., and Mary K. Lovejoy. 1994. *An Ethnographic and Ethnohistoric Literature and Records Search, including Consultations with 13 American*

Indian Tribes, for Dowe Valley, Boulder County, Colorado. Report on file, Colorado State Historic Preservation Office, Denver, Colorado.

Burney, Michael S., and Jeff VanPelt, editors. 2002. *"Híiwes Wiyéewts'etki Paamiláyk'ay Naamiláyk'ay,* It's about Time, It's about Them, It's about Us." *Journal of Northwest Anthropology, Memoir,* no. 6. Moscow.

Burney, Michael S., Jeffrey Van Pelt, and Thomas E. Bailor. 1998. "Native Cultural Resource Management in the Pacific Northwest: The CTUIR Tribal Historic Preservation Program and the Lake Humtepin Experience." *Practicing Anthropology* 20(3):13–17.

Carnett, Carol L. 1995. *A Survey of State Statutes Protecting Archeological Resources.* National Park Service, Preservation Law Reporter Special Report, Archeological Assistance Study, no. 3. USDI-National Park Service, Cultural Resources, Archeological Assistance Division and National Trust for Historic Preservation, Washington, D.C.

Carpenter, Kenneth. 1994. *Paleontological Survey of Dowe Flats, Boulder County, Colorado.* Report prepared for Southwestern Portland Cement Company, Lyons, Colorado.

Carson, Rachel. 1962. *Silent Spring.* Boston: Houghton Mifflin.

Cary, Annette. 2001. "Team Work: Wanapum Band, Hanford Archaeologists Collaborate to Preserve History." *Tri-City Herald,* November 11, C1–2. Kennewick, Washington.

Chatters, James C. 1989. *Hanford Cultural Resource Management Plan.* PNL-6942. Richland, Wash.: Pacific Northwest National Laboratory.

Collier, John. 1947. *Indians of the Americas.* New York: W. W. Norton.

Cummings, Linda Scott. 1991. *Pollen and Phytolith Analysis at 5BL2431: A Stratified Multicomponent Site Near Lyons, Boulder County, Colorado.* Report prepared for Burney and Associates, Boulder, Colorado.

Cushing, Frank H. 1886. *A Study of Pueblo Pottery as Illustrative of Zuñi Cultural Growth.* Bureau of American Ethnology, 4th Annual Report, 467–521. Washington, D.C.

Cushman, David W. 1993. "When Worlds Collide: Indians, Archaeologists, and the Preservation of Traditional Cultural Properties." *Cultural Resource Management* 16:49–54 (Special Issue).

Cypress, Billy L. 1997. "The Role of Archaeology in the Seminole Tribe of Florida." In *Native Americans and Archaeologists: Stepping Stones to Common Ground.* Edited by Nina Swidler, Kurt E. Dongoske, Roger Anyon, and Alan S. Downer, 156–60. Walnut Creek, Calif.: AltaMira.

Darwin, Charles. 1859. *On the Origin of Species by Means of Natural Selection.* London: John Murray.

Deloria, Vine, Jr. 1969. *Custer Died for Your Sins: An Indian Manifesto.* Norman: University of Oklahoma Press.

Dillehay, Thomas D. 1989. *Monte Verde: A Late Pleistocene Settlement in Chile. Vol. 1: The Paleoenvironmental Context.* Washington, D.C.: Smithsonian Press.

DOD. 1994. *Coming in from the Cold: Military Heritage in the Cold War, Department of Defense Legacy Cold War Project.* Washington, D.C.

Dongoske, Kurt E., Mark Aldenderfer, and Karen Doebner. 2000. *Working Together: Native Americans and Archaeologists.* Washington, D.C.: Society for American Archaeology.

Downer, Alan S. 1997. "Archaeologists–Native American Relations." In *Native Americans and Archaeologists: Stepping Stones to Common Ground.* Edited by Nina Swidler, Kurt E. Dongoske, Roger Anyon, and Alan S. Downer, 23–24. Walnut Creek, Calif.: AltaMira.

Downey, Roger. 2000. *Riddle of the Bones: Politics, Science, Race, and the Story of Kennewick Man.* New York: Copernicus.

Doyel, David E. 1982. "Medicine Men, Ethnic Significance, and Cultural Resource Management." *American Antiquity* 47(3):634–42.

Dykman, James L. 1986. "Western Utah." In *Current Status of CRM Archaeology in the Great Basin.* Edited by C. Melvin Aikens, 139–42. Cultural Resource Series, no. 9. Reno: USDI-BLM, Nevada State Office.

Echo-Hawk, Roger C., and Walter R. Echo-Hawk. 1994. *Battle Fields and Burial Grounds: The Indian Struggle to Protect Ancestral Graves in the United States.* Minneapolis, Minn.: Lerner.

Edgerton, Robert B. 1965. "Some Dimensions of Disillusionment in Culture Contact." *Southwestern Journal of Anthropology* 21(1):231–43.

Eiselein, E. B. 1993. *Indian Issues.* Browning (The Blackfoot Nation), Mont.: The Spirit Talk Press.

Evans, Michael J., Alexa Roberts, and Peggy Nelson. "2001 Ethnographic Landscapes." *Cultural Resource Management* 24(5):53–55.

Fagan, Brian. 1993. "The Arrogant Archaeologist." *Archaeology* 46(6)14–16.

Ferguson, T. J. 1996. "Native Americans and the Practice of Archaeology." *Annual Review of Anthropology* 25:63–79.

Ferguson, T. J., Kurt Dongoske, Leigh Jenkins, Mike Yeatts, and Eric Polingyouma. 1994. "Working Together, the Roles of Archeology and Ethnohistory in Hopi Cultural Preservation." *Cultural Resource Management* 16:27–37 (Special Issue).

Ferguson, T. J., Kurt Dongoske, Mike Yeatts, and Leigh Jenkins. 1995. "Hopi Oral History and Archaeology, Part I: The Consultation Process." *SAA Bulletin* 13(2):13–15.

Forsman, Leonard A. 1997. "Straddling the Current: A View from the Bridge over Clear Salt Water." In *Native Americans and Archaeologists: Stepping Stones to Common Ground.* Edited by Nina Swidler, Kurt E. Dongoske, Roger Anyon, and Alan S. Downer, 105–11. Walnut Creek, Calif.: AltaMira.

Fowler, Don D. 1986. "Conserving American Archaeological Resources." In *American Archaeology Past and Future: A Celebration of the Society for American Archaeology 1935–1985.* Edited by David J. Meltzer, Don D. Fowler, and Jeremy A. Sabloff, 135–62. Washington, D.C.: Smithsonian Institution.

Fuller, Reba. 1997a. "A Me-Wuk Perspective on Sierran Archaeology." In *Native Americans and Archaeologists: Stepping Stones to Common Ground.* Edited by Nina Swidler, Kurt E. Dongoske, Roger Anyon, and Alan S. Downer, 143–48. Walnut Creek, Calif.: AltaMira.

Fuller, Reba 1997b. "Aspects of Consultation for the Central Sierran Me-Wuk." In *Native Americans and Archaeologists: Stepping Stones to Common Ground.* Edited by Nina Swidler, Kurt E. Dongoske, Roger Anyon, and Alan S. Downer, 181–87. Walnut Creek, Calif.: AltaMira.

Gearing, Fred. 1960. "The Strategy of the Fox Project." In *A Documentary History of the Fox Project, 1948–1959: A Program in Action Anthropology.* Edited by F. Gearing, R. McC. Netting, and L. R. Peattie. Chicago: University of Chicago, Department of Anthropology.

Gearing, Fred. 1970. *The Face of the Fox.* Chicago: Aldine.

Gilsen, Leland. 1986. "Southeastern Oregon." In *Current Status of CRM Archaeology in the Great Basin.* Edited by C. Melvin Aikens, 99–117. Cultural Resource Series, no. 9. Reno: Bureau of Land Management, Nevada.

Gould, Stephen Jay. 1996. *Mismeasure of Man.* New York: W. W. Norton.

Grant, Marcus. 1990. *Text Excavations at 5BL2431: A Multicomponent Site near Lyons, Boulder, County, Colorado.* Report on file, Colorado State Historic Preservation Office, Denver, Colorado.

Green, Norma. 1969. *Iron Eye's Family: The Children of Joseph La Flesche.* Lincoln: Nebraska State Historical Society.

Green, Thomas J. 1986. "Southern Idaho." In *Current Status of CRM Archaeology in the Great Basin.* Edited by C. Melvin Aikens, 119–36. Cultural Resource Series, no. 9. Reno: USDI-BLM, Nevada State Office.

Green, William, and John F. Doershuk. 1998. "Cultural Resource Management and American Archaeology." *Journal of Archaeological Research* 6(2):121–67.

Hadley, Judy Brunson. 1993. "Traditional Cultural Properties: Pros, Cons, and Reality." *Cultural Resource Management* 16:46–48.

Hallowell, Irving. 1957. "The Backwash of the Frontier: The Impact of the Indian on American Culture." In *The Frontier in Perspective.* Edited by Walker Wyman and Clifton Kroeber, 254–55. Madison: University of Wisconsin Press.

Hardesty, Donald L., Thomas J. Green, and La Mar W. Lindsay. 1986. "Contract Anthropology." In *Handbook of North American Indians: Great Basin,* Volume 11. Edited by Warren L. D'Azevedo, 256–61. Washington, D.C.: Smithsonian Institution.

Harper, Kenn. 1986. *Give Me My Father's Body: Life of Minik, the New York Eskimo.* Iqaluit, Canada: Black Lead Books.

Harrison, Barbara. 2001. *Collaborative Programs in Indigenous Communities: From Fieldwork to Practice.* Walnut Creek, Calif.: AltaMira.

Hart, E. Richard. 1991. *Zuni History, Victories in the 1990s.* Seattle: The Institute of North American West.

Hart, E. Richard. 1993. "The Fence Lake Mine Project: Archaeology as a Traditional Cultural Property." *Cultural Resource Management* 16:38–41 (Special Issue).

Heidenreich, C. Adrian. 1991. *Native American Studies: An Introduction.* New York: McGraw-Hill.

Hester, James J. 1996. "Cultural Resource Management: What, Why, and for Whom?" *High Plains Applied Anthropologist* 1(16):69–75.

Hinshaw, Robert, editor. 1979. *Currents in Anthropology: Essays in Honor of Sol Tax.* The Hague: Mouton.

Hunn, Eugene (with James Selam and Family). 1990. *Nch'I-Wana "The Big River": Mid-Columbia Indians and Their Land.* Seattle: University of Washington Press.

Jackson, Helen Hunt. 1881. *A Century of Dishonor: A Sketch of the United States Government's Dealings with Some Indian Tribes.* New York: Harper & Brothers.

Jackson, Loretta, and Robert H. ("Hank") Stevens. 1997. "Hualapai Tradition, Religion, and the Role of Cultural Resource Management." In *Native Americans and Archaeologists: Stepping Stones to Common Ground.* Edited by Nina Swidler, Kurt E. Dongoske, Roger Anyon, and Alan S. Downer, 135–42. Walnut Creek, Calif.: AltaMira.

Jarvis, T. T., and G. R. Bilyard. 1998. *A Framework for DOE's Stewardship Policy.* Richland, Wash.: Pacific Northwest Laboratory.

Jennings, Jesse D. 1985. "River Basin Surveys: Origins, Operations, and Results, 1945–1969." *American Antiquity* 50(2):281–96.

Johnson, Elden. 1973. "Professional Responsibilities and the American Indian." *American Antiquity* 38(2):129–30.

Josephy, Alvin M., Jr., Joane Nagel, and Troy Johnson. 1999. *Red Power: The American Indian's Fight for Freedom.* Lincoln: University of Nebraska Press.

Karklins, Karlis. 2000. "The J. C. Harrington Medal in Historical Archaeology: Roderick Sprague 2000. *Historical Archaeology* 34(4):1–6.

Katz, Paul R.. 1979. "Cultural Resource Management: Of the People, by the People, and for the People" (abstract). *Thirty-Seventh Plains Conference, Program and Abstracts.* Kansas City, Missouri, November 1–3, 1979.

Kidder, Alfred V. 1962. *Southwestern Archaeology.* New Haven, Conn.: Yale University Press.

King, Thomas F. 1987. "Prehistory and Beyond: The Place of Archaeology." In *The American Mosaic: Preserving a Nation's Heritage.* Edited by R. E. Stipe and A. J. Lee. International Council on Monuments and Sites, Washington, D.C.

King, Thomas F. 1998. *Cultural Resource Laws and Practices: An Introductory Guide.* Walnut Creek, Calif.: AltaMira.

King, Thomas F. 2000. *Federal Planning and Historic Places: The Section 106 Process.* Walnut Creek, Calif.: AltaMira.

Kluth, Rose. 1996. "The Integration of Traditional and Scientific Knowledge on Leech Lake Reservation, Cass Lake, Minnesota." *Society for American Archaeology Bulletin* 14(4):28–30.

Kluth, Rose, and Kathy Munnell. 1997. "The Integration of Tradition and Scientific Knowledge on the Leech Lake Reservation." In *Native Americans and Archaeologists: Stepping Stones to Common Ground.* Edited by Nina Swidler, Kurt E. Dongoske, Roger Anyon, and Alan S. Downer, 112–19. Walnut Creek, Calif.: AltaMira.

Knight, George C. 1979. *Blackfeet Cultural Resources: Management under the American Indian Religious Freedom Act.* Thirty-Seventh Plains Conference, Programs and Abstracts, 22. Kansas City, Missouri.

Knudson, Ruthann. 1986. "Contemporary Cultural Resource Management." In *American Archaeology Past and Future: A Celebration of the Society for American Archaeology, 1935–1985.* Edited by David J. Meltzer, Donald D. Fowler, and Jeremy A. Sabloff, 395–413. Washington, D.C.: Smithsonian.

Kooistra-Manning, Ann, Sherri Deaver, and Tina Quirt. 1993. *Ethnographic Overview of Five Tracts Proposed for Coal Development near Colstrip and Decker, Montana.* Report on file, Ethnoscience, and USDI-Bureau of Land Management, Billings, Montana.

Kroeber, Theodora. 1964. *Ishi in Two Worlds: A Biography of the Last Wild California Indian in North America.* Berkeley: University of California Press.

Laidlaw, Robert M. 1990. "The Evolution of Federal Cultural Resource Management: Native American Cultural and Religious Concerns." In *Preservation on the Reservation: Native Americans, Native American Lands and Archaeology.* Edited by Anthony L. Klesert and Alan S. Downer, 237–43. Navajo Nation Papers in Anthropology, no. 26. Window Rock, Navaho Nation Archaeology Department and the Navaho Nation Historic Preservation Department. Window Rock, Arizona.

Latham, Mark. 2001. *Cultural Resources Management Plan for Lake Sharpe Project Area* (Vol. I of 3 vols.). Report prepared for U.S. Army Corps of Engineers, Omaha District, NE. Report submitted by Burns & McDonnell Engineering Company, Inc., Kansas City, Missouri.

Lazarus, Edward. 1991. *Black Hills White Justice: The Sioux Nation versus the United States, 1775 to the Present.* New York: HarperCollins.

Lederer, Nancy D., and Michael G. Figg. 1994. *Ethnobotanical Literature Review of Plants Found at Dowe Flats and Rabbit Mountain, Boulder County, Colorado.* Report prepared for Southdown, Inc., Lyons, Colorado, and Boulder County Parks and Open Space Department, Boulder, Colorado.

Lipe, William D. 1974. "A Conservation Model for American Archaeology." *The Kiva* 39:213–45.

Longenecker, Julia G., Darby C. Stapp, and Angela M. Buck. 2002. "The Wanapum of Priest Rapids, Washington." In *Endangered Peoples of North America: Struggles to Survive and Thrive.* Edited by Tom Greaves, 137–56. Westport, Conn.: Greenwood.

Longenecker, Julia, and Jeff Van Pelt. 1999. "Training for Law Enforcement: A Tribal Perspective." *Cultural Resource Management* 5:17–18.

Longenecker, Julia, and Jeff Van Pelt. 2000. "Traditional Cultural Values and Non-Indian Advisors." *High Plains Applied Anthropologist* 20(1):90–95.

Lurie, Nancy Oestreich. 1973. "Action Anthropology and the American Indian." In *Anthropology and the American Indian: A Symposium.* Edited by James Officer, 4–15. San Francisco: The Indian Historian Press.

Lurie, Nancy Oestreich. 1999. "Sol Tax and Tribal Sovereignty." *Human Organization* 58(1):108–117.

Lyell, Charles. 1830. *Principles of Geology.* London: John Murray.

Lynott, Mark J., and Alison Wylie, editors. 1995. *Ethics in American Archaeology: Challenges for the 1990s.* Washington D.C.: Society for American Archaeology.

Manners, Robert A. 1974. "Introduction to the Ethnohistoric Reports on the Land Claims Cases." In *American Indian Ethnohistory: Indians of the Northwest.* Edited by David Agee Horr, 17–23. New York: Garland.

Mark, Joan. 1988. *A Stranger in Her Native Land: Alice Fletcher and the American Indians.* Lincoln: University of Nebraska Press.

Martin, Ken. 1971. "Discussant Responding to Omer C. Stewart's 'Anthropologist as Expert Witnesses for Indians: Claims and Peyote Cases.'" In *Anthropology and the American Indian: A Symposium.* Edited by James Officer, 65–66. San Francisco: The Indian Historian Press.

Martin, Rena. 1997. "How Traditional Navajos View Historic Preservation: A Question of Interpretation." In *Native Americans and Archaeologists: Stepping*

Stones to Common Ground. Edited by Nina Swidler, Kurt E. Dongoske, Roger Anyon, and Alan S. Downer. Walnut Creek, Calif.: AltaMira.

Matlock, Staci. 1999. "Picuris Plans Suit Against Mica Mine." *The Taos News,* Thursday, February 18, 1999, A9. Taos, New Mexico.

Maxwell, William. 2001. "Mica Mine's Expansion Plans Raise Ire of Pueblo Residents." *The Taos News,* Thursday, November 15, 2001, A10–11. Taos, New Mexico.

McBride, Kevin A. 1995. "CRM and Native Americans: An Example from the Mashantucket Pequot Reservation." *Cultural Resource Management* 18(3):15–17.

McGimsey, Charles R. III. 1998. "Headwaters: How the Post-War Boom Boosted Archaeology (A Look at the Origins of Public Archaeology)." *Common Ground* 3(2/3):16–21.

McManamon, Francis P., and Fred Wendorf. 2000. "'Dam Good Archaeology— We're Glad It Got Done!'" *Cultural Resource Management* 23(1):41–46.

McNickle, D'Arcy. 1971. *Indian Man: A Life of Oliver La Farge.* Bloomington: Indiana University Press.

Mead, Margaret. 1928. *Coming of Age in Samoa: A Psychological Study of Primitive Youth for Western Civilization.* New York: William Morrow.

Medicine, Beatrice. 1971. "The Anthropologist and American Indian Studies Programs." *The Indian Historian* 4(1):15–18, 63.

Medicine, Beatrice. 2001. *Learning to Be an Anthropologist and Remaining "Native": Selected Writings.* Chicago: University of Chicago Press.

Meighan, Clement W. 1986. *Archaeology for Money.* Clabasas, Calif.: Wormwood.

Meriam, Lewis (Technical Director). 1928. *The Problem of Indian Administration: Report of a Survey Made at the Request of Honorable Hubert Work, Secretary.*

Minesuah, Devon A., editor. 2000. *Repatriation Reader: Who Owns American Indian Remains.* Lincoln: University of Nebraska Press.

Minthorn, Phillip E. 1998. "It Is Good That You Are Listening: The Dynamics of Native American Cultural Resource Management." *Practicing Anthropology* 20(3):31–32.

Morgan, Lewis H. 1851. *League of the Ho-de-no-sau-nee, or Iroquois.* Rochester, N.Y.: Sage and Brother.

Morton, Samuel G. 1839. *Crania Americana; Or a Comparative View of the Skulls of Various Aboriginal Nations of North and South America.* London: Simpkin, Marshall, & Co.

Nash, Philleo. 1973. "Applied Anthropology and the Concept of Guided Acculturation." *The Indian Historian* 6:23–35.

Nelson, Sarah M. 1997. *Gender in Archaeology.* Walnut Creek, Calif.: AltaMira.

Nicholas, George P., and Thomas D. Andrews. 1997. "On the Edge." In *At a*

Crossroads: Archaeology and First Peoples in Canada. Edited by George P. Nicholas and Thomas D. Andrews, 276–79. Simon Fraser University, Department of Archaeology, *Archaeology Press Publication,* no. 24. Burnaby, British Columbia.

Nickens, Paul R., editor. 1998. *Tribal Cultural Resource Studies at the Hanford Site, South-Central Washington.* PNNL-12032. Pacific Northwest National Laboratory. Richland, Washington.

Occhipinti, Frank D. 2002. "American Indian Sacred Sites and the National Historic Preservation Act: The Enola Hill Case." *Journal of Northwest Anthropology* 36(1):3–50.

Officer, James E., editor. 1973. *Anthropology and the American Indian: A Symposium.* San Francisco: The Indian Historian Press.

Ortiz, Alfonso. 1971. "An Indian Anthropologist's Perspective on Anthropology." *The Indian Historian* 4(1):11–14.

Othole, Andrew L., and Roger Anyon. 1993. "A Tribal Perspective on Traditional Cultural Property Consultation." *Cultural Resource Management* 16:42–45 (Special Issue).

Parker, Dorothy R. 1992. *Singing an Indian Song: A Biography of D'Arcy McNickle.* Lincoln: University of Nebraska Press.

Parker, Patricia L. 1993. "Traditional Cultural Properties: What You Do and How We Think." *Cultural Resource Management* 16:1–5 (Special Issue).

Parker, Patricia L., and Thomas F. King. 1990. "Guidelines for Evaluating and Documenting Traditional Cultural Properties." *National Register Bulletin* 38. Washington, D.C.

Parker, Patricia L., and Thomas F. King. 1991. "What Are Traditional Cultural Properties?" *Cultural Resource Management* 14(5):9. Washington, D.C.

Pavlik, Steve. 1998. *A Good Cherokee, a Good Anthropologist: Papers in Honor of Robert K. Thomas* (Contemporary American Indian Issues Series, Vol. 8). Berkeley: University of California.

Relander, Click. 1956. *Drummers and Dreamers.* Caldwell, Idaho: Caxton Printers. (Reprinted 1986. Seattle: Pacific Northwest National Parks & Forest Association.)

Rice, David G. 1980a. *Overview of the Cultural Resources on the Hanford Reservation in South-Central Washington State.* Report on file, U.S. Department of Energy, the Hanford Site, Richland, Washington.

Rice, David G. 1980b. *Hanford Reach of Columbia River, Washington; Cultural Resources Assessment.* Report on file, U.S. Department of Energy, the Hanford Site, Richland, Washington.

Rick, J. 1991. "The Zuni Stanford Anthropology/Archaeology Project." In *Zuni*

History, Victories in the 1990s. Edited by E. Richard Hart. Seattle: Institute of North American West.

Rushmore, Paul. 1994. *A Geomorphic Analysis to Assess the Probability of Buried Archaeological Sites at Dowe Flats, Boulder County, Colorado.* Report prepared for Southwestern Portland Cement Company, Lyons, Colorado (June 20, 1994).

Russo, Kurt W. 2000. *Finding the Middle Ground: Insights and Applications of the Value Orientations Method.* Yarmouth, Maine: Intercultural Press.

SAA. 1995. *Saving the Past for the Future II: Report of the Working Conference.* Washington, D.C.: Society for American Archaeology.

Salazar, Virginia, and Jake Barrow. 2000. "Dialogues." *Cultural Resource Management* 23(9):3.

Salmon, Merrilee H. 1982. *Philosophy and Archaeology.* New York: Academic.

Schlesier, Karl H. 1974. Action Anthropology and the Southern Cheyenne. *Current Anthropology 15*(3): 277–83.

Schlesier, Karl H. 1987. *The Wolves of Heaven: Cheyenne Shamanism, Ceremonies, and Prehistoric Origins.* Norman: University of Oklahoma Press.

Scott, Hugh Lenox. 1907. "The Early History and the Names of the Arapaho." *American Anthropologist,* n.s., 9:545–60.

Sebastian, Lynne. 1993. "Traditional Cultural Properties and Consultation with Traditional Communities." *Cultural Resource Management* 16:15 (Special Issue).

Snyder, Lynn M., Deborah Hull-Walski, Thomas D. Thiessen, and Myra J. Giesen. 2000. "Postwar Partners in Archaeology: The Bureau of Reclamation, the National Park Service, and the River Basin Surveys in the Missouri River Basin (1945–1969)." *Cultural Resource Management* 23(1):17–20.

Sprague, Roderick. 1973. "The Pacific Northwest." In *The Development of North American Archaeology.* Edited by James Fitting, 251–85. Garden City, N.Y.: Anchor Press.

Sprague, Roderick. 1974. "American Indians and American Archaeology." *American Antiquity* 39(1):1–2.

Sprague, Roderick. 1993. "American Indian Burial and Repatriation in the Southern Plateau with Special Reference to Northern Idaho." *Idaho Archaeologist* 16(2):3–13.

Squier, Ephraim G., and E. H. Davis. 1848. *Ancient Monuments of the Mississsippi Valley, Smithsonian Contributions to Knowledge, Vol. 1.* Washington, D.C.

Stapp, Darby C. 2000. "Tribal CRM, Archaeologists, and Action Anthropology." *High Plains Applied Anthropologist* 20(1):72–77.

Stapp, Darby C., and Julie G. Longenecker. 1999. "Learning from the Kennewick Man Controversy." *Anthropology News* (September):10–11. Washington D.C.: American Anthropological Association.

Stapp, Darby C., and Julie G. Longenecker. 1998. "Tribes and Cultural Resource Management in the Mid-Columbia River Region: A Look into the Future." *Practicing Anthropology* 20(3):18–20.

Stewart, Omer C. 1973. "Anthropologists as Expert Witnesses for Indians: Claims and Peyote Cases." In *Anthropology and the American Indian*. Edited by James Officer. San Francisco: The Indian Historian Press.

Stoffle, Richard W. 1983. *Ethnohistory and Native American Religious Concerns in the Fort Carson Piñon Canyon Maneuver Area, Interim Management Report*. University of Wisconsin-Parkside, Applied Urban Field School, Kenosha.

Stoffle, Richard W., and Henry F. Dobyns. 1983. *NUVAGANTU: Nevada Indians Comment on the Intermountain Power Project*. Cultural Resource Series, no. 7. Reno: Bureau of Land Management, Nevada.

Stoffle, Richard W., Henry F. Dobyns, and Michael J. Evans. 1983. *Nungwu-Uakapi: Southern Paiute Indians Comment on the Intermountain Power Project, Intermountain-Adelanto Bipole I Transmission Line*. University of Wisconsin-Parkside, Applied Urban Field School, Kenosaha.

Stoffle, Richard W., and M. J. Evans. 1990. "Holistic Conservation and Cultural Triage: American Indian Perspectives on Cultural Resources." *Human Organization* 49(2):91–99.

Stoffle, Richard W., Henry F. Dobyns, Michael J. Evans, and Omer C. Stewart. 1984. *Toyavita Pivauuhuru Koroin:* Ethnohistory and Native American Religious Concerns in the Fort Carson—Piñyon Canyon Maneuver Area. Report prepared for the U.S. Army. Kenosha: University of Wisconsin-Parkside.

Stoffle, Richard W., and David Halmo, Michael Evans, and Diane Austin. 1996. *PIAPAXA 'UIPI (Big River Canyon)*. Rocky Mountain Regional Office, NPS. Project no. GLCA-R92-0071. Denver.

Stoffle, Richard W., María Nieves Zedeño, and David B. Holmes (editors). 2001. *American Indians and the Nevada Test Site: A Model of Research and Consultation.* DOE/NV/13046-2001/001. Washington, D.C.: U.S. Government Printing Office.

Suagee, Dean B., and Karen J. Funk. 1990. "Enhancing Tribal Roles in Cultural Resources Management: Amendments to the National Historic Preservation Act." In *Preservation on the Reservation: Native Americans, Native American Lands and Archaeology*. Edited by Anthony L. Klesert and Alan S. Downer, 27–59. Navajo Nation Papers in Anthropology, no. 26. Navajo Nation Archaeology Department and the Navajo Nation Historic Preservation Department, Window Rock, Arizona.

Swidler, Nina, Kurt Dongoske, Roger Anyon, and Alan Downer, editors. 1997. *Native Americans and Archaeologists: Stepping Stones to Common Ground.* Walnut Creek, Calif.: AltaMira.

Taylor, Walter W. 1948. "A Study of Archaeology." *American Anthropological Association Memoir* 69. Washington, D.C.

Thomas, David Hurst. 2000. *Skull Wars: Kennewick Man, Archaeology, and the Battle for Native American Identity.* New York: Basic.

Thomas, W. Stephen. 1955. "Arthur Caswell Parker: 1881–1955." *Rochester History* 17(3):1–30.

Toll, Oliver W. 1913. *Report to Oliver Toll on Visit of Arapaho Indians to Estes Park (1913).* Typed Ms. Denver: Colorado Mountain Club. (Copies on file, University of Colorado-Boulder Library and Rocky Mountain National Park Library, Estes Park, Colorado).

Trigger, Bruce G. 1980. "Archaeology and the Image of the American Indian." *American Antiquity* 45(4):662–76.

Trope, Jack F., and Walter R. Echo-Hawk. 1992. "The Native American Graves Protection and Repatriation Act: Background and Legislative History." *Arizona State Law Journal* 24(1):35–77.

Unamuno, Miguel de. 1972. *The Tragic Sense of Life in Men and Nations.* Princeton, N.J.: Princeton University Press.

Utter, Jack. 1993. *American Indians: Answers to Today's Questions.* Lake Ann, Mich.: National Woodlands.

Van Pelt, Jeffrey, Michael S. Burney, and Thomas Bailor. 1997. "Protecting Cultural Resources on the Umatilla Indian Reservation." In *Native Americans and Archaeologists: Stepping Stones to Common Ground.* Edited by Nina Swidler, Kurt E. Dongoske, Roger Anyon, and Alan S. Downer, 167–71. Walnut Creek, Calif.: AltaMira.

Walker, Deward E., Jr. 1991. "Protection of American Indian Sacred Geography." In *Handbook of American Indian Religious Freedom.* Edited by Christopher Vecsey, 100–15. New York: Crossroad.

Walker, Deward E., Jr. (editor). 1998. *Plateau. Handbook of North American Indians, Vol. 12.* Washington, D.C.: Smithsonian Press.

Walker, Deward E., Jr., and Peter N. Jones. 2000. "Anthropology, Tribes, and the Transformation of American Anthropology: A Few Observations." *High Plains Applied Anthropologist* 20(1):67–71.

Warburton, Miranda. 2000. "Who's Program Is It, Anyway?" *High Plains Applied Anthropologist* 20(1):96–99.

Watkins, Joe. 2000. *Indigenous Archaeology.* Walnut Creek, Calif.: AltaMira.

Wax, Rosalie. 1971. *Doing Fieldwork: Warnings and Advice.* Chicago: University of Chicago Press.

Wax, Rosalie, and Robert K. Thomas. 1961. "American Indians and White People." *Phylon: The Atlanta University Review of Race and Culture* 22(4): 305–17.

REFERENCES CITED

Willey, Gordon R., and Jeremy A. Sabloff. 1993. *A History of American Archaeology*. San Francisco: W. H. Freeman.

Winter, Joseph C. 1980. "Indian Heritage Preservation and Archaeologists." *American Antiquity* 45(1):121–31.

Winthrop, Robert H. 1991. *Dictionary of Concepts in Cultural Anthropology*. New York: Greenwood.

Winthrop, Robert H. 1998. "Tradition, Authenticity, and Dislocation: Some Dilemmas of Traditional Cultural Property Studies." *Practicing Anthropology* 20(3):25–27.

INDEX

ABOUT THE AUTHORS

D arby C. Stapp is the director of the Hanford Cultural Resources Laboratory (HCRL), which is operated by Pacific Northwest National Laboratory for the U.S. Department of Energy, Richland Operations. HCRL manages the Department of Energy's Cultural and Historical Resources Program at the Hanford Site, a large federal facility located in southeastern Washington State. Dr. Stapp received his Master's degree from the University of Idaho and a Ph.D. from the University of Pennsylvania. He is a registered professional archaeologist. Dr. Stapp's primary interest is in the area of American Indians and cultural resource protection. In his capacity as director of the Hanford Cultural Resources Laboratory, he oversees Section 106 compliance activities, archaeological surveys, long-term monitoring of site conditions, ARPA compliance, and public education activities. He has worked with the Hanford tribes for over a decade to facilitate their involvement in protecting resources at Hanford and has published widely on this topic. He lives in Richland, Washington.

Michael S. Burney received his B.A. from the University of Idaho in anthropology and his M.A. in western American prehistory from the University of Colorado-Boulder. Since 1975, he has participated in numerous cultural resource management projects in the Pacific Northwest, Great Basin, Rocky Mountain West, and Southwestern United States. Beginning in 1987, he has served as consulting tribal archaeologist for the Confederated Tribes of the Umatilla Indian Reservation, Mission, Oregon, and served as their tribal historic preservation officer from 1996 to 1998. Since 1994, he has been the consulting tribal archaeologist for the Northern Cheyenne Tribe, Lame Deer, Montana, and the Rosebud Sioux Tribe, Rosebud, South Dakota. He also served as consulting tribal archaeologist for the Cocopah Indian Tribe, Somerton, Arizona, and the Oglala Sioux Nation, Pine Ridge, South Dakota. Michael resides in Taos, New Mexico, where he continues to advocate for native cultural resource management, working with tribes that are developing their own programs and assisting tribal staff and attorneys in protecting and preserving archaeological sites, traditional cultural properties, sacred sites, and other ancestral resources.

Breinigsville, PA USA
13 December 2010
251332BV00002B/2/P

9 780759 101050